Citizenship, Migrant Activism and the Politics of Movement

Migration is an inescapable issue in the public debates and political agendas of Western countries, with refugees and migrants increasingly viewed through the lens of security. This book analyses recent shifts in the governing of global mobility from the perspective of the politics of citizenship, utilising an interdisciplinary approach that employs politics, sociology, anthropology and history.

Featuring an international group of leading and emerging researchers working on the intersection of migrant politics and citizenship studies, this book investigates how restrictions on mobility are generating not only new forms of inequality and social exclusion, but also new forms of political activism and citizenship identities. The authors present and discuss the perspectives, experiences, knowledge and voices of migrants and migrant rights activists, in order to better understand the specific strategies, tactics and knowledge that politicised non-citizen migrant groups produce in their encounters with border controls and security technologies. The book focuses the debate of migration, security and mobility rights onto grass-roots politics and social movements, making an important intervention into the fields of migration studies and critical citizenship studies.

Citizenship, Migrant Activism and the Politics of Movement will be of interest to students and scholars of migration and security politics, globalisation, and citizenship studies.

Peter Nyers is Associate Professor of the Politics of Citizenship and Intercultural Relations at McMaster University, Hamilton, Ontario, Canada.

Kim Rygiel is Assistant Professor of Political Science at Wilfrid Laurier University, Waterloo, Ontario, Canada.

Routledge research on the global politics of migration

1 **Globalisation, Migration, and the Future of Europe**
Insiders and outsiders
Edited by Leila Simona Talani

2 **Citizenship, Migrant Activism and the Politics of Movement**
Edited by Peter Nyers and Kim Rygiel

Citizenship, Migrant Activism and the Politics of Movement

Edited by Peter Nyers and Kim Rygiel

LONDON AND NEW YORK

First published 2012
by Routledge
2 Park Square, Milton Park, Abingdon, Oxon OX14 4RN

Simultaneously published in the USA and Canada
by Routledge
711 Third Avenue, New York, NY 10017

Routledge is an imprint of the Taylor & Francis Group, an informa business

© 2012 Peter Nyers and Kim Rygiel for selection and editorial matter;
individual contributors their contribution.

The right of Peter Nyers and Kim Rygiel to be identified as the authors of
the editorial material, and of the authors for their individual chapters, has
been asserted in accordance with sections 77 and 78 of the Copyright,
Designs and Patents Act 1988.

All rights reserved. No part of this book may be reprinted or reproduced or
utilised in any form or by any electronic, mechanical, or other means, now
known or hereafter invented, including photocopying and recording, or in
any information storage or retrieval system, without permission in writing
from the publishers.

Trademark notice: Product or corporate names may be trademarks or
registered trademarks, and are used only for identification and explanation
without intent to infringe.

British Library Cataloguing in Publication Data
A catalogue record for this book is available from the British Library

Library of Congress Cataloging in Publication Data
Citizenship, migrant activism and the politics of movement/edited by Peter
Nyers and Kim Rygiel.
  p. cm. – (Routledge research on the global politics of migration; 2)
  Includes bibliographical references and index.
  1. Immigrants–Political activity. 2. Immigrants–Civil rights.
  3. Emigration and immigration–Political aspects. I. Nyers, Peter. II.
Rygiel, Kim.
  JV6255.C57 2012
  325–dc23

                                                2011036852

ISBN: 978-0-415-60577-9 (hbk)
ISBN: 978-0-203-12511-3 (ebk)

Typeset in Times
by Wearset Ltd, Boldon, Tyne and Wear

Contents

List of contributors	vii
Acknowledgements	xi

Introduction: Citizenship, migrant activism and the politics of movement   1

PETER NYERS AND KIM RYGIEL

1 **Securitised migrants and postcolonial (in)difference: the politics of activisms among North African migrants in France**   20

ALINA SAJED

2 **Claiming rights, asserting belonging: contesting citizenship in the UK**   41

RUTH GROVE-WHITE

3 **Ungrateful subjects? Refugee protests and the logic of gratitude**   54

CAROLINA MOULIN

4 **'We are all foreigners': No Borders as a practical political project**   73

BRIDGET ANDERSON, NANDITA SHARMA AND CYNTHIA WRIGHT

5 **Ethnography and human rights: the experience of APDHA with Nigerian sex workers in Andalusia**   92

ESTEFANÍA ACIÉN GONZÁLEZ

vi *Contents*

6 **Moments of solidarity, migrant activism and (non)citizens at global borders: political agency at Tanzanian refugee camps, Australian detention centres and European borders** 109

HEATHER JOHNSON

7 **Building a sanctuary city: municipal migrant rights in the city of Toronto** 129

JEAN McDONALD

8 **Taking not waiting: space, temporality and politics in the City of Sanctuary movement** 146

VICKI SQUIRE AND JENNIFER BAGELMAN

9 **Undocumented citizens? Shifting grounds of citizenship in Los Angeles** 165

ANNE McNEVIN

Index 184

Contributors

Editors

Peter Nyers is Associate Professor of the Politics of Citizenship and Intercultural Relations in the Department of Political Science at McMaster University, Hamilton, Ontario. His research focuses on the social movements of non-status refugees and migrants, in particular their campaigns against deportation and detention and for regularisation and global mobility rights. He is the author of *Rethinking Refugees: Beyond States of Emergency* (Routledge 2006), co-editor (with E.F. Isin and B.S. Turner) of *Citizenship between Past and Future* (Routledge 2008) and editor of *Securitizations of Citizenship* (Routledge 2009). He has published research articles in the journals *Citizenship Studies*, *Economy & Society*, *European Journal of Cultural Studies*, *International Political Sociology*, *Millennium: Journal of International Studies* and *Third World Quarterly*.

Kim Rygiel is Assistant Professor in the Department of Political Science at Wilfrid Laurier University, Waterloo, Ontario. Her research focuses on citizenship as a globalising regime of government in relation to regulating mobility through border controls within North America and Europe. Her current research examines activism of non-citizen migrant groups and migrant rights organisations in relation to migrant and refugee camps. She is the author of *Globalizing Citizenship* (University of British Columbia Press 2010) and co-editor (with Krista Hunt) of *(En)Gendering the War on Terror: War Stories and Camouflaged Politics* (Ashgate 2006). She has published research articles in *Citizenship Studies* and has contributed chapters to several books, including 'Abject Spaces: Frontiers, Zones and Camps' (with E.F. Isin) in *The Logics* of *Biopower and the War on Terror: Living, Dying, Surviving* (Palgrave Macmillan 2007).

Contributing authors

Estefanía Acién González is the Coordinator of the Working Group on Prostitution for the Asociación Pro Derechos Humanos de Andalucía (APDHA – Human Rights Association of Andalusia), Spain, and a researcher for that organisation. She is also a doctoral candidate at the University of Almería and viii *Contributors*

has researched and published on the topics of migration and border controls, especially relating to woman migrants and sex workers. She is a member and researcher at the Laboratorio de Antropología Social y Cultural (Laboratory of Social and Cultural Anthropology) at the University of Almería (since 1998), member of the Centro de Estudio de las Migraciones y las Relaciones Interculturales (Center for the Study of Migrations and Intercultural Relations, CEMyRI) at the same university and a member since 1993 of the NGO Acción en Red (Action Network).

Bridget Anderson is a Senior Research Fellow at the Centre on Migration, Politics and Society at the University of Oxford, UK. Her research interests include migration, low-waged labour markets, 'victimhood', and immigration enforcement. Her work examines the relation of the state to the construction of certain categories of person as being worthy of protection or of work and others as threatening or dishonourable, and also considers migrant subjectivity and theories and practices of citizenship. She has worked as an adviser and activist with a range of migrants' organisations and trade unions. She has edited special issues of the journals *Refuge*, *Subjectivity* and *Population, Space and Place* and is the co-editor (with Martin Ruhs) of *Need for Migrant Labour? An Introduction to the Analysis of Staff Shortages, Immigration and Public Policy* (Oxford University Press 2010).

Jennifer Bagelman is a doctoral candidate in the Department of Politics and International Studies at The Open University, UK. Her research focuses on questions of sovereignty and critical citizenship practices. Her particular interest is in exploring the borderland of sanctuary cities as a complex site of power relations and resistance, with an emphasis on understanding the role of sanctuary 'recipients' as political.

Ruth Grove-White is a Policy Officer at the Migrants' Rights Network (MRN), a UK charity launched in 2006, which works to support the rights of all migrants, and campaigns for progressive immigration policies in the UK. She is responsible for managing the MRN's policy and parliamentary work, including advocacy, policy analysis and the work of the All Party Parliamentary Group on Migration. Ruth regularly presents the MRN's perspectives at conferences and training sessions and in the media, as well as contributing to publications by think-tanks and NGOs relating to migration policy in the UK. Ruth graduated with an MSc in Political Sociology from the London School of Economics. Before joining MRN in 2008 she worked as a project coordinator at the International Organization for Migration in Bosnia-Herzegovina and as the Programme Manager of European Dialogue in the UK.

Heather Johnson is Assistant Professor in the Department of Political Studies at Trent University, Peterborough, Ontario. Her research examines the ways in which the cross-border migration of refugees impacts global hierarchies of power and the sovereignties of nation-states, and how the related practices of border control affect understandings of political agency for non-citizens. She also has interests in the fields of irregular migration and the visual representation of political subjects, globalisation studies and interdisciplinarity. She has published her research in *Third World Quarterly* and as book contributions.

Jean McDonald holds a SSHRC post-doctoral fellowship at the Institute on Globalization and the Human Condition at McMaster University, Hamilton, Ontario. Her research focuses on processes of illegalisation and barriers facing non-status immigrants attempting to access services in Toronto. In addition, she has extensive activist and community organising experience with the social movement group No One Is Illegal and has been a key figure in organising Don't Ask Don't Tell campaigns in Toronto, furthering rights for non-status undocumented migrants. She is the author of 'Citizenship, Illegality and Sanctuary' in *Interrogating Race and Racism* (University of Toronto Press 2007).

Anne McNevin is Lecturer in International Studies and Research Fellow at the Global Cities Research Institute at RMIT University, Melbourne, Victoria. She is the author of *Contesting Citizenship: Irregular Migrants and New Frontiers of the Political* (Columbia University Press 2011) and is the co-editor (with Manfred Steger) of *Global Ideologies and Urban Landscapes* (Routledge 2011). Her research spans migration, citizenship theory, globalisation, neoliberalism and critical political geography and has been published in *The Australian Journal of Political Science, Citizenship Studies, Globalizations, New Political Science* and *Review of International Studies*. She is Assistant Editor of the journal *Citizenship Studies*.

Carolina Moulin is Assistant Professor of International Relations at the Institute of International Relations, PUC-Rio, Brazil. She has published journal articles in *International Political Sociology, Alternatives: Global, Local, Political* and *Refuge*. Her research interests include critical international relations theory, political agency, human mobility, and refugee studies.

Alina Sajed is Assistant Professor of International Relations at the University of Hong Kong. Her core research interests are postcolonial approaches to international relations, globalisation and transnationalism, the politics of the Global South, and critical security issues. She has published articles in *Citizenship Studies, Review of International Studies* and *Cambridge Review of International Affairs*. Her book, *Postcolonial Encounters in International Relations: The Politics of Transgression in the Maghreb*, will be published by Routledge in 2012.

Nandita Sharma is Associate Professor in the Department of Sociology at the University of Hawai'i at Manoa, Honolulu, Hawai'i. Her research interests address themes of human migration, migrant labour, national state power, ideologies of racism and nationalism, processes of identification and self-understanding, and social movements for justice. Sharma is an activist scholar whose research is shaped by the social movements she is active in, including

x *Contributors*

No Borders movements and those struggling for the commons. She is the author of *Home Economics: Nationalism and the Making of 'Migrant Workers' in Canada* (University of Toronto Press 2006) and co-editor (with Bridget Anderson and Cynthia Wright) of a special issue of the journal *Refuge* on 'No Borders as Practical Politics'.

Vicki Squire is RCUK Research Fellow at the Department of Politics and International Studies and the Centre for Citizenship, Identities and Governance, The Open University, UK. Her research is located at the intersections of migration studies, citizenship studies and critical security studies. She examines political struggles over migration as a way to critically diagnose and intervene in contemporary practices of the governing of mobility. In addition to writing articles and book chapters on issues of migration, citizenship and security, she is author of *The Exclusionary Politics of Asylum* (Palgrave 2009), editor of *The Contested Politics of Mobility: Borderzones and Irregularity* (Routledge 2011) and Assistant Editor of the journal *Citizenship Studies*.

Cynthia Wright teaches in the School of Women's Studies, as well as the Departments of Geography and History, at York University, Canada. Her diverse research interests include the historical production of immigration controls; migrant justice movements (especially among non-status and undocumented people); and twentieth-century 'international history from below'. With Bridget Anderson and Nandita Sharma, she was co-editor of a special issue of *Refuge* on 'No Borders as Practical Politics'.

Acknowledgements

We would like to thank the people and institutions without whose help this project and book would not have been possible. The book is the product of a workshop, 'Putting Citizenship in Motion', held at McMaster University, Hamilton, Ontario, in October 2009. The workshop was made possible with financial assistance from the Institute on Globalization and the Human Condition at McMaster University and the Social Sciences and Humanities Research Council of Canada. We would like to thank both for their assistance. We would also like to thank Will Coleman for his support throughout the project, and workshop participants whose insights have contributed to the high quality of the chapters presented here, including William Walters, Sharry Aiken, Audrey Macklin, Sarah Batten, Jen Vermilyea, Sonya Zikic and Branka Marijan. For editorial assistance, we appreciate the help of Shealah Stratton and Caitlin Craven. We have benefited from the assistance of the team at Routledge including Heidi Bagtazo and Alexander Quayle. All images in Chapter 5, 'Ethnography and human rights', are reproduced with permission from Estefanía Acién González. An earlier version of Chapter 4, ' "We are all foreigners" ', appeared in the journal *Refuge* 26:2 and we thank the journal for permission to reproduce parts of it in a different version here.

Finally a big thanks to our families and to our respective partners Oona Pagham and Feyzi Baban.

Introduction

Citizenship, migrant activism and the politics of movement

Peter Nyers and Kim Rygiel

This book investigates the possibilities and impossibilities of migrant activism in the context of securitised sovereignties and regimes that restrict mobility. As implied by the title, our aim is to bring together three major themes into a critical dialogue: the forms of *citizenship* that have emerged in the context of transformations in the global migration regime; the forms of *migrant activism* that have emerged to contest this migration regime; and the implications these two processes have for how we theorise and conceptualise the *politics of movement*. We have asked each of the contributors to reflect, in their own way, on these themes in their individual chapters. The result is a rich collection of empirically grounded and theoretically attuned analyses of migrant activism in different contexts around the world.

Our aim in this Introduction is to elaborate on the three themes and explain how each chapter addresses them. We start with the theme of citizenship because it has become such a focal point of debates about borders, sovereignty and migration. Anxieties over the fate of national citizenship in the context of global migrations have led to stricter rules on conferring citizenship, such as the spread of citizenship tests and innovations in legal (and extralegal) ways of revoking citizenship. The accompanying discourse – i.e. that Western states are being overrun by migrants and refugees from the Global South – is remarkable for how often, quickly and effectively it can be mobilised. This is despite the fact that the right to mobility within and between rich countries has been overwhelmingly granted to citizens of other rich countries. A major empirical study of visa controls has confirmed this bias and concludes that access to the mobility regime is highly uneven and differential (Mau 2010). Given this state of affairs, it is not surprising that many have concluded that citizenship is no less than 'a conspiracy against the rest of the world' (Hindess 2000: 1489; cf. Shachar 2009; Stevens 2009). While we acknowledge the importance of this, our primary interest in these regimes that restrict mobility and citizenship does not lie with the exclusions they generate. Rather, we wish to emphasise how the practice and experience of mobility – even when restricted – is itself productive of new forms of citizenship and of being political.

The focus on how political subjectivity can be enacted in various ways in the context of the global mobility regime is the second major theme of the book.

2 P. Nyers and K. Rygiel

This theme investigates the social and political responses to restrictions on mobility and citizenship. While we see how these restrictions and controls are generating new forms of inequality and social exclusion, our primary focus is on the contestation of these controls. What new forms of political activism, citizenship identities, and openings for different concepts of citizenship are emerging in this context? Our perspective is that citizenship is more than a legal and political institution, because it includes moments of political engagement such that those lacking formal citizenship status, by acting and claiming rights to citizenship, in effect practise citizenship (Isin 2009). The chapters of this book explore how, through various strategies of claims-making, non-citizen migrant groups are involved in practices and ways of engaging in citizenship even when lacking formal citizenship status. Taken together, we hope the chapters contribute to an understanding of how migrant activism is a key site for reconceptualising citizenship.

Finally, the third theme elaborates on the significance that the politics of mobility and movement has for emerging citizenship spaces and forms. Our aim here is to conceptualise migrant citizenship 'from below' – that is, from the perspectives, experiences, knowledge and voices of refugees, migrants and migrant rights activists. Indeed, many of our contributors are both academics and activists, who not only research and write about migrant rights, but who are also actively engaged in these movements. They bring a focus from the point of view of the grass roots and social movements – migrant citizenship seen 'from below' – to the discussions around border security, migration, mobility rights and the politics of citizenship. The result is a deeply contextual understanding of the specific strategies, tactics and knowledges that migrant groups mobilise in their encounters with border controls and security technologies.

Redefining citizenship through mobility rights

Mobility is widely regarded as a defining feature of globalisation. It is now commonplace to recognise the increased importance and intensification of cross-border movement and exchanges among peoples, cultures, goods and information. Important research has been done on how this enhanced mobility has significantly reorganised space, time, identity and politics across the globe. At the same time, however, mobility is increasingly seen as a problem in need of regulation and control. Over the past 10 years, various reforms to migration and border control have been institutionalised in the name of security across industrialised countries, particularly in Europe and North America. We are interested in how this regulation of mobility has provoked new ways of conceptualising borders and governing the mobility of people. For example, borders are now conceptualised in diverse forms as 'borderscapes' (Rajaram and Grundy-Warr 2007), 'networked' borders (Rumford 2006), or as 'filters' (Walters 2006) in the 'social sorting' of populations (Lyon 2003). Borders are at once externalised and delocalised, such that they perform a kind of 'remote control' policing (Zolberg 2002; Bigo 2002; Salter 2003; Lahav and Guiraudon 2000). Most importantly, as several of the chapters in this book point out, border and migration controls change the status of people within states and thus have a direct bearing not only on rights to movement, but also on a whole series of related rights having to do with access to employment, housing and social services within a country. As Anderson, Sharma and Wright explain in Chapter 4:

> The greater, though less studied, effect of restrictive immigration policies has been to restrict the rights and entitlements that migrants can claim once they are *within* national states. In practice, rather than simply restricting movement, restrictive immigration policies have enabled states to shift the status they accord migrating people. Fewer people are now given a status that comes with rights (e.g. 'permanent resident' or 'refugee') and more and more are legally subordinated (e.g. through the status of 'illegal') or are forced to work in unfree employment relations (including through the status of 'temporary foreign worker').

Borders thus make certain populations governable by rendering their status more vulnerable to bordering practices, for example by placing people in conditions of 'deportability' (De Genova 2002), or by enabling their 'differential inclusion' rather than overt exclusion (Andrijasevic 2009). We conclude, therefore, that the regulation of mobility plays a key role in articulations of citizenship and who can and cannot be a citizen.

Examining the 'top-down', state-initiated control of mobility is certainly crucial for understanding the mobility-citizenship nexus. However, we believe it is insufficient for understanding how these regulations are actually producing new ways of being mobile and new subjectivities that are defined in and through the condition of mobility. Our aim is therefore to emphasise how the institutionalisation of more restrictive policies regulating mobility can also be understood as constitutive of new ways of 'being political' (Isin 2002). New political subjectivities may reflect different ways of organising political community through a condition of mobility, in which values of equality, justice and recognition come to be redefined from the perspectives of mobile subjects. It is these latter aspects that are the focus and concern of the chapters in this book.

An examination of the regulation of rights to mobility (defined here as a right to move, including throughout domestic space, a 'right to escape' [Mezzadra 2004b], to return, *and to stay*) and of mobile populations, particularly refugees and irregular migrants, illustrates that mobility is also *productive* of subjectivity. Individuals and populations are constituted as certain types of subjects through the regulation of their movement and through their access to mobility as a resource, as well as their abilities to make claims to rights to movement. As such, the governing of mobility is directly connected to constructions of citizenship, not only as a legal and political institution and status, but also related to practices, daily living and subjectivities related to and constitutive of being political. This relationship between mobility and the production of citizen subjectivities can take on more institutionalised forms related to immigration programmes

4   P. Nyers and K. Rygiel

that create a 'gradation' in status (Goldring, Berinstein and Bernhard 2009). Rather than the binaries of non-citizen/citizen and non-status/status subject positions, the reality is often much more complex, with policies regulating movement producing variations of 'less than full' citizenship statuses (ibid.). Confusing simple legal/illegal binaries, people often move in and out of pathways of irregularity (Squire 2011). For example, the use of point systems in Canada and the UK constitutes notions of skilled workers that define which skills are deemed worthy of citizenship status. Temporary foreign workers programmes (such as Canada's Seasonal Agricultural Worker Program) and other specialised programmes such as Canada's Live-In Caregiver Program, directed at specific groups like domestic workers, create categories of gendered and classed temporary migrant worker statuses. Similarly, legal instruments such as the Palermo protocol, directed at regulating trafficking, are also productive of (non)citizenship statuses and subjectivities. By identifying women migrants working as sex workers as victims of trafficking, they also constitute them as irregular migrants that should be excluded from the state and state support as victims of crime or labour exploitation (Andrijasevic 2009: 399). In addition to these more formalised ways, mobility systems are also constitutive of non-citizen subjectivities in less formal ways where mobility is an integral part of processes of making and unmaking citizen-subjects (Nyers 2006b, 2008, 2010; Rygiel 2010). New travel regulations using biometric and risk-profiling technologies, for example, are constitutive of not just high and low risk subjects but also first- and second-class citizenships (Nyers; Rygiel 2010).

Citizenship is also constituted through mobility in a much more ontological and biopolitical sense. Here we are interested in how the condition of mobility (and stasis) is itself a fundamentally constitutive binary of citizenship. For, as Barry Hindess (2000) has argued, the institution of citizenship is responsible for dividing the world's population into respective states and can be described as involving the 'international management of populations'. To be recognised as a citizen with rights requires a certain degree of stasis, on the one hand, since rights, in practice, materialise mostly as citizenship rights through membership within a particular political community, defined predominantly through the bounded territorial space of the nation-state system. The condition of immobility is then, in this sense, constitutive of modern liberal citizenship. But this also means that the condition of im/mobility is integral to the constitution of citizenship in a biopolitical sense, as Moulin outlines in Chapter 3. States have a biopolitical investment in the identification of desirable and undesirable populations, often defined through their productive capability. Migration and border controls become an important means for states to control this productive capacity of population. Governments may facilitate the mobility of business workers and domestic workers, for example, if such workers bring resources into the state in the form of capital, knowledge, skills or remittances. Individuals and groups deemed less productive or desirable are by the same logic prevented from entry or longer-term settlement, or regulated more restrictively as with refugee and temporary worker classes. However, somewhat paradoxically, at the same time

Introduction 5

modern liberal citizenship has also come to be constituted through the very experience of freedom, which, in the late twentieth century and the early twenty-first, has come to be defined in part through the experience of international mobility (Rygiel 2012), such as, for example, through the institutionalisation of the international passport system (Salter 2003).

In addition to these intersections between mobility and citizenship, the contributors to this book also draw attention to yet another way in which mobility is productive of citizenship by taking mobility as the key analytic. Within critical migration, citizenship and security scholarship, interest and thinking about citizenship in relation to mobility as an analytic has emerged, in large part, as a result of challenges posed by the field of autonomous migration literature (Hardt and Negri 2000; Mezzadra 2004a, 2004b; Mezzadra and Neilson 2003; Mitropoulos and Neilson 2006; Papadopoulos *et al.* 2008; Rodriguez 1996). This literature uses migrant agency as a lens through which to understand border controls, citizenship and migration. Mobility is portrayed as a resource employed by migrants. From this perspective, border controls are a response to order the potential power that migrants' ability to move enacts. Many of the contributors to this book share this approach, in which 'migration is a potentially creative social movement capable of confounding and destabilising the distributions and markings of social power' (Walters 2008: 184). Such an approach challenges scholars working at the intersection of scholarship on citizenship, migration, borders and security to take mobility as an analytic through which to analyse and reconceptualise each of these concepts. In a special issue of the journal *Subjectivity*, Andrijasevic and Anderson (2009: 366) explore 'subjectivity as related to migration and agency'. In it, they argue, 'emerging migrant collective subjectivities through political mobilisations have direct bearing on our understanding and conceptualisation of citizenship. Migrants' claims for justice and the contestation of ascribed/prescribed categories challenges the presupposition that citizenship cannot be enacted by non-citizens.' Thus while we recognise the importance of much of the recent work around mobility/migration, citizenship and security, which has been top-down and focused on the prevention of movement by border controls, the chapters collected here aim to contribute to the smaller but emerging critical literature that reflects on how border controls respond to migrant mobility in the first place, by placing mobility, rather than control, at the centre of analysis. Thus we can ask: In what ways can the current intensification of the regulation of mobility and rights to movement in many industrialised countries be understood as responses to preceding pathways of migration? Moreover, we can simultaneously consider how migrants use their im/mobility as a resource to renegotiate their status, belonging and subjectivity. The contributors to this book consider the issue of the increased securitisation of migration and mobility that has occurred throughout Europe, North America, Australia and North Africa in recent years. They also reflect in different ways on how fundamental rights to movement (right to move, right to escape, right to return, right to stay) are being reconfigured and how citizenship gets redefined as a result, in particular in relation to non-citizen migrants and their differential access to mobility rights. The

6 P. Nyers and K. Rygiel

contributors also consider the implications of regulating movement for certain groups and their ability to access rights and resources through a change in citizenship status.

Further to such reflections, the autonomous migration perspective asks us to reflect on the very concepts and binary of citizen/non-citizen through an analytic of mobility. One such way is to recognise that mobility as an analytic disrupts the dichotomy of non-citizen/citizen. For example, in her discussion of irregular migration, Squire (2011) notes that mobility is fundamental to the creation of distinctions between non-citizens and citizens through the creation of pathways of irregularity. She argues (ibid.: x) that it is thus necessary to '*politicise* mobility through examining how the movement of people, in particular the "irregular" movement of people, is constituted as an object of and as a subject of politics'. Yet it is equally important to consider how '*mobilising* politics means to render politics mobile through exploring how the "irregular" movement of people entails a shift in what it means to be political'.

Within the social sciences, in what has become known as the 'mobility turn', mobility has come to be regarded as an object of analysis and an analytic in its own right rather than simply a 'black box' (Urry 2007: 6). The analytic power of this mobility turn lies in its challenge to one of the key organising principles within the social sciences – the distinction between the 'territorial' or 'sedentary' and movement – through the idea that place and space are created through social relations, processes and movement (Hannam *et al.* 2006: 2). Viewed from the perspective of mobility as an analytic, it is not so much that people move into a space but rather that space is created and constructed as a result of the flows of people, goods, services, systems and the interactions between them (ibid.). Viewed this way, mobility as an analytic forces us to discard our usual notions of spatiality and scale and their relation to temporality. Rather than fixed locations contained in space and time, places are conceptualised as dynamic spaces of flow, that is 'places of movement that are about relationships and the placing of peoples, materials images and systems of difference that they perform in relation to each other' (ibid.: 13). Finally, from this perspective, movement is no longer problematised as that which challenges the perceived normality of the ontological condition of stasis or semi-permanent location in a fixed place such as a city or state. Rather, mobility is privileged as a way of life. It is a condition of being mobile in which all participate through degrees of access to mobility and within the context of other hierarchies such as race, gender, class, age and sexuality (Hyndman 2004). If we put mobility forward as the primary analytic, thinking citizenship through mobility in this sense means to conceptualise citizenship 'in motion' and raises the question of whether the ontological condition of mobility can put citizenship as a concept 'in motion' (Mezzadra 2004a). Can thinking citizenship through mobility (that is the experiences and perspectives of being mobile) challenge the foundational precepts central to modern citizenship, starting with such binaries as stasis/mobility, citizen/non-citizen, belonging/exile, insider/outsider, legal/illegal, documented/undocumented and status/non-status? Finally, if we take seriously people's

Introduction 7

experiences of living in motion, can we conceptualise citizenship as a practice and status differently, in a way that does not necessarily privilege stasis as a condition for belonging, status, identity and rights? Can we conceptualise citizenship through mobility in ways that take seriously the movement of people in and through space and the creation of social networks in and in relation to space as flows? And what different types of political subjectivities, forms of political community and ways of being political would emerge as a result? These are some of the concerns central to this book.

Migrant citizenship 'from below'

The recent increased restrictions on movement have by no means gone unchallenged. A study on the theme of refugees and resistance provides a list of a number of recent protests by refugees:

> Dramatic coordinated resistance has also been present in camp settings as demonstrated by the massive rejection of camp 'security' in Honduras in 1987, in which 4,500 refugees walked out of their camp in favor of wartime repatriation, pointing to the failure of UNHCR and the host government to secure protection for the refugees; the organisation of Guatemalan refugees in Mexico to protest their handling at the hands of UNHCR, the Mexican government, and the Guatemalan government; the occupation of a border settlement by Roma refugees in Macedonia protesting return to Kosovo and unlivable circumstances in Macedonia; and the organised protest march of 800 refugees from Krisan camp in Ghana to the Ivorian border, to draw attention to what they considered unlivable conditions and to push for resettlement. While these examples represent primarily non-violent techniques, violence has been employed in desperate circumstances. In Bangladesh, where Rohingya refugees were facing systematic refoulement coordinated in conjunction with the Burmese government, resistance to armed repatriation police lead to widespread detention and protest that injured both refugees and police. Ultimately, refugees were permitted to protest the action in a nonviolent sit-in, with the support of UNHCR. Similarly, clashes between camp administration and refugees lead to violence in a series of protests in Saudi Arabia in the 1990s – leading to hunger strikes that ultimately killed three people and left 104 hospitalised in critical condition.
>
> (Lewis 2006: 8–9)

The list is, of course, far from complete and could be expanded to include many more examples of refugee protests (e.g. Moulin and Nyers 2007). While the instances of refugee and migrant resistances are as long as they are varied, they have yet to take a firm root in the collective imagination. Why is it that we do not hear more about these acts of resistance by refugees and migrants? Like most enactments of resistance, they exist at the margins of awareness of mainstream society and media. This does not, however, diminish their significance.

8 *P. Nyers and K. Rygiel*

The element of contestation is never far from the phenomenon of migration. The figure of the refugee, for example, has historically had a close relationship to resistance. The act of taking flight from circumstances that have become intolerable – the 'well founded fear of persecution' of the UN Refugee Convention – is itself a political act. It is political in the sense of being a strategic counter-measure to real or perceived persecution. It is political also in the sense that the process of becoming someone new – a refugee – is simultaneously the act of refusal, as the flight signifies a lack of legitimacy of state from which he or she flees. The resistive dimension to refugees is often forgotten in the various discursive regimes that claim to speak for refugees. The refugee is caught between two competing, and at times overlapping, discursive regimes: humanitarianism and securitisation. On the one hand, the humanitarian regime of the UNHCR, major international NGOs, and human rights groups have institutionalised the figure of the refugee as a humanitarian figure whose abject victimage has silenced their voice and emptied their subjectivity of agency (Malkki 1996; Rajaram 2002; Nyers 2006a). On the other hand, politicians and governments have targeted refugees and asylum seekers as objects of securitisation, representing them as harbingers of threats, dangers and social ills (Watson 2009). The opportunity to enter into a dialogue with the public in this context is severely constrained, and the risks of speaking out against mistreatment can be high. As one recent study of refugee protests concluded: 'Through affiliation with a protest or resistance movement, refugees in hosts states often risk their hard won legal status, and quite possibly their safety and livelihood since host states, depending upon domestic policy, may imprison or deport refugees who have violated local law or the conditions of their resident status. The result in often considerable submission and quiet powerlessness on the part of refugees when it comes to claiming basic rights, demanding better treatment, and voicing grievances' (Lewis 2006: 4–5).

Significant social movements of migrants at various levels of legality (refugees, temporary workers, asylum seekers, undocumented migrants) have emerged across the globe. The forms of migrant activism that are emerging are diverse, ranging from conventional forms of public campaigns, research and petitions, to newer tactics of anti-deportation and sanctuary campaigns (Nyers 2003), border camps and caravans (Walters 2006), and creative art projects (Padgham 2005). General strikes by undocumented workers have been seen in the United States and elsewhere. Detention facilities, notorious for their role in restricting global mobility rights, are not only sites of confinement and control, but can also be investigated as sites of political action, as places where mobilisations occur, subjectivities are formed, and contestations of the regimes governing mobility are enacted (Rygiel 2011). Dramatic acts of protest are not uncommon. To emphasise the voicelessness of being labelled a refugee, many acts of protests focus on the body – self-immolation, public hunger strikes and suicide attempts, suturing lips, ears and mouths – according flesh instead of voice the means to establish one's status as a speaking subject.

The specific form of refugee and migrant mobilisation, as well as the content of the claims made, will of course vary across geographies, contexts, and

Introduction 9

material conditions (Monforte and Dufour 2011). While these movements and campaigns do not dominate media headlines, their significance is nonetheless worth investigating. For example, Ellerman (2010) argues that it is precisely the lack of formal status to make rights claims that makes the claims of undocumented migrants so powerful. As some of the most interesting work in the area of critical citizenship studies has revealed, the significance of refugee and migrant activism is that it breaks down the distinction between citizen and non-citizen and problematises the ontological divide between these two categories (McNevin 2011; Squire 2011; Bosniak 2008; Dauvergne 2008). The chapters in this volume build upon this literature by exploring various acts, strategies and moments of migrant activism that emerge in response to the securitisation of migration and mobility. The authors look at how groups of non-citizen migrants and migrant rights activists engage, contest, transform, and otherwise resist new ways of regulating mobility and in doing so enact a migrant citizenship 'from below'.

Emerging citizenship spaces and subjectivities

Migrant activism in its diverse forms, as discussed in the previous section, opens up the possibility of transforming our thinking about citizenship subjectivities and spaces. The third theme of this book aims to outline concrete strategies, campaigns and 'moments' of activism initiated by migrants and those working in solidarity with them. The shift presented in this book, of re-thinking citizenship – a concept normally identified with stasis or location in a particular political community – through movement, draws our attention to new spaces of citizenship that potentially enable both new ways of being political and new visions for the type of politics we wish to imagine in the world. Many of the examples discussed here of emerging migrant subjectivities that enact a form of citizenship 'from below' present various demands for social justice conceived differently from the current order. For example, sanctuary movements, No Border politics and Don't Ask Don't Tell campaigns put forward different normative visions of the future, in which notions of belonging and entitlement to rights are founded on criteria of residence, participation in community, and social relations developed in space and in relation to 'the commons'. This is in contrast to the current liberal measure for citizenship and entitlement grounded in legal status, stasis and location in bounded space, documentation, exclusion, and private property.

As noted above, non-citizen migrants engage in making claims to belonging, to rights and to being political through a variety of strategies. In doing so they enact a form of citizenship 'from below'. In other words, non-citizen migrants enact themselves as political beings and de facto as citizens, despite lacking legal status, political membership or documentation of belonging. In fact, there is now a burgeoning literature spanning several disciplines, including anthropology, political geography, urban studies and political science, that reflects on 'spaces of abjection' (Isin and Rygiel 2007), in which peoples who are disenfranchised

10 *P. Nyers and K. Rygiel*

from citizenship (whether formally through status or informally through poverty and war) are finding new ways of claims-making in such spaces. Displaced peoples, slum-dwellers, refugees, non-status and irregular migrants and the Sans-papiers (Appadurai 2001; McNevin 2011; Nyers 2003, 2008; Squire 2009), as well as grass-roots organisers in shantytowns and 'the squatter citizen' (Dawson 2004), are all examples of the new types of citizen subjectivities emerging in relation to im/mobility. Engin Isin uses the term 'activist citizenship' to characterise these newly emerging types of citizen subjectivities in contrast to the 'active citizen' more traditionally associated with the politics of modern liberal citizenship. Isin (2009: 380) argues that in contrast to the 'active citizen', identified with traditional citizenship roles such as voting, military service and paying taxes, 'activist citizenship' refers to struggles and acts that present a 'sense of making a break, a rupture, a difference'. In other words, what the focus on mobility here illustrates is that rather than viewing non-citizens as always being, by definition, external to the political community and Other to the citizen subject, this reading instead shows a co-constitutive relationship between non-citizen migrants and citizens. Placing mobility and migrant perspectives in the foreground has the power to disrupt this binary in favor of a more fluid exchange between subject positions. In campaigns like Don't Ask Don't Tell, the point is to render the relative statuses of non-citizens and citizens less important in terms of daily living practices, such that this becomes a less important criterion in our daily interactions with people living together in community and ultimately in the basis upon which to recognise legal rights such as access to social welfare provisions.

But focusing on reading citizenship through migrant agency also works to create citizen subjectivities that might be antithetical, or at least ambivalent, to the notion of the citizen subject as a desirable subject position. Such is the case with the discussion of migrant women workers working in the Los Angeles migrant cooperative, Magic Cleaners, that Anne McNevin discusses in Chapter 9 of this book. As McNevin argues here, it is important also to

> imagine a political practice that leaves open the possibility of opting out of citizenship as a mode of resistance. Such a practice would expose the limits of citizenship in prevailing *or altered* forms, to reflect the range of political subjectivities and practices that are possible and/or desirable. I am thinking here of a refusal to justify one's political subjectivity in terms that make sense within existing socio-spatial vocabularies and conceptual limits.

A similar point is made by Papadopoulos and Tsianos (2007: 166) who note that migrants may prefer strategies of 'de-identification', remaining 'underground' as undocumented persons without status rather than necessarily obtaining citizenship status. The recognition that putting citizenship in motion can entail its refusal raises yet another question regarding the very framing of migrant activism in terms of citizenship. Do we impose a category of citizenship subjectivity on peoples whose actions may not necessarily be framed in this way? And, if so,

Introduction 11

do we eclipse other ways of being political? The answer here must necessarily be yes and no. The question is a significant one that cannot be treated lightly. In fact, Barry Hindess (2004: 307) raises such a question when he asks 'What's so great about citizenship?' and argues for the need to not simplistically assume citizenship to be a progressive institution within which all peoples wish to be incorporated. As Hindess (ibid.) explains,

> It is not difficult to find cases in which people appear to have preferred a way of life that did not involve citizenship, or involved it only in a weaker form. Many Greeks of the classical period lived under Persian rule in Asia Minor, and, while there were certainly some revolts against Persian rule, we have no reason to suppose that they would all have preferred the citizenship enjoyed by those who lived in the free cities.

So, too, one could argue that for some indigenous peoples, citizenship might be regarded as antithetical to their own ways of being political, grounded in ecocentric rather than androcentric ways of living in the world; citizenship is understood in its modern sense as being tied to territoriality, state sovereignty and histories of colonisation, which were and continue to be destructive of indigenous knowledges and lifestyles.

Yet, on the other hand, if we read citizenship outside of its temporal and spatial specificity of the nation-state to consider the term, instead, as that which best evokes the notion of political subjectivity, we might argue otherwise. Rather, reading migrant activism through the lens of citizenship does not necessarily eclipse other ways of being political, but opens up the possibility to think about citizenship and the basic ontology between self and other in more profound and perhaps less violent ways. For the language of citizenship is still that which best encapsulates the language of political subjectivity. As Jacques Rancière (2004: 307) points out with respect to his understanding of politics as *dissensus*, perhaps what is as important as the acquisition of legal status is what citizenship mobilises in its name. As Rancière notes, politics is mobilised in the 'gap' or discrepancy between the desire and belief of 'a right to have rights' and the absence of the materialisation of those rights where certain groups of people fail to have 'the rights that they have' (ibid.: 302). In other words, the language of citizenship can inspire movement forward in the aspirations of greater social justice, rights and equity, formulated in the absence, discrepancy or 'gap' between the ideal of citizenship and its absence on the ground. It is this gap in which citizenship motivates a language of alternative futures, an ideal that represents its usefulness in the end. Thus we believe that citizenship both as an analytic and as a subjectivity is useful for its capacity to mobilise people for social justice, and so it is useful to retain the term as opposed to abandoning it altogether.

Finally, migrant activism opens up new spaces in which subjects can enact themselves as political beings and through which people can conceptualise political community. Political geographers such as Doreen Massey (1994) and

12 *P. Nyers and K. Rygiel*

Edward Soja (1996) have noted that not only are social relations productive of space but our conceptualisation of space is also constitutive of the types of relations we are able to build. Several chapters of this book investigate different types of space, from the 'mobile enclaves of sanctuary' in the UK, to 'housebars' in Almería, Spain, to non-status migrant cooperatives in Los Angeles, to city spaces, as important sites of citizenship. The focus on creative new spaces such as these opens up discussion of new ways of being political that challenge the privileging of the state and the nation as the site of citizenship. Furthermore, insights from critical geography and border studies illustrate how borders are multiple and complex and take various forms as virtual, technological and delocalised, and thus produce new ways of managing populations. If this is the case, then attention to migrant activism enables us to focus on how border politics can also be used as a resource by migrants. If borders can be re-imagined in new ways to manage mobility based on the exclusion of non-citizen migrants then so too can they be re-imagined for their democratic inclusion. Part of the challenge, then, in reflecting upon citizenship through mobility lies in thinking about spatial strategies that promote different understandings of what citizenship can be about, and the different relationships between self and other that can be built on relational rather than hierarchical and exclusionary ontologies that pit 'insiders' against 'outsiders'. Inspired by such a perspective, several chapters in this collection explore how migrant forms of activism challenge the way we conceptualise the relationship between mobility, rights and status that are so fundamental to concepts of modern citizenship. These chapters explore the way non-citizen migrants and migrant rights organisations and social movements use the issue of mobility and mobility rights to rearticulate new forms of citizen subjectivities. In the process they also inquire into the space and place in which citizenship is practised and investigate whether emerging forms of non-citizen migrant activism can offer new ways of thinking about space and subjectivities.

Overview of the book

Each of the chapters in this collection considers the themes of citizenship, migrant activism and the politics of movement in its own way. The first three chapters explore the way migrant activism in diverse contexts – France, the UK and Brazil – emerges in response to state-driven border and immigration controls. In Chapter 1 Alina Sajed examines the constraints that acts of securitisation place on migrant activism among immigrant Muslim communities. To demonstrate these constraints, Sajed looks at North African Muslim communities within France, who find themselves at the intersection of various transnational links, such as those of migrant labour, postcolonial (in)difference, the global politics of knowledge, and shifts in citizenship. The chapter explores both the impact of securitisation on Muslim identities, and the tensions inherent in practices of migrant activism, as well as their implications for understanding mobile citizenship. Sajed takes her inspiration from Françoise Lionnet and Shu-mei Shih's conceptualisation of 'minor transnationalism', and investigates

Introduction 13

both the necessity for a new theoretical vocabulary in understanding transnational mobility and the need to explore the complex terrain of minority interactions in Western societies. Sajed emphasises the diversity of forms through which such activism can be enacted, including Islamic activism undertaken by migrants and 'second-generation' migrants, and the feminist activism taken on by North African women living in France.

In Chapter 2, Ruth Grove-White details changes in UK immigration and citizenship policy around the debate of 'earned citizenship' and the social responses generated by this shift. She analyses various migrant rights campaigns in the UK, including the Strangers into Citizens campaign in support of the regularisation of migrants, as well as the work of grass-roots human rights organisations such as the Migrant Rights Network, with which she is affiliated. Since the inclusive provisions of the 1948 British Nationality Act, UK citizenship policy has changed almost beyond recognition. The new 'earned citizenship' process makes naturalisation as a British citizen an increasingly selective and expensive process, rewarding those who can show they have 'British values'. In this chapter, Grove-White traces the emergence of 'earned citizenship' by focusing on the reworking of British values and asking about the nature and impact of their inclusion in citizenship law. Grove-White poses some critical questions to this form of citizenship, asking whose values and 'shared standards' this project represents, and how far the 'values-based' notion of citizenship effectively represents a continuation of more overtly racialised nationality policies of the past 60 years. She concludes that 'earned citizenship' is a project that is unlikely to result in the assimilation of diverse communities in the UK. Rather, it will likely generate friction and politicise a system of control that increasingly fails to accommodate difference or generate a sense of belonging among migrant communities.

Chapter 3, by Carolina Moulin, investigates the political mobilisation of Palestinian refugees in Brazil as reflective of the difficult dilemmas of a politics of non-citizenship in the context of South–South migrations. Once the refugees began to make rights claims on their host country, a process of constructing them as 'ungrateful subjects' took root. Moulin critically explores the politics of gratitude in this context of refugees, who are expected to be grateful to their hosts, and what happens when such communities refuse these terms.

Building on the first three chapters, Chapter 4, by Bridget Anderson, Nandita Sharma, and Cynthia Wright, outlines a detailed foundation for a call to a No Borders politics. The chapter makes a powerful argument for No Borders as a practical political project and draws our attention to the ways in which mobility acts as an analytic from which to conceptualise politics and political subjectivity differently. The authors propose the concept of the 'commons' – as opposed to territorially and nationally defined communities and private property regimes – as a way to orient a No Border politics. They begin with the paradox that as nation-states across the world enact ever more restrictive immigration policies, there exists, simultaneously, a large and growing international movement of people. They note that this paradox has led to a growing recognition of the ideological character of

14   *P. Nyers and K. Rygiel*

border controls: what is restricted is not migration per se but the rights and protections available to those who move across and into nationalised spaces. For these authors, such a situation calls into question the purposes served by the entire array of contemporary migration controls – the totality of which has made many migrants more vulnerable and their lives and livelihoods more precarious. This chapter examines the emergence of calls for No Borders and reflect on the politics of No Border social movements across North America and Europe.

The idea that migrant activism can be understood in terms of emergent forms of migrant citizenship 'from below' is explored in Chapter 5, where Estefanía Acién González outlines the experiences of the Spanish organisation Asociación Pro Derechos Humanos de Andalucía (APDHA), with which she is affiliated. The chapter focuses on the organisation's work with Nigerian women migrants, who work as sex workers in Andalusia in Southern Spain, and with those in transit in Morocco. González outlines the work that APDHA does in support of and in solidarity with migrants to further the rights of migrants. In particular, she looks at how APDHA approaches the reality of migration using ethnographic work through two lenses: assisting individuals in their migratory processes, and denouncing the human rights violations that affect them. The chapter provides a rich source of ethnographic information about the migratory experiences of Nigerian women to the South of Spain. Of particular importance is the focus in this chapter on the 'house-bar' that accommodates employment in sex work for Nigerian women and hospitality that services the larger Nigerian community working in the agricultural industry in Almería. Within the larger context of the themes of this book, the chapter raises questions as to whether we can conceptualise the 'house-bar' as a form of political activism of migrant women, given that the example demonstrates the agency of women migrants to navigate the situation they find themselves in as a result of borders and border controls. The site of the 'house-bar' also raises interesting questions about the potential of other locations beyond the state and city – those traditionally associated with citizenship – as a potentially emerging space in which women migrants enact themselves as citizens in spite of their disenfranchisement from the formal legal Spanish citizenship regime. The chapter also raises questions about many of the assumptions foundational to citizenship that are often dependent upon political engagement in a public sphere, raising awareness about the gendered nature of assumptions about space that often inform our notions of citizenship. Here, the 'house-bar' acts as a private but also quasi-public space for the Nigerian community for developing community and building integration of migrant communities.

In Chapter 6, Heather Johnson reflects similarly on quieter or smaller 'moments' of citizenship, activism and political voice but within the politics of asylum. Focusing on empirical research from camps in Tanzania and Morocco, and detention centres in Spain and Australia, Johnson works to understand how solidarities among and between migrants and citizens emerge to shape a politics of resistance within securitised and temporary moments of migration. Johnson is particularly interested in how these moments can speak across time and space to shape our knowledge of migration. The chapter explores questions around what

Introduction 15

is meant by activism, assumptions about the location of political agency in the political subjectivity of the citizen, and the quieter and more individual ways that political agency is exerted in everyday life by non-citizens but in ways that through the compilation of moments create fundamental change.

The final three chapters all take the city as a creative and important space of emergent forms of migrant citizenship 'from below'. These chapters examine creative forms of city politics in which migrants enact themselves as citizens and through which emergent forms of citizen subjectivities materialise. Chapter 7 by Jean McDonald and Chapter 8 by Vicki Squire and Jennifer Bagelman examine campaigns to build sanctuary cities that enable migrant rights to the city. In her chapter, Jean McDonald examines the work of the migrant justice organisation, No One Is Illegal–Toronto, with which she is affiliated, and its 'access without fear' campaign. She argues that the city is a strategic location for an emergent and active citizenship. McDonald examines how a campaign for 'access without fear' to local community and social services such as health care, education, emergency services, shelters, housing and food banks is conceptualised as a kind of 'regularisation from below' by migrant justice activists. This campaign works to address the everyday borders that arise as people living with precarious status try to access services and community supports. McDonald argues that by looking at internal borders, which arise in the realm of service provision, one can see how a challenge to these internal borders may also pose a challenge to processes of illegalisation, and thus to the production of migrant illegality itself. The political importance of the campaign to build a sanctuary city, she suggests, may very well lie in its challenge to how borders work to subordinate people within national borders rather than simply keeping people out.

Vicki Squire and Jennifer Bagelman's chapter explores the UK City of Sanctuary movement, which is characterised by emerging relations of mutuality within 'mobile enclaves', and asks about the potential of such campaigns to uncover shifting forms of political engagement through which sanctuary is dynamically constituted in anti-statist forms. In this chapter the authors argue that the concept and practice of sanctuary that we have inherited inscribes a strong division between those in need of care and those who are able to provide care – a division which maps relatively easily onto the inscribed divisions between the citizen and the migrant or refugee. Such an articulation of sanctuary, the authors argue, is important for questions of citizenship and mobility because it rests on the assumption that recipients seek sanctuary within fixed or enclosed sites, with those who 'receive' sanctuary conceived of as immobile and those who 'provide' sanctuary conceived of as able to move freely. This tendency to see mobility as split would seem to parallel that which informs statist understandings of citizenship regimes, in which there is a perceived division between those who are free to move and others who are denied such rights. In order to engage with questions around citizenship and mobility through an analysis of sanctuary, this chapter questions the statist assumption that sanctuary necessarily entails the practice of enclosure and a form of 'split mobility', while also developing some analytical tools for a re-thinking of sanctuary through mobility.

16   *P. Nyers and K. Rygiel*

Chapter 9 by Anne McNevin looks at forms of migrant citizenship 'from below' emerging from undocumented migrants, or 'undocumented citizens'. Focusing on three cases of undocumented migrant activism (student activism, worker cooperatives, and parent mobilisation in the school system) this chapter investigates contestations of citizenship made by undocumented migrants in Los Angeles. McNevin makes two claims about the contemporary dynamics of citizenship. She argues first that the city (as opposed to the nation-state) is the locus of new kinds of citizenship struggles, and second, that struggles far less ambitious than those asserting an unconditional claim to citizenship may nevertheless destabilise citizenship boundaries in subtle but significant ways. In making these claims, McNevin takes up the notion of 'citizenship in motion' with respect to migrant activism but also with respect to changing spatial scales of sovereignty, governance and political subjectivity in the context of globalisation. The chapter presents profound examples of how those without legal citizenship status can practise citizenship through 'acts of citizenship'. However, at the same time McNevin raises the question of whether forms of migrant agency might also produce subjectivities that choose to 'opt out' of citizenship or are at least ambivalent to the pursuit of citizenship as a desirable political project.

Bibliography

Andrijasevic, R. (2009) 'Sex on the Move: Gender, Subjectivity and Differential Inclusion' *Subjectivity* 29 (1): 389–406.

Andrijasevic, R. and B. Anderson (2009) 'Conflicts of Mobility: Migration, Labour and Political Subjectivities' *Subjectivity* 29 (1): 363–366.

Appadurai, A. (2001) 'Deep Democracy: Urban Governmentality and the Horizon of Politics' *Environment and Urbanization* 13 (2): 23–43.

Bigo, D. (2002) 'Security and Immigration: Towards a Critique of the Governmentality of Unease' *Alternatives: Global, Local, Political* 27 (1): 63–92.

Bosniak, L. (2008) *The Citizen and the Alien: Dilemmas of Contemporary Membership*, Princeton: Princeton University Press.

Dawson, A. (2004) 'Squatters, Space, and Belonging in the Underdeveloped City' *Social Text* 81 22 (4): 17–34.

Dauvergne, C. (2008) *Making People Illegal: What Globalization Means for Migration and Law*, Cambridge: Cambridge University Press.

De Genova, N. (2002) 'Migrant "Illegality" and Deportability in Everyday Life' *Annual Review of Anthropology* 31: 419–447.

Ellermann, A. (2010) 'Undocumented Migrants and Resistance in the Liberal State' *Politics & Society* 38 (3): 408–429.

Goldring, L., C. Berinstein and J. Bernhard (2009) 'Institutionalizing Precarious Immigration Status in Canada' *Citizenship Studies* 13 (3): 239–265.

Hannam, K., M. Sheller and J. Urry (2006) 'Editorial: Mobilities, Immobilities and Moorings' *Mobilities* 1 (1): 1–22.

Hardt, M. and A. Negri (2000) *Empire*, Cambridge: Harvard University Press.

Hindess, B. (2000) 'Citizenship in the International Management of Populations' *American Behavioural Scientist* 43 (9): 1486–1497.

Hindess, B. (2004) 'Citizenship for All' *Citizenship Studies* 8 (3): 305–315.

Introduction 17

Hyndman, J. (2004) 'The (Geo)politics of Mobility' in L.A. Staeheli, E. Kofman and L. Peake (eds) *Mapping Women, Making Politics: Feminist Perspectives on Political Geography*, New York and London: Routledge.

Isin, E.F. (2002) *Being Political: Genealogies of Citizenship*, Minneapolis: University of Minnesota Press.

Isin, E.F. (2009) 'Citizenship in Flux: The Figure of the Activist Citizen' *Subjectivity* 29: 367–388 [special issue: R. Andrijasevic and B. Anderson (eds) *Conflicts of Mobility: Migration, Labour and Political Subjectivities*].

Isin, E.F. and K. Rygiel (2007) 'Abject Extrality: Frontiers, Zones and Camps' in E. Dauphinee and C. Masters (eds) *The Logics of Biopower and the War on Terror: Living, Dying, Surviving*, Houndmills, Basingstoke: Palgrave.

Lahav, G. and V. Guiraudon (2000) 'Comparative Perspectives on Border Control: Away from the Border and Outside the State' in P. Andreas and T. Snyder (eds) *The Wall Around the West: State Borders and Immigration Controls in North America and Europe*, Lanham, MD: Rowman and Littlefield.

Lewis, M. (2006) 'Nothing Left to Lose? An Examination of the Dynamics and Recent History of Refugee Resistance and Protest', paper presented at the 4th annual Forced Migration Post-graduate Conference, University of East London, London, UK, 18–19 March.

Lyon, D. (ed.) (2003) *Surveillance as Social Sorting: Privacy, Risk and Digital Discrimination*, London and New York: Routledge.

Malkki, L. (1996) 'Speechless Emissaries: Refugees, Humanitarianism, and Dehistoricization' *Cultural Anthropology* 11 (3): 377–404.

Massey, D. (1994) *Space, Place and Gender*, Minneapolis: Polity Press.

Mau, S. (2010) 'Mobility Citizenship, Inequality, and the Liberal State' *International Political Sociology* 4 (4): 339–361.

Mezzadra, S. (2004a) 'Citizenship in Motion' *Makeworlds* paper no. 4, 4 April, available at www.makeworlds.org/node/110 (accessed 24 March 2010).

Mezzadra, S. (2004b) 'The Right to Escape' *Ephemera: Theory and Politics in Organization* 4 (3): 267–275.

Mezzadra, S. and B. Nielsen (2003) 'Né qui, né altrove – Migration, Detention, Desertion: A Dialogue' *borderlands e-journal* 2 (1), available at www.borderlands.net.au/ (accessed 13 April 2010).

Mitropoulos, A. and B. Neilson (2006) 'Exceptional Times, Non-governmental Spacings, and Impolitical Movements' *Vacarme* 34, available at www.vacarme.org/article484.html (accessed 12 April 2010).

McNevin, A. (2006) 'Political Belonging in a Neoliberal Era: The Struggle of the Sans-Papiers' *Citizenship Studies* 10 (2): 135–151.

McNevin, A. (2007) 'Irregular Migrants, Neoliberal Geographies and Spatial Frontiers of the "Political"' *Review of International Studies* 33: 655–674.

McNevin, A. (2011) *Contesting Citizenship: Irregular Migrants and New Frontiers of the Political*, New York: Columbia University Press.

Monforte, P. and P. Dufour (2011) 'Mobilizing in Borderline Citizenship Regimes: A Comparative Analysis of Undocumented Migrants' Collective Actions' *Politics & Society*: 1–30.

Moulin, C. and P. Nyers (2007) ' "We Live in the Country of UNHCR": Refugee Protests and Global Political Society' *International Political Sociology* 1 (4): 356–372.

Nyers, P. (2003) 'Abject Cosmopolitanism: The Politics of Protection in the Anti-Deportation Movement' *Third World Quarterly* 24 (6): 1069–1093.

18 *P. Nyers and K. Rygiel*

Nyers, P. (2006a) *Rethinking Refugees: Beyond States of Emergency*, New York: Routledge.

Nyers, P. (2006b) 'The Accidental Citizen: Acts of Sovereignty and (Un)making Citizenship' *Economy and Society* 35 (1): 22–41.

Nyers, P. (2008) 'No One Is Illegal between City and Nation' in E.F. Isin and G.M. Nielson (eds) *Acts of Citizenship*, London and New York: Zed Books.

Nyers, P. (2010) 'Irregular Forms of Citizenship' in V. Squire (ed.) *Contesting the Securitisation of Migration: Borderzones and Irregularity*, London: Routledge.

Padgham, O. (2005) 'Drawing Detention: A Conversation with No One Is Illegal' *Fuse Magazine* 28 (2): 15–19.

Papadopoulos, D., N. Stephenson and V. Tsianos (2008) *Escape Routes: Control and Subversion in the Twenty First Century*, London: Pluto Press.

Papadopoulos, D. and V. Tsianos (2007) 'How to Do Sovereignty Without People? The Subjectless Condition of Postliberal Power' *Boundary 2: International Journal of Literature and Culture*, 34 (1): 135–172.

Pojmann, W. (ed.) (2008) *Migration and Activism in Europe since 1945*, Houndmills: Palgrave Macmillan.

Rajaram, P.K. (2002) 'Humanitarianism and Representations of the Refugee' *Journal of Refugee Studies* 15(3): 247–264.

Rajaram, P.K. and C. Grundy-Warr (2007) *Borderscapes: Hidden Geographies and Politics at Territory's Edge*, Borderlines vol. 29, London and Minneapolis: University of Minnesota Press.

Rancière, J. (2004) 'Who Is the Subject of the Rights of Man?' *South Atlantic Quarterly* 103 (2/3): 297–310.

Rodriguez, N. (1996) 'The Battle for the Border: Notes on Autonomous Migration, Transnational Communities, and the State' *Social Justice* 23 (3): 21–37.

Rumford, C. (2006) 'Introduction: Theorizing Borders' *European Journal of Social Theory* 9 (2): 155–169.

Rygiel, K. (2010) *Globalizing Citizenship*, Vancouver: University of British Columbia Press.

Rygiel, K. (2011) 'Bordering Solidarities: Migrant Activism and the Politics of Movement and Camps at Calais' *Citizenship Studies* 15 (1): 1–19.

Rygiel, K. (2012) 'Mobile Citizens, Risky Subjects: Security Knowledge at the Border' in S. Ilcan (ed.) *Mobilities, Knowledge, and Social Justice*, Montreal and Kingston: McGill-Queen's University Press.

Salter, M. (2003) *Rights of Passage: The Passport in International Relations*, Boulder and London: Lynne Rienner.

Shachar, A. (2009) *The Birthright Lottery*, Cambridge, MA: Harvard University Press.

Soja, E. (1996) *Thirdspace: Journeys to Los Angeles and Other Real-and-Imagined Places*, Malden, MA: Blackwell.

Squire, V. (2009) *The Exclusionary Politics of Asylum: Migration, Minorities, Citizenship*, Basingstoke: Palgrave.

Squire, V. (2011) 'The Contested Politics of Mobility' in V. Squire (ed.) *The Contested Politics of Mobility: Borderzones and Irregularity*, London: Routledge.

Stevens, J. (2009) *States without Nations: Citizenship for Mortals*, New York: Columbia University Press.

Urry, J. (2007) *Mobilities*, London: Polity.

Walters, W. (2006) 'No Border: Games With(out) Frontiers' *Social Justice* 33 (1), 21–39.

Walters, W. (2008) 'Acts of Demonstration: Mapping the Territory of (Non)citizenship' in E.F. Isin and G.M. Nielson (eds) *Acts of Citizenship*, London and New York: Zed Books.

Watson, S. (2009) *The Securitisation of Humanitarian Migration: Digging Moats and Sinking Boats*, New York: Routledge.

Zolberg, A. (2002) 'Guarding the Gates' available at www.ncwschool.edu/icmec/guardingthegates.html

1 Securitised migrants and postcolonial (in)difference

The politics of activisms among North African migrants in France

Alina Sajed

In January 2005, French feminist activists congregated in Reims to celebrate the thirtieth anniversary of the Veil law (*loi Veil*), which decriminalised abortion in 1975. The demonstration was massive, colourful and dynamic, but it was marked by one significant incident. Alain Lipietz, a French economist and politician, currently a Member of the European Parliament for the Green Party, related on his blog how several weeks before the demonstration a group of headscarved Muslim women activists had visited the organisers to express their wish to join in (www.lipietz.net). The Muslim women wanted to wear arm bands in support of abortion and contraception. The organisers refused to put their names down and allow them to march with other women. The Muslim activists, nonetheless, did come to the event, and were placed at the very end of the demonstration 'behind the anarchists' (Lipietz 2005). This incident, seen as minor by many at that demonstration, carries enormous significance as it highlights the complex and ambivalent politics of activisms in France. It encapsulates the post/neo-colonial intersections between ideals and practices of French citizenship, civic and political activism, migration flows, racial politics, and gender dimensions. Lipietz mentions that the largely secular crowd welcomed Catholic activists showing their support of abortion policies, but not the veiled Muslim women. The incident is thus not about the discomforts of championing publicly one's religious identity in a 'hyper-secular society' (Khosrokhavar 2010: 232), but about the role of and space for the racialised *other*, whose visibility and stubborn *difference* disturbs cherished homogenous and universalist ideals of political community, belonging and citizenship.

This chapter examines activisms of North African (Maghrebian) Muslim communities in France, who find themselves at the intersection of various trans-national links, such as those of migrant labour, postcolonial (in)difference, the global politics of knowledge, and shifts in citizenship. I focus on two types of migrant activisms: one revolves around the creation of a Muslim diasporic identity through engagement in Islamic activist organisations, and the other focuses on North African women's activisms that attempt to navigate the ambivalent terrain of women's rights practices and Muslim identities in a secular society. Politically, such a comparative perspective would also provide a needed intervention into a discussion of Muslim identities by emphasising a plurality of

Securitised migrants 21

positions and identities. I argue that these various political expressions of migrant activisms are instances of minor transnationalisms emerging in an era of globalised flows (see JanMohamed and Lloyd 1990; Lionnet and Shih 2005).

By 'minor transnationalism' I mean the various 'micropractices' undertaken by minority and diasporic communities through which they negotiate and challenge the ambivalent boundaries of nation, citizenship and belonging (Lionnet and Shih 2005: 6–7). Such a conceptualisation of transnationality indicates the 'transversal' formations engendered by migrant mobilisations, whose projected sense of community and belonging draws on affiliations and loyalties that exceed the limits of the national. By going beyond the binary of dominant versus resistant identities, this chapter aims to illustrate the complicated and contradictory practices through which various minor transnationalisms (and their intersections) reconfigure the narrow confines of the citizen versus non-citizen binary. As Lionnet and Shih remark, '[w]e study the centre and the margin but rarely examine the relationships among different margins' (2005: 2). By focusing on women's mobilisations and Islamic activism, I seek to emphasise the mobile character of migrants' political engagement and the politics of movement that attend it. The examination of different (and sometimes conflicting) subject positions – such as secular or Muslim feminists, Islamic activists or de-colonial activists – entails both a movement towards the transnational (via larger feminist or Islamic networks), and a reconfiguration of citizenship. Such a dual focus allows for an understanding of citizenship as a set of multifaceted practices, which sometimes push at its rigid boundaries and sometimes reinforce them. The relationships between various transnational phenomena such as the securitisation of Muslim communities, Islamic activisms, women's mobilisations, flows of migration, and state-centric discourses of citizenship reconfigure the notion of citizenship in the Franco-Maghrebian borderland in unexpected ways.

Migrant mobilisations acquire here a double meaning: they point both to the migrants' political articulations of migratory experiences, but also to the migrants' engagements with transnational political movements. Such a double movement helps to destabilise the facile opposition between citizen and non-citizen, and serves to illustrate that citizenship is not a stable category with solidified boundaries. Rather, through an examination of migrants' experiences, a more ambivalent picture of citizenship emerges, which involves negotiation, accommodation, resistance, and transformation. The chapter begins by offering some background on the processes of the securitisation of Islam in France, and on how such processes impact migrant mobilisations and migrants' perceptions of identity and community. The practices securitising North African Muslim communities predate 9/11, and go back to the Algerian War of Independence (1954–1962) and to the Algerian civil war (1991–2004). In France, the terms 'Muslim' and 'immigrant' are almost synonymous (Cesari 1994, 1998, 2010a), which highlights both the visibility of the Muslim *other*, and the never-ending debate over the possibility of the *integration* of these groups within French society. This overlap explains why in Europe there is a tight link between immigration policies, securitisation measures and anti-terrorist legislations (Coolsaet

22   *A. Sajed*

2008; Pargeter 2008; Cesari 2008, 2010a; Khosrokhavar 2010). The marginalisation of North African migrants within French society, and the various securitisation policies implemented throughout the decades, cannot be understood outside of the (post)colonial project that has bound France to North Africa (particularly Algeria) in intimate and violent ways (Balibar 2004 and 2009). It is not surprising, then, that a number of significant acts of legislation adopted in 'postcolonial' France, which have attempted to tackle the Maghrebian 'issue' (whether pertaining to citizenship, anti-terrorist measures or violence in the *banlieues*), stem from French colonial laws (Cesari 1994: 12; Ezekiel 2008: 246).

Thus securitisation measures have profoundly altered the self-perceptions of North African Muslim migrants and reconfigured the possibilities of mobilisation, association and activism. Jocelyne Cesari has argued that Islamic activism has created new forms of citizenship among North African migrants by 'disentangling political and national identifications' and thus producing a *civil* practice of citizenship (meaning grass-roots local participation in social and political initiatives) rather than a *civic* one (entailing a recognition of and allegiance to public authorities and centralised universal political institutions) (2002: 43–44). The second part of this chapter thus looks at various Islamic organisations and their methods of mobilisation. The plethora of Muslim-based organisations active in France evinces deep transnational links that shape activists' notions of political community, belonging and citizenship. However, attention to gender brings into focus the underlying power relations and complicities that are crucial to grasping the complicated terrain of migrant activisms. In the last part of the chapter, an analysis of the headscarf debate becomes the basis for investigating the ambivalent and uneasy relationships between migrant women's rights activism and Muslim-based mobilisations. The spotlight on this link highlights both the possibilities and the limits of contesting the rigid boundaries of citizenship within the Franco-Maghrebian borderland (see Sajed 2010). Such a link is further complicated by the emergence of new types of migrant activisms that embrace the activists' status as *indigènes* (natives) of the (Post/Neo)Colonial Republic (*République Post/Neo/Coloniale*), and use it as a rallying cry for the actualisation of a decolonial politics. Theirs is a transnational political consciousness that draws on solidarities with other minor transnationalisms, thus de-legitimising the universality of the French republican model.

The securitisation of Islam in France: from 'ratonnades' to the 'war on terror'

Securitisation, as a concept associated with the Copenhagen School of Security Studies, has been defined as the removal of certain issues from the political sphere of democratic negotiation and contestation to that of security, away from public scrutiny (see Buzan *et al.* 1998). An issue is securitised when it is perceived to pose an existential threat to the survival of a society or community. Thus, the ongoing discussion in the literature on the securitisation of migration refers to the process whereby migration becomes a security issue, one that

Securitised migrants 23

threatens the very survival of political communities.[1] In the case of France, the securitisation of North African Muslim immigrants has been a politically controversial process that started after the Second World War. Even before the war, North African labourers had a significant presence in French society due to their status as French colonial subjects (see Blanchard and Bancel 1998). With the end of the Second World War, the number of North African labourers increased dramatically (ironically, especially after the independence of Algeria) due to a high demand for cheap (and disposable) labour needed for the reconstruction of French society. This post-war generation of North African labourers was largely a masculine migration from rural areas. Scholars indicate that this particular group of migrants was in a precarious position not only in terms of their living conditions (sordid shanty-towns known as *bidonvilles* on the peripheries of urban areas), but also because politically they inhabited an extremely marginal and fragile location. They were frequently targeted both by police raids and by racist attacks known as *ratonnades* (Noiriel 1996; Ben Jelloun 1997; Blanchard and Bancel 1998; Gastaut 2004).[2]

The securitisation of North African migration in France is inseparable from the anti-colonial struggle of the Algerians in the 1950s and 1960s, as France was waging an extremely violent war against Algerian independence movements. Perhaps one of the most memorable and bloodiest *ratonnades* in the history of North African migration in France occurred on 16–17 October 1961 and became known as the Paris Massacre of 1961. A pro-Algeria demonstration in Paris, organised by the Algerian Front for National Liberation and attended by thousands of migrants and French supporters, was violently repressed by the French police, leaving hundreds dead, most of them Algerian. Thousands of demonstrators, mostly from shanty-towns around Paris, and designated as 'Français musulmans d'Algérie' (French Algerian Muslims), were taken by the police to various locations, where they were beaten and violently assaulted. In his vivid account of this episode, historian Jean-Luc Einaudi (1991) describes the horror witnessed by members of medical teams, social services, and even by some police members as they looked on at the physical abuse of the demonstrators by the police. Einaudi suggests that this is one of the most dismal moments in the history of the Fifth French Republic. It is perhaps no small detail that the chief of police who ordered the violent repression against the Algerian migrants was Maurice Papon, former senior police official of the Vichy government. When in 1997 he was prosecuted by the French state, it was for his role in the Vichy government between 1942 and 1944, and not for the violent repression of a peaceful demonstration of North African migrants. The 'anti-Algerian pogrom', as it is called by Pierre Vidal-Naquet (quoted in Einaudi 1991: 330), was conveniently left aside.[3]

Between the 1950s and 1970s, there was a general feeling that the North African migrants would end up by being assimilated into French society, thus erasing their difference and embracing the homogenising lure of French citizenship. The laws on family regrouping (*regroupement familial*) adopted by Jacques Chirac in 1976, which allowed migrants to bring their families to France, officialised this sentiment. But the change effected to the Code of Nationality (*Code*

24   A. Sajed

de Nationalité) in 1993 (also known as the Pasqua Laws, named after the then Interior Minister, Charles Pasqua) attempted to reverse the immigration trend. In fact, Pasqua declared that the goal was for France to attain zero immigration. The Pasqua legislation stipulated that children born in France of foreign parents would no longer be automatically granted citizenship. This reversal of immigration policies had started much earlier, in the 1970s, when France was hit by oil-price shocks and therefore attempted to close its doors to migrants (see Doty 2003). It is now common knowledge that the 1993 reforms of the Code of Nationality specifically targeted North African and African migrants, that is, racialised populations from the former colonies of France. In the (post)colonial French context, the legacy of the Algerian War (and later on the spillover effects of the Algerian civil war) has amplified anti-Arab racism. More specifically, the term *immigré*, which in English is usually translated as 'migrant', encapsulates, in the French context, very specific racial and class connotations. Thus *immigré* actually designates individuals of North African background, Muslim, uneducated, and working as low-skilled labourers. Following Blanchard and Bancel (1998), Albert Memmi (2004) and Hafid Gafaiti (2003), I thus understand the term *immigré(e)* to designate not only a racial difference, but also a class difference in the constitution of North African migrants as a racialised social category (see Sajed 2010).

Thus the category of *immigré*, in this particular case, points to the location of the North African migrant as a racialised category, within a society whose imagination is haunted by its recent colonial past, and by its concurrent aspiration to a unitary and undisturbed national identity. Speaking about 'l'arabe' in France is inextricable from colonial history and memory, from postcolonial (in)difference, and from the ensuing rhetoric on immigration and security. As Albert Memmi insightfully suggests in *Portrait du décolonisé*, 'the North African migrant [*le Maghrébin*] is not a Russian or Romanian migrant, a stranger arrived there by chance, he is the illegitimate child [*le bâtard*] of the colonial affair, a living reproach or a permanent disillusion' (2004: 97).[4]

Historian Benjamin Stora remarks that the Algerian War represents a founding moment not only for the new modern French nation (see Ross 1995), but also for what he labels as 'Confederate Nationalism under a Republican Mask' (2006: 157). This 'confederate imaginary' emerges periodically in various guises and relies on the assumption that there is a clear and unambiguous incompatibility between Islam and French values as embodied in the national ideology of *laïcité* (French secularism). Jocelyne Cesari remarks that the 1993 reforms to the Code of Nationality were strangely reminiscent of colonial laws (1994: 12). The laws promulgated by Napoleon III in 1865 required Muslim subjects of French Algeria who desired *full citizenship* to give up the jurisdiction of Islamic law in terms of personal status and submit themselves fully to the jurisdiction of French law (Weil 2005 and 2008). The current ideal of French citizenship whereby the nation is one and indivisible, homogeneous and universalistic (meaning blind to differences) requires no less than the erasure of any signs of difference so that those visibly different can pose no danger to this idealised unity. Therefore, the

Securitised migrants 25

Pasqua laws can be read as 'the return of [the] colonial situation to the heart of the hexagon' (Cesari ibid.). It is not coincidental, then, that in 2005 when riots erupted in the *banlieues* (suburban estates) involving mainly French Muslims of North African descent, the first reaction of the French government was to dig up a 1955 state of emergency colonial law, which had been originally designed to repress the Algerian independence movement (Ezekiel 2008: 245).

This discussion thus aims to draw attention to the colonial provenance of current policies concerning the securitisation of migration in postcolonial France, and the securitisation of Muslim communities in particular. The spectre of Islam as an object of security in France was raised when Algeria was in the throes of civil war in the 1990s. When in 1991 the Islamist party (Front of Islamic Salvation, FIS) was set to win both parliamentary and local elections, the Algerian government cancelled the elections, arrested the leaders of the Islamist movements and instituted a state of emergency (International Crisis Group 2004). What followed was a violent civil war between governmental forces and Islamist groups, which took a heavy toll on civilians. Since Berber activists, Algerian intellectuals and journalists were among the main targets of Islamist groups, a significant number of Algerians took refuge in France. The spillover effects of the Algerian civil war in France became apparent when the GIA (*Groupe Islamique Armé*, Islamic Armed Group) extended its attacks to French soil in 1994 by hijacking an Air France flight, and in 1995 through a series of bombings and attempted bombings. The GIA used the marginalised spaces of the French *banlieues* as fertile ground for the recruitment of young Muslims who would wage war either on French or Algerian soil. Farhad Khosrokhavar notes that rampant marginalisation and poverty in the suburbs prompted a small number of youths to enrol in various jihadist networks (2010: 230). Khaled Kelkal, a young man of Algerian descent from the *banlieue* of Vaux-en-Velin outside Lyon, attained notoriety when he was hunted down and shot dead by French police because of his involvement in several GIA bombings in France in 1995. Similarly, Mourad Benchellali, taken to Guantanamo Bay in 2001, came from the suburbs of Lyon (Roy 2004: 146). These incidents created in France (and more generally in Europe) the perception of Islam as a dangerous doctrine fostering fundamentalism and violence, and of North African migrants as potential terrorists. The *banlieues* or suburban ghettoes have been seen as spaces of jihad, that is as fertile breeding-grounds of Muslim extremism (see Kepel 1991), even though the number of youths involved in extremist groups is very low.

The response of the French government to these incidents crystallised in the activation of security and anti-terrorist legislation known as 'Vigipirate'. Vigipirate constitutes France's national security alert system, and was put in place in 1978 by President Valéry Giscard d'Éstaing In 1995, after the GIA bombings in France, the Vigipirate system was activated, consisting of a 'plan of vigilance, surveillance, and the centralisation of information' drawing on the joint permanent participation of the army, the police and the *gendarmerie* (the French military police) (www. defense.gouv.fr/ema/forces_interarmees/missions_interieures/vigipirate/vigipirate). Thus, after 1995, the securitisation of Muslim communities increased as the

26   *A. Sajed*

government linked the issue of Muslim immigration more tightly to that of terrorism and violence. In 2001, after 9/11, the French government implemented the Law on Everyday Security, which strengthens police powers through an expansion of search and surveillance policies. Moreover, immigration legislation adopted in 2003 makes it easier for individuals to be deported if they are suspected of criminal activities or if they are seen as potential disruptors of public order, not to mention tougher sanctions on illegal immigration and the introduction of controversial data-gathering systems (Cesari 2010a: 21). This increased securitisation of the *banlieues* explains the siege mentality of many young people of Maghrebian descent, for whom the police have become an identifiable adversary and object of loathing (Cesari 1994: 167). Constant aggressive police intervention thus also creates mobilisation among North African migrants in France, whether in the form of Islamic organisations or civic associations, as is explored in the next section.

Globalised Islam? On the formation of a Muslim diasporic identity among North African migrants[5]

Since the early 1980s French society has been the scene of vigorous migrant activism, especially as initiated by the children of North African migrants. Their emerging political consciousness has attempted to break both with what they perceived to be the resignation of their parents to a life of discrimination and marginalisation, and with mainstream understandings of French citizenship, which seemed to find no place for different ways of being French. This young generation, also known as second generation or as *beurs* (slang for Arabs), mobilised around a strong anti-racist agenda, but also targeted the socio-economic marginalisation of migrants in terms of their housing conditions and lack of access to education and social services. This was a generation that was fed up with the 'immigration problem' rhetoric and desired to insert itself into the public and political sphere by becoming *visible*. North African youth were seen as symbols of the 'immigrant problem': young people agonising between the traditions of their parents and the modernity of French society, unable to accomplish a successful integration without erasing the former (Silverstein 2004: 26). The aim of the *beur* movements of the 1980s was to inscribe new ways of citizenship into the national imagination, which allowed *difference* to be accepted and recognised. The challenge posed by the postcolonial migration was thus to delink the hyphen between nation and citizenship in the French Republic.

The 1983 March for Equality and Against Racism (also known as *Marche des Beurs*), when thousands of young people from the *banlieues* and anti-racist activists marched from Marseilles to the Place de la République in Paris, stands out as one of the most memorable anti-racist mobilisations in France. The march was initiated in protest against a series of violent attacks against North African migrants perpetrated by police or by French citizens. In his controversial *French Hospitality*, Tahar Ben Jelloun (1997) makes an inventory of all those injured or killed by racist attacks in the decades of the 1970s and 1980s,

Securitised migrants 27

among them two North African children shot dead by a French neighbour (with a .22-calibre hunting rifle) who was irritated by the noise of their play. It was precisely this type of murderous attack that prompted the 1983 March. As Paul Silverstein remarks, '[t]he image of the .22 calibre rifle – serving as a token for the attack as a whole – became a recurrent trope in second-generation activist writing and political mobilisation that would respond to this anti-immigrant racism' (2004: 159). Several organisations were born of this march, the most famous perhaps being SOS Racisme. SOS Racisme initally embraced a rhetoric of the 'right to difference', which aimed to promote a multicultural and multiracial France where everyone belonged. *Beur* activists celebrated the arrival of a multicultural hybridised (*métissée*) identity (see Sebbar *et al.* 1988). However, the *beur* movement was also severely criticised for falling into the trap of rightwing rhetoric (à la Jean Marie Le Pen's National Front), who saw North African Muslim communities as essentially *different* and thus incompatible with French values. Moreover, some blamed the failure of the *beur* movement on its tooclose association with Marxist organisations, which had a deeply secular character, and therefore were not keen on accommodating religious identities. These associations with political parties also served to launch successful political careers for many of the leaders of the movement, who were now perceived as having been co-opted into the political mainstream (they were dubbed the new *beurgeoisie*).[6]

Several scholars point to the paradoxes of anti-racist discourses in France, especially as championed by groups such as SOS Racisme and France Plus.[7] First, the anti-racist discourse advocated by the *beur* movement did not challenge the hyper-secular nature of French society. On the contrary, by and large, the *beur* movement was a secular movement entrenched in an Enlightenment-inspired discourse of equality and human rights. Second, their discourse of cultural *difference* was later on co-opted by right-wing movements, who justified the further ghettoisation of Muslim migrants by employing the types of cultural essentialisms that had been used strategically by *beur* activists (Silverstein 2004: 173). In response to this manipulation, SOS Racisme dropped their 'right to difference' slogan and adopted instead the motto 'right to resemblance' (which for many critics translated into 'right to indifference'). What this change of tone meant was an intensification of the pressures to assimilate and thus an attempt to domesticate *difference* by making it non-threatening to the French republican model. Jocelyne Cesari remarks that the rage of the third generation, who started mobilising around ethnic and religious dimensions, is the expression of their frustration with being caught between their passive and submissive families, on the one side, and 'political institutions (such as unions, political parties, anti-racist associations) who, according to them, do not respond to their expectations and dissolve the *specificity of their 'here and now'* condition into general strategies they do not understand' (1994: 183; added emphasis). Farhad Khosrokhavar (2010: 244n11) goes even further and suggests that the increasing Islamic radicalisation of young North Africans during the 1990s and the first decade of the new millennium is a direct consequence of the failure of anti-racist discourses to

28   *A. Sajed*

break the link between Muslim/Arab/marginalisation/discrimination on the one side, and Frenchness/*laïcité*/homogenising practices of citizenship on the other.[8]

While mainstream French political discourse suggests that the increasing visibility of mosques, Islamic associations, Muslim cemeteries and prayer halls (not to mention headscarves) translates into radicalised Muslim communities inhabiting the *banlieues*, Cesari remarks that in fact such a visibility of religious signs indicates a different reality. She suggests that the increasing visibility of Islamic signs in the 1990s does not necessarily suggest increased radicalisation, but rather a resignation on the part of those newly arrived migrants to make France their home. Since they came to France as temporary migrants, the desire and the prospect of returning home to North Africa had always been on their social and emotional horizon. However, due to their precarious position both in their countries of origin and in France, their return plans did not materialise. Their 'symbolical investment in Islam ... appears as a way of recovering their lost unity and of compensating for the social consequences of the impossibility of their return' (Cesari 1994: 11). Therefore, the proliferation of mosques, Muslim cemeteries and prayer halls represents their attempt to build a home away from home, and their manner of socially integrating within larger French society (Cesari 1994 and 2002).

On the other hand, for the younger generations, a return to Islam and to a Muslim identity has had a different significance. For most of those who were born in the *banlieues* – spaces of social and political exclusion characterised by some researchers and activists as neocolonial theatres (see Cesari 1998; Silverstein 2004; Lapeyronnie 2005) – French citizenship translates into the marginalisation of difference, ghettoisation, and invisibility. As many have pointed out, this is a generation of rage (*haine*), no longer interested in the social contract of French citizenship (Cesari 1994: 16–17). This is also a generation that has understood and felt, better than anyone, the exclusivity of the French citizenship allegiance, and their reaction was a refusal of this allegiance. In both cases, the older and the younger generation's 'symbolic investment in Islam' gestures towards a specific tension within the politics of citizenship. The former's enactment of the right to stay and the latter's desire to escape disrupt visions of citizenship as static. Rather this tension appears to indicate that a politics of movement and mobility is inescapably linked to citizenship. Both generations understand their relationship with French citizenship and belonging in terms of their right to mobility. This particular minor transnationalism reconfigures citizenship as a process of accommodation and resistance that inevitably transforms idealised visions of 'how to be French' (see Weil 2008).

To understand the relationship between the formation of a diasporic Muslim identity and the marginalisation of North African migrants in France it is important to take into consideration certain transnational dimensions, which have significantly influenced not only the subject-formation of these young people, but also their relation to French citizenship. Undoubtedly one explanation for the religious radicalisation of certain Maghrebian youths is their rejection of and rebellion against Frenchness (Cesari 1998; Khosrokhavar 2010: 231). Since

France does not want them, they do not want it in return. No wonder that during a soccer game at the famous Stade de France, thousands of young *Maghrébins* whistled in protest as the national hymn of France, 'La Marseillaise', was being sung (Memmi 2004: 145; Sajed 2010: 372). Given that the ideal of French citizenship posits the *indivisibility* of the nation and a perfect overlap between nation and political community, the young North African Islamic activists imagine their community elsewhere, across and beyond the borders of the French nation. Their new political community is no longer the nation, but an imagined *umma* – a community without fixed or concrete borders, conjured into existence by the linked fates of Muslims around the world (see Mandaville 2001; Roy 2004; Khosrokhavar 2010).

The emergence of an imagined *umma*, or the 'neo-*umma*' as Khosrokhavar calls it, among young North African migrants in France is inseparable from the emergence of a pan-Islamic ideology, whose bases have been laid by Muslim scholars in the midst of anti-colonial and anti-European struggles in the nineteenth and twentieth centuries. The rise of a globalised Islamic ideology (Roy 2004) has been spearheaded by various transnational Islamic movements, whose scope of activities has ranged from an apolitical educational orientation (aiming to draw Muslims closer to a purer form of Islam), to radical, politically engaged, jihadist groups (targeting Western and anti-Islamic interests through violent means). In France, some Islamic groups are based on social activism and on a reformism that aims to make Islamic tenets compatible with modernity and secularism (Cesari 2002: 47). Organisations such as the Union of Islamic Organisations in France (UOIF) and French National Federation of Muslims (FNMF) accept the dominance of secular laws over religious ones (Khosrokhavar 2010: 241), and are most active through secular associations outside the mosques. Thus they focus on issues such as drug addiction, crime and unemployment. Moreover, with the increased securitisation of Muslim communities, associations such as UOIF and FNMF find it more efficient and prudent to channel their activities through secular grass-roots organisations in the *cités* (housing estates) away from the scrutiny and monitoring of the police and intelligence agencies. While they embrace an anti-Western and anti-imperialist rhetoric, they are also eager to de-link the perceived connections between Muslim activism and terrorism. Theirs is an activism which produces new forms of citizenship emphasising the *civil* dimension more than the *civic* one (Cesari 1994, 1998, 2002). The former implies recognition of the social spaces of the neighbourhood, the school and the suburban housing estate as the loci of action and transformation, by attempting to address long-standing issues such as delinquency, drug addiction and social alienation. The latter involves a primacy accorded to those political institutions (such as the unions, political parties, electoral processes), which claim a centralised and universal vocation as public spaces (Cesari 1998: 124).

Others become active in more puritanical and radical organisations, such as Tabligh wa Dawa (TD, Foi et Pratique, Faith and Practice). This type of activism tends to be more inward-looking, more ascetical and puritanical, claiming to draw people to a purer Islam and to a more pious and devoted life. Many disaffected North African youth from poorer districts are attracted towards this type of Islamic practice. This organisation, self-described as apolitical, focuses on drawing young people away from a life of crime to one of devotion and practice. The aim of their activities is to educate young Muslims to respect Islamic precepts and transform their lives through piety and devotion. Although disseminating a puritanical type of Muslim practice, organisations such as TD also adhere to a rhetoric of empowerment through education. These types of Islamic activism, as practised by UOIF, FNMF and TD, help produce new forms of French citizenship insofar as they emphasise both the religious dimension of the individual, and their active insertion in and participation within the larger society. Moreover, their main focus is on the type of education and instruction that produces both a good *Muslim* and a good *French citizen* without the two dimensions being contradictory. In this sense, they succeed in transcending the constrictions of the 'right to difference'/'right to resemblance' dichotomy that had subverted the *beur* movements of the 1980s. However, as the discussion on gender and race in the next section illustrates, this positioning does not come without its paradoxes and erasures.

The most radical type of Islamic activism is associated with salafist organisations. Salafism has been defined as the most radical type of pan-Islamism, an ideology that exalts the strict adherence to the *purity* of Islam as practised by the Prophet and his followers, uncompromised and untainted by Western ideas or principles or by any other type of innovation and interpretation. In France, this type of fundamentalism attracts young people who feel rejected by and disembedded from their social environment, and for whom such a total immersion in Islam expresses their radical rejection of Frenchness, or as Farhad Khosrokhavar puts it, their 'anti-Frenchness' (2010). What is interesting about such movements is that their ideology shares common elements both with Marxist/leftist movements (in their anti-Western and anti-imperial rhetoric) and with right-wing movements (in terms of their conservative social outlook, extolling patriarchal values and excluding any alternative interpretations of religious teachings).

The types of Islamic activism described above draw on profoundly modern and transnational pan-Islamic discourses. Their modernity is illustrated by their individualised understanding and interpretation of Islam, which translates into a voluntarist adoption and practice of Islamic tenets based solely on the individual's willingness to embrace them and unmediated by the traditional elucidation of Islamic clergy and scholars. The individual as the new locus of interpretation and practice represents a wholly modern technique of experiencing religion in a secular world, or, as Olivier Roy sees it, a post-modern 'triumph of the self' (2004: 38). This *privatisation* of religion is accompanied by its *deterritorialisation*, whereby Islam is no longer tied to ethnicity or locale, but is emancipated from the particularistic local traditions that had infused various Islamic practices throughout the world (see Roy 2004; Mandaville 2001 and 2007). To put it differently, the types of pan-Islamic ideologies mentioned above see Islam no longer as attached to a particular culture but rather as a global or translocal set of practices purged of superstitions, local traditions and rituals. For a group such as the young Maghrebian immigrants – considered an underclass in France and in Europe more generally (Cesari 2002; Khosrokhavar 2010) – the lure of a pan-Islamist community, the *umma*, promises the hope of belonging and recognition denied to them by French society. The imagined *umma* allows them to connect to other Muslims across the world and to invest themselves politically in global/transnational issues they find relevant for their transnational community, such as the fate of Muslims in Bosnia, Chechnya, Afghanistan, Iraq and Palestine. For them, these are the new contours of their imagined political community, not the rigid borders of the French nation-state, whose unyielding overlap between nation and state sees them as undesirable persons, quasi-citizens (inhabiting the limbo between belonging and exclusion). It is this transnational dimension – or what Paul Silverstein calls *transpolitics* – that reconfigures citizenship in the Franco-Maghrebian borderland. Following Balibar's theorisation of Europe as a borderland (2009), I understand the Franco-Maghrebian borderland to be constituted of overlapping (hi)stories of colonial violence, conquest, cultural exchanges, (post)colonial migratory flows and activisms. Thus the citizenship reconfigured by Islamic activisms in postcolonial France is a transnational one, which negotiates the strictures of *laïcité* in creative ways that render Muslim *others* as visible and complex social/political agents.

The politics of 'muslimwoman':[9] race, gender and activism in a hyper-secular context

As Jocelyne Cesari (1994: 180) and Étienne Balibar (1994) have remarked, the paradox of the equality envisioned by the French citizenship framework is that it has produced a generation of young people fed on a diet of 'equality' and 'social opportunities' who cannot find a space for their equality claims due to their status as 'illegitimate children of the colonial affair' (Memmi 2004: 97). However, when taking into consideration the gendered dimensions of migrant activisms in France, 'equality' becomes an even more fragile and contested ideal. To insert gender into a discussion on citizenship and activism is to expose, as Cathie Lloyd so aptly illustrated, the 'normative maleness' that infuses discourses and practices of citizenship (Llyod 1998 and 2003). In the French context, the norm of *fraternité* (brotherhood) from the famous '*liberté, égalité, fraternité*' slogan (much touted by various anti-racist and immigrant activist groups) imagines the legitimate political subject of citizenship as a male figure. As noted by many feminist scholars, the normative maleness of citizenship enforces a divide between public man, as an empowered political agent, and private woman, an unproductive individual tucked away within domesticity and always acted upon (see Pateman 1990). Although this divide has been contested by several generations of feminists, the intersection between race and gender complicates both feminist and anti-racist struggles.

Within French society, one recurrent image that seems to haunt not only the national imagination but also feminist discourses is that of the veiled Muslim woman. The veil has thus become not only a symbol of an essentialised

32   A. Sajed

Muslim femininity, but also a fetishised symbol of the French woman's desire to rescue the dignity of her othered sisters. Debates over the 'right' or 'wrong' character of the veil have been ongoing for the last couple of decades within France, and the overall dichotomy created is that between autonomy/freedom and oppression. Jane Freedman, in an analysis of the French headscarf debate (*l'affaire du foulard*), remarks that while some Muslim women adopt a more Western feminist point of view and reject the veil as oppressive, '[f]or others, the wearing of the headscarf is an autonomous decision, a key part of their identity' (2006: 184; see also Freedman 2007). In spite of its perceptive discussion on French Muslim women's subjectivity, Freedman's analysis glosses over a number of significant implications of the headscarf debate.

First, by exploring the issue of the headscarf within an autonomy-versus-oppression binary, many feminist analyses fail to see how the veil operates politically in various contexts. Although the veil stands for a particular vision of Muslim femininity, it is also fair to claim that it represents an epiphenomenal manifestation of certain socio-political configurations. Frantz Fanon's (1965) analysis of the political valences of the veil within colonial Algeria indicates a more complex reality. During colonialism, the veil had been not only a symbol of the patriarchal configuration of Algerian society, but also an interdict preventing European colonialists from penetrating the sacred sphere of the colonised family (Fanon 1965: 47). With the Algerian War, however, the veil became a means, an instrument (Fanon 1965: 63), which allowed Algerian women to conceal weapons and carry them unhindered through French security check-points. But the same women were quick to let go of their veils as soon as the anti-colonial strategy changed. Gillo Pontecorvo's *Battle of Algiers* explores the controversial issue of the *porteuses de bombes* (women bomb-carriers), who used European clothes and hairdos in order to slip by check-points unnoticed. Pontecorvo is careful to underline the blurred boundaries of autonomy and oppression, self-determination and dependence. His *porteuses de bombes* are undoubtedly strong women, but they are also fragile parts of complex networks of local patriarchies and of a rather masculine vision for national liberation.

Similarly, current French debates on the right/wrong character of the headscarf (which emerged in 1989, 1998 and 2004) reiterate, in a postcolonial/neocolonial setting, the complex intersections between women's agency, enduring patriarchal structures, racial hierarchies, and contesting visions of citizenship and belonging. Women activists of North African descent who supported the ban on the headscarf have been vehemently criticised by (Western) feminists for their endorsement of a discriminatory and illiberal policy. Freedman's article, for example, quotes Souad Benani, founding member of the Nanas-Beurs, who stated: 'To legitimise the wearing of the headscarf is to put under pressure those who are fighting for their emancipation and their liberty' (quoted in Freedman 2006: 184; also Freedman 2007: 40). Nanas-Beurs is a feminist organisation formed by second-generation Maghrebian women in 1985 who wanted to draw attention to the gendered dimensions of the immigrant experience. Their mission has been to make visible the specificity of migrant women's lived experience in

France, and to address the continuing marginalisation and discrimination of Maghrebian communities from a feminist perspective (Mélis 2003). More specifically, their activities and manifestos convey the message that anti-racist and feminist struggles should be inseparable. One of the problems indicated by associations such as Nanas-Beurs and Ni Putes Ni Soumises (NPNS, Neither Whores Nor Submissives) was that anti-racist mobilisations in France had produced gender-blind approaches based on universalistic claims to equality and *fraternité* (see Lloyd 1998: 71 and 2003). Such approaches obscured the gendered violence within migrant communities and rendered women's rights as secondary to anti-racist struggles. Thus, when Souad Benani endorsed the ban on the headscarf, something more complex is going on in her statement that cannot be reduced to her being a Westernised aggressive feminist and hence an 'inauthentic woman of colour' (Ezekiel 2008: 245). Both Nanas-Beurs and NPNS were founded as a reaction against several waves of violence against Maghrebian women in the *banlieues* perpetrated by Maghrebian men. After 17-year-old Sohane Benziane was burned alive by her former boyfriend in the Parisian *banlieue* of Vitry-sur-Seine in 2002, a March of Women (*Marche des Femmes*) happened in 2003 linking 23 towns (Fayard and Rocheron 2009: 1).[10]

These feminist or women's-rights-based mobilisations of Maghrebian women supported the ban on the headscarf, but highlighted that excluding veiled girls from school was not the answer. Their support was prompted by a concern with the rise of violence against women in the *banlieues*, but also with the impact of transnational Islamic activist networks on migrant women's social and economic status in France. To associations such as Nanas-Beurs, NPNS and Expressions Maghrébines au Féminin (EMAF), the headscarf was the symbol of Islamist violence during the Algerian civil war directed at unveiled women who were seen as impure and hence legitimate targets (see International Women's Human Rights Law Clinic and Women Living Under Muslim Laws 1999). It is not coincidental that the second headscarf debate happened just as Algeria was in the throes of a violent civil war, where women were among the main victims. Many of the women activists were recent Algerian migrants or of Algerian background, and thus fully aware of the betrayal of Algerian women's rights causes both by the postcolonial Algerian government and by Islamist groups. The competition between the Algerian government and Islamist forces resulted in the implementation in 1984 of a family code that significantly diminished women's rights pertaining to divorce and inheritance, which they had gained with the independence of Algeria (Lloyd 1998; Cesari 2010b). As Judith Ezekiel aptly suggests (2005: 232), a debate simply about the emancipatory or repressive character of the veil does not encompass the issues around the veiled girls in the French 'hijab story', who embody the intersection of various transnational processes such as women's right activism and various feminisms, Islamic transnational networks, anti-racist mobilisations, contested visions of citizenship and political agency.

As the incident presented in the introduction of this chapter suggests, the picture is yet even more complex. Pan-Islamic networks, Olivier Roy's globalised Islam, have created different political subjectivities for both men and

34   *A. Sajed*

women. French Muslim women who don the veil assign it various meanings: they can do it under the pressure of their families, but they can also choose the veil to avert their families' criticisms with regards to their respectability and thus to have access to education and public institutions. But they can also choose to wear the veil on account of a religiosity, whose tenets they themselves have interpreted and actualised, as explained in the previous section. To what category shall we assign veiled Muslim women who join a feminist demonstration in support of abortion and contraception? And what shall we make of the French feminists' refusal to include them? The incident indicates that what is at stake in the headscarf debate is not simply a collision between different visions of modern femininity, but between different political subject-positions and different visions of community and citizenship. For organisations such as Nanas-Beurs, NPNS, EFAM and others, citizenship means transcending racial and gender divides both by drawing attention to the racial discrimination and socio-economic marginalisation experienced by Maghrebian communities, and by highlighting the specificities of migrant women's lived experience. These activist groups do not reject the French republican model of citizenship. Rather they attempt to inflect it with the kind of gender and racial articulations that do not endanger its claims to universality. Perhaps this is why these organisations have been severely criticised for attempting to marry 'professed socialist and feminist ideas to a certain narrow idea of French republicanism and citizenship' (Kemp 2009: 21). Moreover, they seem to construct an ideal of the emancipated French woman who, very much like her male counterpart, can *only* be secular and unencumbered by traditions or community. The universal ideal of femininity posited by such organisations can be limiting and exclusionary.

Perhaps a more promising alternative stems from activist movements such as the Mouvement des Indigènes de la République (MIR, Movement of the Natives of the Republic), who champion their status as *indigènes* (which was the racialised term used by French colonisers to refer to subjected local populations, natives). On the website of their organisation, the slogan is 'Va t'faire intégrer' (Go integrate yourself), which is a play on the common curse 'Va t'en faire foutre' (Go f— yourself) (see www.indigenes-republique.fr). This is an uncompromising position vis-à-vis French citizenship, expressing a refusal to toe the line of French republicanism – a refusal performed neither in the style of Islamic activism (with its emphasis on patriarchal values and withdrawal into piety) nor in the manner of French feminist organisations (with their exclusive focus on secularism and 'liberation'). MIR is an umbrella movement which encompasses various organisations whose purported mission is to create an autonomous space for an anti-racist and decolonial politics. One of the participating feminist movements is Blédardes (again, a reference to colonial terminology)[11] who describe themselves as *'féministes indigènes'* (native feminists). This type of anti-colonial feminism is open in nature[12] and produces a type of political subjectivity that is antithetical to French republicanism and welcomes women and men who are committed to a decolonial politics, irrespective of their (secular and religious)

Securitised migrants 35

persuasions. More specifically, this emerging type of 'native feminism' or anti-colonial feminism adheres to an ethics of decolonisation, whereby the link between Islam and feminism is not a taboo issue nor a contradiction, but an opportunity to discuss and negotiate one's position as a woman and a Muslim. The discourse emerging from MIR activities, publications and manifestos poses a significant challenge to mainstream ideals of French citizenship through their complex analyses of and solidarity with other (post)colonial margins, whether in France or abroad. *Their* Republic is the *Postcolonial/Neocolonial* Republic (not the *French* Republic) whose history and imagination is in urgent need of decolonisation.

Towards a decolonial transnational citizenship

The type of citizenship emerging from MIR is a transnational one forged through an engagement both civil and civic. Recently, MIR announced the establishment of the Parti des Indigènes de la République (PIR, Party of the Natives of the Republic), which aims to represent the interests of the 'natives' of the Republic by paying tribute to their 'migrant parents and to [their] colonised and deported predecessors'.[13] Refusing to join traditional 'white' parties, PIR aims to create an autonomous space for decolonial struggle capable of influencing policies at national and transnational levels. MIR political engagement draws on anti-colonial and decolonial texts by Frantz Fanon, Malcolm X, Martin Luther King and others, and thus posits itself as a translocally engaged movement forging solidarity links with other minor transnationalisms such as the Palestinian cause, Black Power movements, Islamic activist networks, migrant activist groups such as the Sans-papiers, and others. Their activism attempts to transcend the false dilemma posed earlier (and concomitantly) by anti-racist, Islamic activist and women right's mobilisations between anti-sexism and anti-racism. However, as explained above, the types of migrant mobilisation championed by MIR, SOS Racisme, France Plus, NPNS, Nana-Beurs, UOIF, FNMF and others are circumscribed by the ideals of the French republican model (either by embracing it or resisting it).

Such mobilisations also represent responses to the crisis of the universal in France (see Cesari 1998: 93–95). The limits of the universal become painfully apparent when looked at from the prism of postcolonial migrations and their activisms. The false promises of universal citizenship – far from gesturing towards a welcoming political community eager to embrace difference – materialise into an 'official recolonisation' of postcolonial migrants whose difference must be either tamed and ultimately erased or securitised and ghettoised. This citizenship conundrum inevitably reconfigures the types of mobilisations that are possible within the Franco-Maghrebian borderland. This chapter's focus on the relationship between the various minor transnationalisms active in France exposes the limits but also the possibilities of migrant activisms. It also illustrates that relationships between the margins are themselves structured by power hierarchies and inequalities (Lionnet and Shih 2005). One of the

36   *A. Sajed*

major divisions between migrant activist movements in France is the pitting of political agendas of anti-sexism and anti-racism against each other. As some scholars and activists have remarked, this is a false choice – one that cannot possibly capture or justly address the complex historical conditions of the ongoing marginalisation and securitisation of Maghrebian Muslim communities in France. Therefore, the political activism of migrant movements such as MIR expresses a desire and an attempt to draw on solidarities within and beyond the borders of the French nation. By grounding their platform in their post/neo-colonial condition, such movements have developed a *transnational* political consciousness allowing them to insert themselves into a *translocal* politics, which promises to help them more effectively challenge the rigidity of French citizenship.

Notes

1 For in-depth analyses of the issue of the securitisation of migration in the EU see Huysmans (2000 and 2006) and Ceyhan and Tsoukala (2002).
2 *Ratonnade*, literally meaning 'rat hunting', is a racist expression used to describe violent attacks against North African migrants. 'Raton' (rat) was a racist term referring to Maghrebian migrants.
3 Einaudi was called upon by various civil parties to testify against Maurice Papon and to make public the latter's orchestration of the massacre (Einaudi 1991: 357). Later, Papon sued Einaudi for defamation, and lost the trial. It was Einaudi's testimony that brought this episode under public scrutiny at the end of the 1990s.
4 French sources quoted in this chapter are my own translations unless otherwise specified.
5 I use the term 'North African migrants' to refer more generally both to people born outside of France who migrated there, and to those born in France of migrant families. Within French society, those born of immigrant parents are themselves perceived as migrants (usually qualified as second or third generation migrants). Although there are differences among the experiences of these various groups, I choose to identify them as 'migrants' to underline their precarious position vis-à-vis practices of citizenship and belonging.
6 *Beurgeoisie* refers to those prominent leaders in the *beur* movement who, after active engagement in migrant activist organisations, moved on to become successful politicians, professionals and civil servants.
7 France Plus is an association established in 1984 by Maghrebian young people, fighting for the 'right to resemblance', meaning the right to integrate and civic rights.
8 The picture of Maghrebian migrant activism in France is further complicated if we add the types of activisms that coalesce around specific ethnic identities marginalised by 'mainstream' Maghrebian groups, such as the Berber movements. The Berbers see themselves as the indigenous people of North Africa with distinct linguistic and socio-cultural traditions. They have mobilised against the postcolonial nationalist projects in North Africa, which adhere to totalitarian nation-building policies by privileging 'Arabitude' and Islam, and marginalising and oppressing the multiplicity of the Maghreb (see Toumi 2002 and Silverstein 2004).
9 'The muslimwoman' is the title of an article by Miriam Cooke. For Cooke, 'muslimwoman' stands for the 'representative visibility' of Muslim women as symbols of Muslim *otherness* and gestures towards the 'erasure of [the] diversity' of their experience (2007).
10 NPNS, initially established as an anti-racist feminist organisation in 2002 by Fadela

Amara, has been severely criticised for becoming a mouthpiece for the French government. Critics point to how NPNS propagates the type of racial stereotypes of young Maghrebian men as violent and backward, which anti-racist organisations have struggled to dismantle. NPNS rose rapidly to national fame due to their innovative mix of anti-racism and feminism, and attracted a massive following, many of whom have since been disillusioned with the organisation's instrumental co-optation by the French government. Recently, Fadela Amara was appointed Secretary of State for Urban Policies in Sarkozy's conservative government. For a critique of NPNS as an ideological apparatus of mainstream French republicanism, see Marteau (2006) and Kemp (2009).

11 In North Africa (especially Algeria), *bled* is the 'native' village, but in French it has a connotation of isolation and backwardness.

12 Charactarisation of the Blédardes as 'open' needs to be qualified. The best-known voice and face of the Blédardes and of MIR is Houria Bouteldja whose public statements have attracted criticisms from the left and the right for endorsing anti-Semitism and Islamic extremist groups in the name of resistance. Moreover, certain feminists have accused Bouteldja of sacrificing the women's rights cause on the altar of Islamist resistance and anti-racism, thus positing a false choice between anti-sexism and anti-racism (see Ezekiel 2008: 246; Hamel and Delphy 2006).

13 www.indigenes-republique.fr/statique?id_article=189

Bibliography

Balibar, É. (2004) *We, the People of Europe? Reflections on Transnational Citizenship,* Princeton: Princeton University Press.

Balibar, É. (2009) 'Europe as borderland', *Environment and Planning D: Society and Space,* 27 (2): 190–215.

Ben Jelloun, T. (1997) *Hospitalité française: Racisme et immigration maghrébine,* Paris: Éditions du Seuil.

Blanchard, P. and N. Bancel (1998) *De l'indigène à l'immigré,* Paris: Gallimard.

Buzan, B., O. Waever and J. de Wilde (1998) *Security: A New Framework of Analysis,* Boulder: Lynne Rienner.

Cesari, J. (1994) *Être musulman en France: Associations, militants et mosquées,* Paris: Éditions Karthala et RÉMAM.

Cesari, J. (1998) *Musulmans et républicains: Les jeunes, l'islam et la France,* Bruxelles: Éditions Complexe.

Cesari, J. (2002) 'Islam in France: The shaping of a religious minority' in Y.Y. Haddad (ed.) *Muslims in the West: From Sojourners to Citizens,* Oxford: Oxford University Press, 36–51.

Cesari, J. (2008) 'Muslims in Europe and the risk of radicalism' in R. Coolsaet (ed.) *Jihadi Terrorism and the Radicalization Challenge in Europe,* Aldershot: Ashgate, 97–107.

Cesari, J. (2010a) 'Securitization of Islam in Europe' in J. Cesari (ed.) *Muslims in the West After 9/11: Religion, Politics, And Law,* London and New York: Routledge, 9–27.

Cesari, J. (2010b) '*Shari'a* and the future of secular Europe' in J. Cesari (ed.) *Muslims in the West After 9/11: Religion, Politics, and Law,* London and New York: Routledge, 145–175.

Cooke, M. (2007) 'The muslimwoman', *Contemporary Islam,* 1: 139–154.

Coolsaet, R. (ed.) (2008) *Jihadi Terrorism and the Radicalization Challenge in Europe,* Aldershot: Ashgate.

38   *A. Sajed*

Doty, R. (2003) *Anti-Immigrantism in Western Democracies: Statecraft, Desire, and the Politics of Exclusion*, London and New York: Routledge.

Einaudi, J.-L. (1991) *La bataille de Paris: 17 octobre 1961*, Paris: Éditions du Seuil.

Ezekiel, J. (2005) 'Magritte meets Maghreb: This is not a veil', *Australian Feminist Studies*, 20 (47): 231–243.

Ezekiel, J. (2008) 'French dressing: Race, gender, and the hijab story' in W. Pojmann (ed.) *Migration and Activism in Europe since 1945*, New York: Palgrave Macmillan, 233–249.

Fanon, F. (1965) 'Algeria unveiled' in *A Dying Colonialism*, New York: Grove Press.

Fayard, N. and Y. Rocheron (2009) '*Ni putes ni soumises*: A republican feminism from the *quartiers sensibles*', *Modern & Contemporary France*, 17 (1): 1–18.

Freedman, J. (2006) 'The headscarf debate: Muslim women in Europe and the "war on terror"' in K. Rygiel and K. Hunt (eds) *(En)Gendering the War on Terror: War Stories and Camouflaged Politics*, Aldershot: Ashgate, 169–190.

Freedman, J. (2007) 'Women, Islam and rights in Europe', *Review of International Studies*, 33 (1): 29–44.

Gafaiti, H. (2003) 'Nationalism, colonialism, and ethnic discourse in the construction of French identity' in T. Stovall and G. van den Abbeele (eds) *French Civilization and its Discontents: Nationalism, Colonialism, Race*, New York: Lexington Books, 189–212.

Gastaut, Y. (2004) 'Les bidonvilles, lieux d'exclusion et de marginalité en France durant les trente glorieuses', *Cahiers de la Méditéranée*, 69, available at http://cdlm.revues. org/index829.html#tocto1n4 (accessed 19 June 2010).

Government of France (2011) 'Interarmées', available at www.defense.gouv.fr/ema/forces_interarmees/missions_interieures/vigipirate/vigipirate (accessed 2 May 2011).

Hamel, C. and C. Delphy (2006) 'On vous a tant aimé-e-s! Entretien avec Houria Bouteldja', *Nouvelles Questions Féministes*, 25 (1): 128–129.

Huysmans, J. (2000) 'The European Union and the securitization of migration', *Journal of Common Market Studies*, 38: 751–77.

Huysmans, J. (2006) *The Politics of Insecurity: Fear, Migration, and Asylum in the EU*, London and New York: Routledge.

International Crisis Group (2004) 'Islamism, violence and reform in Algeria: Turning the page', *ICG Middle East Report* no. 29, Cairo/Brussels, available at www.crisisgroup. org/~/media/Files/Middle%20East%20North%20Africa/North%20Africa/Algeria/Islamism%20Violence%20and%20Reform%20in%20Algeria%20Turning%20the%20Page.ashx (accessed 22 June 2010).

International Women's Human Rights Law Clinic and Women Living Under Muslim Laws (1999) 'Shadow Report on Algeria Submitted to the Committee on the Elimination of Discrimination Against Women', available at www.wluml.org/sites/wluml.org/files/import/english/pubs/pdf/misc/shadow-report-algeria-eng.pdf (accessed 22 June 2010).

JanMohamed, A.R. and D. Lloyd (1990) 'Introduction: Toward a theory of minority discourse: What is to be done?' in A.R. JanMohamed and D. Lloyd (eds) *The Nature and Context of Minority Discourse*, New York and Oxford: Oxford University Press, 1–16.

Kemp, A. (2009) 'Marianne d'aujourd'hui? The figure of the *Beurette* in contemporary French feminist discourse', *Modern & Contemporary France*, 17 (1): 19–33.

Kepel, G. (1991) *Les banlieues de l' Islam: Naissance d'une religion en France*, Paris: Édition Points.

Khosrokhavar, F. (2010) 'Islamic radicalism in Europe' in J. Cesari (ed.) *Muslims in the*

West After 9/11: Religion, Politics, and Law, London and New York: Routledge, 229–244.

Lapeyronnie, D. (2005) 'La banlieue comme théâtre colonial ou la fracture coloniale dans les quartiers' in P. Blanchard, N. Bancel and S. Lemaire (eds) *La fracture coloniale: La société française au prisme de l'héritage colonial*, Paris: La Découverte, 213–222.

Lionnet, F. and S.-M. Shih (2005) 'Introduction: Thinking through the minor, transnationally' in F. Lionnet and S.-M. Shih (eds) *Minor Transnationalism*, Durham, NC: Duke University Press, 1–23.

Lipietz, A. (2005) 'Les Verts, loi Veil: un week-end difficile', available at http://lipietz. net/spip.php?page=blog&id_breve=35 (accessed 18 June 2010).

Lloyd, C. (1998) 'Rendez-vous manqués: Feminisms and anti-racisms in France', *Modern & Contemporary France*, 6 (1): 61–73.

Lloyd, C. (2003) 'Women migrants and political activism in France' in J. Andall (ed.) *Gender and Ethnicity in Contemporary Europe*, Oxford: Berg, 97–116.

Mandaville, P. (2001) *Transnational Muslim Politics: Reimagining the Umma*, London and New York: Routledge.

Mandaville, P. (2007) *Global Political Islam*, London and New York: Routledge.

Marteau, S. (2007) 'Ni putes ni soumises: Un appareil idéologique d'état', *Mouvements des Idées et des Luttes*, available at www.mouvements.info/Ni-Putes-Ni-Soumises-un-appareil.html (accessed 21 June 2010).

Mélis, C. (2003) 'Nanas Beurs, voix d'elles rebelles et voix de femmes: Des associations au carrefour des droits des femmes et d'une redéfinition de la citoyenneté', *Revue Européenne des Migrations Internationales*, 19 (1): 81–100.

Memmi, A. (2004) *Portrait du décolonisé arabo-musulman et de quelques autres*, Paris: Gallimard.

Noiriel, G. (1996) *The French Melting Pot: Immigration, Citizenship, and National Identity*, transl. G. de Laforcarde, Minneapolis: University of Minnesota Press.

Pargeter, A. (2008) *The New Frontiers of Jihad: Radical Islam in Europe*, London: I.B. Tauris.

Pateman, C. (1990) *The Disorder of Women: Democracy, Feminism, and Political Theory*, Stanford: Stanford University Press.

Ross, K. (1995) *Fast Cars, Clean Bodies: Decolonization and the Reordering of French Culture*, Cambridge, MA: MIT Press.

Roy, O. (2004) *Globalized Islam: The Search for a New Ummah*, New York: Columbia University Press.

Sajed, A. (2010) 'Postcolonial strangers in a cosmopolitan world: Hybridity and citizenship in the Franco-Maghrebian borderland', *Citizenship Studies*, 14 (4): 363–380.

Sebbar, L., A. Gaye and É. Favereau (1988) *Génération métisse*, Paris: Syros Alternatives.

Silverstein, P.A. (2004) *Algeria in France: Transpolitics, Race, and Nation*, Bloomington and Indianapolis: Indiana University Press.

Stora, B. (2006) 'The Algerian war in French memory: Vengeful memory's violence', transl. P.A. Silverstein, in U. Makdisi and P. Silverstein (eds) *Memory and Violence in the Middle East and North Africa*, Bloomington and Indianapolis: Indiana University Press, 151–174.

Toumi, A. (2002) *Maghreb Divers*, New York: Peter Lang.

Weil, P. (2008) *How to be French: Nationality in the Making Since 1789*, transl. C. Porter, Durham, NC: Duke University Press.

Online sources

Alain Lipietz' blog: www.lipietz.net
La Commission Islam & Laïcité: www.islamlaicite.org
Mouvement des Indigènes de la République: www.indigenes-republique.fr
Vigipirate (French Ministry of Defense): www.defense.gouv.fr/ema/forces_interarmees/
  missions_interieures/vigipirate/vigipirate

2 Claiming rights, asserting belonging

Contesting citizenship in the UK

Ruth Grove-White

Greater global mobility presents new and compelling challenges to the traditional model of citizenship, which is understood as a formal tie between individual and state, with specific rights and responsibilities attached. As a result, both politicians and scholars have given considerable attention to the exercise of citizens' rights and responsibilities in a more mobile world, the reworking of the notion of national communities, and the continued exclusion of groups from the attainment and practice of formal citizenship (Balibar 2002; Croucher 2004; Yuval-Davis *et al.* 2005).

The naturalisation of a growing number of non-citizens living outside their home country is a key area undergoing political change. Some scholars have considered the ways that states can open up naturalisation in order to better meet the needs and interests of a more mobile global population. Could increased migration widen the scope for new forms of transnational citizenships, extending political membership beyond state boundaries (Baubock 1994)? Perhaps states can most effectively respond to internal social diversity by making national citizenship more inclusive, with lower requirements for entry, and room for local, national, and international status (Soysal 1996). The recent acceptance of dual or multiple citizenships by some states, and the development of European citizenship within the European Union, have been described as 'beginning to dilute the particular formalisation [of citizenship and nationality] coming out of European history' (Sassen 2002a: 8). According to some scholars, this indicates a shift toward a more cosmopolitan approach by states in the future (Leitner and Ehrkamp 2006).

In contrast to this more optimistic reading, recent developments indicate that the dominant response within many liberal democracies has been to take a more restrictive approach to the attainment of formal citizenship by migrants. Controlling access to formal citizenship is viewed as a significant tool within the armory of state immigration control mechanisms. It not only impacts the inflow and stay of migrants but also social policy, determining the rights and responsibilities of those settled in the country. Citizenship is also increasingly becoming a symbolic status in the context of debates about national identity, with many national governments making efforts to re-nationalise citizenship and promote cohesive political and social communities.

42   R. Grove-White

Within this context, naturalisation in many states (such as Australia, Denmark and the Netherlands) is becoming a more difficult and highly charged process. The wider context is a shift to highly politicised calls for the integration of diverse communities, reflected in charged public debates, the rising popularity of the far right, and the implementation of prohibitive social policies, such as those emerging across Europe in relation to Islamic symbolism. Changes to the naturalisation process, which I will explore in relation to the development of 'earned citizenship' in the United Kingdom, increasingly frame citizenship as having to be 'earned' by a display of migrants' 'integration'. This thinking places the onus on migrants to adhere to state-determined criteria in order to attain the social belonging, political recognition and, in the words of Hannah Arendt (1968: 297), 'the right to have rights' associated with formal citizenship.

The recent developments in citizenship policy have demanded a focus on formal, legal citizenship status as the primary site of rights and entitlements. In particular, as the position of migrants in the UK has become increasingly precarious, the potential instrumental and symbolic importance of this status has grown. The distinction between 'us' (citizens) and 'them' (non-citizens) inherent to citizenship (Croucher 2004) is formalised in naturalisation criteria, which set the framework for attainment of access to full rights and entitlements. Tightening up citizenship requirements deliberately squeezes the space available to migrants to exercise their individual rights and interests, resulting in differential entitlements between migrants and citizens according to immigration status. The result is a splintering of rights, with some migrants – particularly those (including many temporary and undocumented migrants) for whom access to citizenship is often officially prohibited – rendered more vulnerable, more excluded and more disenfranchised than others.

State power to define, restrict and control the pathways to formal citizenship relies upon the subjects having little capacity for resistance, or for carving out shared alternative social and political agendas, which assert a different notion of identity and interests to that of the state narrative. Political and civic activity among non-citizens is increasingly viewed as presenting a challenge to this paradigm, described by some as a form of 'informal citizenship' (Sassen 2002b). As states attempt to consolidate their grip over the meaning of and access to formal citizenship, how far can non-citizens stake their own claims to rights and recognition using political activism and social engagement?

Over the past decade in the UK, the growth of dynamic political activity involving migrant communities has been marked by the launch of a number of new organisations which openly advocate the interests of migrants. Much of this work frames the issues in terms of the rights of non-citizens, drawing together individuals and groups across the boundaries of immigration status and nationality, and organising with a view to developing formal political influence and voice. In particular, reference within these activities to the underlying principles of universal human rights – defined and shared across international boundaries – has the potential to be significantly disruptive to the formal state citizenship agenda. By seeking to claim rights rather than to 'earn' them as the state demands, migrant advocacy increasingly demands political and public space by asserting rights that transcend state boundaries.

The observations in this chapter are drawn from my work as policy officer for the Migrants' Rights Network (MRN). MRN is a UK-based network of organisations working in support of migrants, whose work is framed in terms of a human rights approach to migration. In this chapter, I have chosen not to explore the work of MRN in any great detail, but rather to focus on observations about some of the groups we work with. In particular, I examine the Strangers into Citizens campaign organised by Citizens UK, and the wider advocacy work of migrant activists and groups working in support of migrants in the UK, which adopts the language and framework of a 'rights-based approach'.

'Earning citizenship' in the United Kingdom

During the Labour Party's 13 years in government in the UK, a reworking of the naturalisation process came to occupy a position of symbolic significance in national immigration policy. By the time Labour was voted out in May 2010, it was on the verge of introducing a new 'earned citizenship' system aimed at significantly tightening up access to British citizenship for foreign nationals. Although this policy was subsequently dropped by the new government, 'earned citizenship' represented a shift in political thinking about access to citizenship which continues to inform policymaking in this area in a substantial way.

When Labour came to power in 1997, it seems that it had no firm intention to make significant changes to the naturalisation process in the UK, or indeed to wider immigration policy (with the possible exception of the asylum system).[1] Historically, the legacy of the British Empire had led the UK to take what would now be considered a liberal approach toward citizenship. Until 1983, acquisition of citizenship was relatively attainable for most people within the Commonwealth, and no knowledge of the UK or the English language was required in order to do so. The majority of the UK's substantial ethnic minority populations from across Asia, the West Indies and Africa arrived in the country with the knowledge that they would likely be able to settle there with minimal fuss. This process was marked by a broadly tolerant multiculturalist response toward ethnic diversity, which Labour, whether by design or by accident, initially continued.

A series of developments around the turn of the twenty-first century, however, led the Labour Government to develop a more prescriptive approach toward immigration, ethnic diversity, and citizenship (Flynn 2003, Yuval-Davis *et al.* 2005). The 2001 race riots in the north of England, and the post-9/11 (and later 7/7) security agenda, led to rising political concern about the UK's ethnically diverse populations (Spencer 2007). Had successive governments been too casual about the way that diverse communities were coexisting? Were minority communities really fitting into the British way of life and sharing the same values, or should more be required from them to 'integrate'? A rejection of multiculturalism – seen as too laissez-faire – was pushed forward by the new Commission on Integration and Cohesion and, to some degree, by the Commission for Racial Equality.

44 R. Grove-White

Political preoccupation with the UK's ethnic and cultural diversity at this time was also fed by growing public anxiety over the steady rise in net immigration to the UK. Press coverage of asylum and immigration was increasingly hostile, feeding concerns about the level and impact of immigration in the country. Although many new arrivals did settle in the UK during the early 2000s, attaining British citizenship was clearly not a significant goal for all of them; 60 per cent of people eligible for citizenship in 2006, for example, had reportedly chosen not to apply for it, perhaps because they saw minimal benefits accruing from this status (Rutter *et al.* 2008). There was political suspicion that citizenship had diminishing meaning for newer arrivals as well as the settled population, and was not fulfilling its potential to act as a common link which could connect diverse communities (Kelly and Byrne 2007). Ministers moved toward viewing naturalisation as a milestone, at which point migrants could and should be expected to do more to demonstrate their willingness to fit in.

Labour's reworking of access to citizenship began in 2004, with the introduction of 'a new life in the UK' test, aimed at measuring applicant awareness of British history, politics, and customs. The test included an English language requirement for those applying for settlement and/or British citizenship. The following year, Labour launched a comprehensive immigration plan which outlined how immigration policy would be reworked with a view to increasing the benefits for the UK. Citizenship was at the heart of this strategy, with the aim of building 'among migrants and the settled population a stronger sense of social participation and shared values' (Home Office 2005: 24).

Identifying the 'shared values' and sense of Britishness to which migrants should be required to conform was a more difficult task. Ministerial uncertainty about what this actually meant in practice was indicated by the then chancellor Gordon Brown when he mused: 'if we are clear about what underlies our Britishness ... we can be far more ambitious in defining for our time the responsibilities of citizenship' (Brown 2006). The identification of core social principles and values which could be used as a benchmark for drawing together Britain's diverse communities turned out to be more elusive, perhaps, than politicians had hoped. This was reflected in, for example, the outcome of a *Daily Telegraph* 'Call Yourself British' campaign which was launched in 2007.[2] Building on public inputs, the newspaper came up with what it claimed were ten features of Britishness. However, the list included respect for the rule of law, personal freedom and private property – values that could be applied to virtually any Western democracy. Perhaps unhelpfully for the political project underway, one core 'British value' which many people could agree on was 'tolerance of difference'.

In 2008, a formal government enquiry into British citizenship laid out the steps that could be taken to foster 'active citizenship' among a general population which seemed increasingly politically and socially disengaged, with minority communities a key focus (Goldsmith Citizenship Enquiry 2008). In the same year, a government green paper titled 'The Path to Citizenship' was released, which laid out the terms of a new 'earned citizenship' proposal (Home Office 2008). It outlined the thinking behind a radical reworking of the naturalisation process in the UK planned for the future, and a redefinition of the underlying demands made of migrants seeking to attain citizenship under this system.

The idea that citizenship should be 'earned' appears to have been inspired by a new set of policy proposals developed by the Migration Policy Institute in the United States, which put forward the idea of an 'earned regularisation' in 2005 as an alternative approach for bringing undocumented migrants back into the system (Papademetriou 2005). However, the British government sought to extend this approach to *all* migrants wishing to settle or naturalise in the UK. As the name of the policy suggests, 'earned citizenship' descibed a more lengthy and difficult naturalisation process which would be introduced for migrants, requiring them to show a 'more visible and more substantial contribution' to the UK before they could become British citizens. The policy was framed as a new approach to accessing citizenship, requiring migrants to develop and demonstrate 'shared values' and 'join in with the British way of life' (Home Office 2008). The claim made was that the new system would bring about a stronger sense of national belonging and identity among those attaining formal citizenship by introducing a new set of costs and requirements for migrants.

In practical terms, the 'earned citizenship' proposal would make the naturalisation process significantly longer than under pre-existing regulations. A migrant from outside the European Union applying to become either a British citizens or a permanent resident would be required to spend an additional period of temporary residence in the UK as a 'probationary citizen'. For most migrants, including refugees, this would extend the UK's standard qualifying period for citizenship from the five-year minimum already in place to an eight-year period. Throughout probationary citizenship, migrants would not have access to non-contributory social welfare benefits such as housing and council-tax benefits and child tax credits – all benefits previously available to migrants after a minimum of four years in the UK if they attained indefinite leave to remain.

Reflecting the debate about integration and community cohesion, the 'earned citizenship' policy was underpinned by an emphasis on 'British values' and required migrants to 'contribute a bit extra' in order to earn citizenship. The only way that migrants would be able to shorten their period as probationary citizens would be to undertake regulated community volunteering, monitored by local authorities. This would be explicitly aimed at getting migrants to engage with people and causes outside of their own communities, with the government suggesting that this could include activities such as running local scout groups (UK Government 2009). Research carried out into this policy by charities suggests that migrants do spend substantial amounts of time volunteering, often but not always restricted to their local communities (Grove-White 2010). However, given the guidelines for the scheme and the high level of monitoring required by the government in order to operate it, it seemed very unlikely that casual or community-based volunteering would be included under the earned citizenship system. Further, the government made it clear that very few migrants, regardless of their circumstances (refugees, women, the disabled or the elderly), would be exempt from the volunteering dimension of earned citizenship (UK Government 2009).

46   *R. Grove-White*

Despite the fact that citizenship would be more difficult to attain, Labour hoped that a new earned citizenship system would increase its value for those who were eligible for citizenship but might previously have chosen not to apply for it. The new system would not leave migrants to 'languish in limbo', as they were said to do by the then home secretary Jacqui Smith (Home Office 2008), but instead would push eligible migrants towards applying for citizenship. This would be achieved by extending the time taken to attain settlement in the UK from four years up to a maximum of ten years – even longer than the time needed to progress to citizenship.

Following the release of the 'Path to Citizenship' green paper, a series of public consultations were launched by the Home Office during 2008–2009. However, there seemed to be little attempt to sample and include the perspectives of migrant communities on the fundamental issues of identity, values and belonging which had emerged as central to the policy, or to debate some burning questions about the underlying meanings and assumptions of these concepts. What is Britishness? Whose values were included and represented in the earned citizenship policy, one clearly built around a values agenda? Was the government looking for a two-way integration of migrants, or did it have a more coercive and assimilatory agenda? There were real questions about why this direction was being taken. The underlying logic that increasing the hurdles to citizenship would foster the 'shared values' claimed by the government seemed to be a backward way to approach the issue. Surely this project and its accompanying rhetoric, which had excluded migrants from its development and would place new burdens on them, would have the opposite effect: it would instead generate mistrust, insecurity and resentment among non-citizens.

Labour ministers followed this development with another announcement: a new 'points-based test' for citizenship would also be built into the earned citizenship framework after July 2011. This test would be used as a new barrier to vet potential citizens, including the possibility that migrants could be stalled from moving toward citizenship on the grounds of 'failure to integrate' or 'active disregard for UK values'. Labour Immigration Minister Phil Woolas agreed that acts that would lower a migrant's score could include participation in peaceful street demonstrations, as people keen to show their willingness to naturalise could be legitimately required to 'keep their heads down' before becoming citizens (Sparrow and Vikram 2009). This dimension of the policy framework seemed designed to inhibit migrants from claiming political rights or voice, echoing the distinction between citizens and non-citizens. In addition, it would further increase the uncertainty of the naturalisation process for those moving through it.

Attempts by civil society, including migrant organisations, to question the Government more closely about the implications of these proposals (Runnymede Trust 2008, Equality and Diversity Forum 2008 and Migrants' Rights Network 2008 and 2009) did not lead to substantial change in the design of 'earned citizenship', and the core elements of the policy were adopted into law under the Borders, Immigration and Citizenship Act (2009). However, it was not destined to come into force – at least not in the form envisaged by the Labour Government. Although it was announced that the system would become operational on or after July 2011, the change of government in May 2010 preceded its introduction. The new government, a coalition between the Conservative and Liberal Democrat parties, announced in November 2010 that 'earned citizenship' would be abandoned, describing it as 'too complicated and bureaucratic'. A new review of access to settlement and citizenship is currently underway in the UK, but there is no sign that the thinking around these issues will differ from the perspective underpinning 'earned citizenship'.

The legacy of Labour's 'earned citizenship' policy remains significant. It reflects how diversity has come to be viewed and accommodated by politicians in the UK, and shows the direction these beliefs may be moving in. Labour framed its perspective in terms of the meaning and practice of formal citizenship in the UK, and by reinforcing a hierarchy between migrants and citizens. Its approach rested on the idea that citizenship, and thereby the political and social rights associated with formal citizenship, should be earned by newcomers. This approach had significant implications for wider dimensions of migrant life in the UK, relating to the recognition of migrants by the state as part of local and national communities, their capacity to lead life in security, and their sense of belonging in the UK. It undermines the notion that rights can be claimed – instead, they are a prize for conformity and alignment with a national agenda.

Regularising status, earning citizenship

The reworking of access to formal citizenship has been contiguous in the UK with the emergence of competing claims to citizenship using the language of human rights, from within migrant communities and across wider civil society. Campaigns for the regularisation of undocumented migrants in the UK have emerged as a particularly prominent opposition to government policy. Their position has been of particular interest to scholars, in terms of the apparent contradiction they present to the formal model of citizenship. Officially, undocumented migrants have few rights. However, this does not mean that they have been without public or political voice, leading some to consider whether political claims-making or an identity as an (irregular) resident can be considered in itself to be the exercise of informal citizenship (Anderson 2008: 2010). Regularisation movements have also been considered as 'acts of citizenship' – a concept describing the moments in which people may seek to claim rights and responsibilities through identifying sites of struggle (Isin 2008).

Looking at the UK in particular, it is estimated that around 625,000 people living there are undocumented, and as such lack all formal status, rights or responsibilities (Gordon *et al.* 2009). Their presence within state policies is as 'illegal migrants' for whom life should be made as difficult as possible before their eventual removal from the country. In 1998, campaigners managed to win a time-limited regularisation programme for migrant domestic workers; the quiet, ongoing regularisation of certain undocumented migrants also takes place via the 14-year concession within the Immigration Rules. But campaigns for a wider

48 R. Grove-White

resolution to the status of undocumented migrants in the UK have not yet been successful in bringing about more far-reaching changes to their status and rights.

The most vocal regularisation campaign since 1998 has been the Strangers into Citizens campaign, led by the prominent community-organising body Citizens UK, which demands a 'pathway to citizenship' for undocumented migrants. Citizens UK, affiliated with the Industrial Areas Foundation in the United States, draws together people of different faith and community activist orientations, and different nationalities, around common goals. Although not migrant-led, it has managed to attract strong support among migrant communities, particularly through connections with the Catholic Church in the UK (Ivereigh 2009). Its activities are heavily informed by pragmatic as well as idealistic considerations, in order to increase the likelihood of campaign 'wins'.

The launch of Strangers into Citizens in 2006 built on the advocacy work of a number of civil society organisations in preceding years, in order to campaign for a regularisation of some of the UK's undocumented migrant population. Its main policy demand is for all irregular migrants who can demonstrate that they have been resident in the UK for a minimum of four years to be given a two-year temporary work permit in order to 'earn' their right to apply for British citizenship. A core component of the campaign message has been that this would be a one-off measure and, as such, would not be a 'pull factor' for future migrants seeking British citizenship, a common concern among policymakers. Interesting questions are raised by the campaign demand that migrants be given a chance to 'earn' their regular status. This again echoes the pragmatic approach toward regularisation outlined by the Migration Policy Institute in 2005. Calls to regularise undocumented migrants in the UK are likely to situate themselves within this framework in order to have the best chance of gaining political credibility and a resulting 'win'.

The campaign has sought to increase public support around its principle aim, building its work around an annual demonstration on May Day in London's Trafalgar Square. The public demonstrations in 2007 and 2009[3] attracted an estimated 10,000 people, and generated significant media and political exposure for the issue. Citizens UK leaders have also sought political support within London, with some degree of success. The emphasis the campaign places on the high proportion of undocumented migrants living in the capital has meant that political purchase has also been gained with the city's administration, through the endorsement of the Conservative mayor Boris Johnson and the Greater London Authority.

Political influence has also been sought at the national level, although responses have been varied. At the Liberal Democrat Party conference in September 2007, the party formally adopted a form of regularisation into its policy. This success has not been repeated with either Labour or the Conservative Party. In February 2009, an Early Day Motion was lodged, expressing 'support for the debate on regularisation', with specific mention of Strangers into Citizens. It was signed by 106 Members of Parliament from across the three main political parties.[4] The issue was also raised at a national-level Citizens Assembly held in May 2010, three days before the UK general election, where all three party leaders were publicly asked to support the policy. Although the event succeeded

Claiming rights, asserting belonging 49

in bringing attention to the issues and the campaign, no new political endorsements were secured.

The Strangers into Citizens campaign raises significant problems for government policies such as earned citizenship, which attempts to increase the hurdles people must overcome to attain formal citizenship. By demanding that formal citizenship be opened up for those with no legal status in the UK, the campaign brings a relatively hidden group of migrants, who currently fall outside of all possibilities of attaining citizenship, into the debate about access and entitlements. Formal citizenship is presented by the campaign as an instrumental status for migrants themselves, and its proponents stress the security and legitimacy that it could bring to people without regular status in the UK.

The campaign also presents access to formal citizenship as a question of morality. It claims that undocumented migrants *already are* a form of citizen, and that it would be wrong not to recognise this 'substantial sub-class of citizen' as such (Strangers into Citizens 2010). This echoes Sassen, for example, who considers that 'the practices of ... undocumented migrants are a form of citizenship practices and their identities as members of a community of residence assume some of the features of citizenship identities' (2002a: 13) According to these arguments, a regularisation of status would simply be a recognition of pre-existing rights.

Migrant mobilisation: a rights-based approach

A further broad and emergent challenge to the thinking behind the UK's state citizenship project is likely to be presented by the growth of wider migrant rights movements and activities in the UK. Moving on from the temporal concept of actions specifically concerned with attaining formal citizenship status, and specific 'acts of citizenship' – the discontinuous and potentially unintended enactment of political citizenship (Isin 2008) – there is scope to consider the significance of a wider emergent social activism around and within migrant and refugee communities. The significance of this work lies in its advocacy of the human rights of migrant communities in the UK, regardless of their formal citizenship or immigration status. This activity is likely to be particularly significant because it promotes the public engagement and political involvement of migrants in the UK – rights normally associated with formal legal citizenship.

Civil society action in support of migrants is, of course, not a new development. The UK has a well-established history of trade union activism, community organising, and advocacy for specific groups of migrants, in many ways building upon the solid foundations laid by the race equality movement which emerged in the 1970s and continues today. The basis of much race equality work in the language of civil rights located it upon different, and possibly firmer, footing compared to that of migrant and refugee advocacy work, which often finds itself battling against migrants' lack of formal or substantive entitlements. Work at the local, regional, and national levels in the UK ranges from providing community support and advice to campaigning and advocacy work. The latter kind of

50   *R. Grove-White*

campaigning has been particularly prominent in support of refugees in the UK, with charities such as the Refugee Council, Refugee Action and Asylum Aid all active in the field. The work of immigration lawyers, drawn together by groups such as the Immigration Law Practitioners Association and the Joint Council for the Welfare of Immigrants around the legal challenges to the position of migrants in the UK, has also contributed meaningful support to migrants in the UK.

However, although a wide range of effective advocacy work has been carried out in support of migrants and refugees in the UK, those organisations that do this work have not formed into a cohesive movement with a strong, national voice advocating for the rights of migrants, nor has such a movement been led by prominent actors from migrant communities. Some of the work developed in recent years is likely to address this, in terms of a new character and agenda for migrant community organising (Però 2008 and 2009). This is being reflected and adapted in areas across the UK by the recent emergence of a number of migrant-led, rights-based organisations, which hold the explicit aim of gaining political traction in the UK. Much of the work these groups do seeks to avoid drawing distinctions between migrants on the basis of national or ethnic background or immigration status, choosing instead to promote the shared experiences and values of migrant communities.

For example, Migrants' Rights Scotland (MRS), a migrant-led community network launched in early 2010, aims to bring migrant communities, trade unions, voluntary sector groups and others together in a coalition in support of migrants across Scotland. The MRS has an overtly political set of goals, aiming to 'work alongside migrants and their community organisations for a rights-based approach to migration, supporting their engagement in developing the policies and procedures which affect their lives in Scotland and the UK'. In spring 2010, MRS conducted a series of focus groups across Scotland to produce a migrant-led response to a Scottish government enquiry into immigration, leading to participation in an evidence-gathering session at the Scottish Parliament.

The development of new work also aims to address the lack of migrant presence and perspectives in media coverage about immigration. A new national-level organisation called Migrant Voice also launched in early 2010 aims to 'transform how migrants are seen and heard in the media: from passive, disempowered and marginalised victims, to makers of their own media content' (Migrant Voice 2010). The key activity of the group since its launch has been to produce a newspaper, also called *Migrant Voice*, a print and Web publication aiming to communicate the concerns of migrants via a series of articles by migrants and their supporters. Wider aims include increasing the skills and confidence of migrant community members to speak for themselves, and providing a platform for debate which acts as a counterbalance to negative media coverage about immigration in the UK. Migrants' Rights Network and others act to support this work; the focus on migrant rights is also a common thread across the work of community-based groups across the country, such as Migrants Supporting Migrants in the Northwest, the Migrant Rights Centre in Bristol, the Migrant and Refugee Communities Forum in West London, and the Wolverhampton-based Refugee and Migrant Centre.

Conclusion

It is early days for this work, and we are still far away from being able to talk about a consolidated migrants' rights movement. However, the adoption of a human rights discourse by groups advocating for the interests of migrants is significant. Most extensively developed and considered in the context of work in the development sphere, a rights-based approach is described by the Danish Council of Human Rights as

> a framework that integrates the norms, principles, standards and goals of the international human rights system into the plans and processes of development. It is characterised by methods and activities that link the human rights system and its inherent notion of power and struggle with development.
>
> (Kirkemann Boesen and Martin 2007: 9)

In this context, a rights-based approach has been used in order to define an alternative way to provide aid and development, which asserts the rights of the individuals and the obligations of the state toward them.

This approach has particular significance within the context of international immigration because migrants are so often excluded from the political, legal and cultural means of securing human rights that are reserved for citizens (Flynn 2006). Migrants' rights activism in the UK questions whether formal citizenship is a prerequisite for dynamic and political social action, or for the assertion of rights and alternative values. By exploring how interests, rights and social capital can be developed and exerted regardless of citizenship, this work stakes out new and significant ground.

In particular, the overt adoption of a human rights discourse and agenda in relation to the position of migrants and refugees in the UK is challenging. By substituting individual rights for collective values, the state has sought to close down the space of alternative claims to citizenship. But through work which re-emphasises the primacy of human rights and entitlements, perhaps it will be possible to identify a space for migrant interests within which social engagement, a sense of belonging, and a willingness to engage politically have the potential to introduce a new meaning to citizenship altogether.

Notes

1 Roche (2010).
2 See *Daily Telegraph* comment (2007).
3 No demonstration was held in 2008, and there were only small-scale actions in 2010 due to the impending general election.
4 Find the Early Day motion online at http://edmi.parliament.uk/EDMi/EDMDetails. aspx?EDMID=37768&SESSION=899.

52   R. Grove-White

Bibliography

Anderson, B. (2008) 'Illegal immigrant: Victim or villain?', *Working Paper No. 64*, Oxford, UK: ESRC Centre on Migration, Policy and Society, University of Oxford.

Arendt, H. (1968) 'The decline of the nation-state and the end of the rights of man' in *The Origins of Totalitarianism*, San Diego, New York and London: Harcourt Inc, 266–302.

Balibar, E. (2002) *Politics and the Other Scene*, New York: Verso.

Baubock, R. (1994) *Transnational Citizenship: Membership and Rights in International Migration*, Cheltenham, UK: Aldershot, Edward Elgar.

Brown, G. (2006) 'The future of Britishness', speech given on 14 January 2006, Imperial College, London, available at www.fabians.org.uk/events/speeches/the-future-of-britishness (accessed 2 May 2011).

Croucher, S.L. (2004) *Globalisation and Belonging: The Politics of Identity in a Changing World*, Lanham, MD: Rowman and Littlefield Publishers.

Daily Telegraph (2007) 'We must never forget to call ourselves British' [comment], 10 December, available at www.telegraph.co.uk/comment/3644609/We-must-never-forget-to-call-ourselves-British.html (accessed 2 May 2011).

Equality and Diversity Forum (2008) 'Response to "The Path to Citizenship": The next steps in reforming the immigration system', available at www.edf.org.uk/EDFpubs.php?action=fullnews&id=1001.

Flynn, D. (2003) *Tough as Old Boots? Asylum, Immigration and the Paradox of New Labour Policy*, London: Joint Council for the Welfare of Immigrants.

Flynn, D. (2006) *Migrant Voices, Migrant Rights: Can Migrant Community Organizations Change the Immigration Debate in Britain Today?* London: Barrow Cadbury Trust.

Goldsmith Citizenship Enquiry (2008) *Citizenship: Our Common Bond*, London: COI.

Gordon, I., K. Scanlon, T. Travers and C. Whitehead (2009) *Economic Impact on the London and UK Economy of an Earned Regularisation of Irregular Migrants to the UK*, London: London School of Economics.

Grove-White, R. (2010) *Engage to Change: Should Citizenship be Earned through Compulsory Volunteering? Migrant and Refugee Voices on Active Citizenship*, London: Migrant & Refugee Community Forum.

Home Office (2005) *Controlling our Borders: Making Migration Work for Britain: A Five Year Strategy for Asylum and Immigration*, London: COI.

Home Office (2008) *The Path to Citizenship: Next Steps in Reforming the Immigration System*, London: COI.

Isin, E.F. (2008) 'Theorizing acts of citizenship' in E.F. Isin and G. Nielsen (eds) *Acts of Citizenship*, New York: Zed Books Ltd.

Ivereigh, A. (2009) *Faithful Citizens: A Practical Guide to Catholic Social Teaching and Community Organising*, London: Darton Longman & Todd.

Kelly, R. and L. Byrne (2007) *A Common Place*, London: Fabian Society.

Kirkemann Boesen, J. and T. Martin (2007) *Applying a Rights-based Approach: An Inspirational Guide for Civil Society*, The Danish Institute for Human Rights, available at http://humanrights.inforce.dk/international (accessed 2 May 2011).

Leitner, H. and P. Ehrkamp (2006) 'Transnationalism and migrants' imaginings of citizenship', *Environment and Planning A*, 38: 1615–1632.

Migrants' Rights Network (2008) *The Path to Citizenship: Comments on the Home Office Green Paper*, briefing paper, available at www.migrantsrights.org.uk/downloads/briefingpapers/pathtocitizenship.pdf (accessed 2 May 2011).

Migrants' Rights Network (2009) *Citizenship Provisions in the Borders, Citizenship and*

Claiming rights, asserting belonging 53

Immigration Bill, briefing paper, available at www.migrantsrights.org.uk/downloads/briefingpapers/briefingpaper_on_citizenship.pdf (accessed 2 May 2011).

Migrant Rights Scotland (2011) 'Mission' and 'Aims', available at http://migrantsrightss-cotland.org.uk/#/about-us/4539496622 (accessed 2 May 2011).

Migrant Voice (2010) 'Welcome to Migrant Voice', 17 July, available at www.migrantvoice.org (accessed 2 May 2011).

Papademetriou, D.G. (2005) *The 'Regularization' Option in Managing Illegal Migration More Effectively: A Comparative Perspective*, Policy Brief no. 4, September 2005, Washington, DC: Migration Policy Institute.

Però, D. (2008) 'Political engagement of Latin Americans in the UK: Issues, strategies, and the public debate', *Focaal*, 2008 (51): 73–90.

Però, D. (2009) 'Migrants' mobilisation and anthropology: Reflections from the experience of Latin Americans in the United Kingdom' in D. Reed-Danahay and B.C. Brettell (eds), *Citizenship, Political Engagement and Belonging: Immigrants in Europe and the United States*, Chapel Hill, NC: Rutgers University Press.

Roche, B. (2010) 'Making the best of immense challenges' in T. Finch and D. Goodhart (eds) *Immigration Under Labour*, London: Institute for Public Policy Research.

Runnymede Trust (2008) written consultation response to *The Path to Citizenship: Next Steps in Reforming the Immigration System*, available at www.runnymedetrust.org/uploads/policyResponses/PathToCitizenship.pdf (accessed 2 May 2011).

Rutter, J., M. Latorre and D. Sriskandarajah (2008) *Beyond Naturalisation: Citizenship Policy in an Age of Super Mobility: A Research Report for the Lord Goldsmith Citizenship Review*, London: Institute for Public Policy Research.

Sassen, S. (2002a) 'The repositioning of citizenship: Emergent subjects and spaces for politics', *Berkeley Journal of Sociology*, 46: 4–24.

Sassen, S. (2002b) 'Towards post-national and denationalized citizenship' in E.F. Isin and B.S. Turner (eds) *Handbook of Citizenship Studies*, London: Sage, 277–291.

Soysal, Y.N. (1996) 'Changing citizenship in Europe: Remarks on post-national citizenship and the nation state' in D. Cesarani and M. Fulbrook (eds) *Citizenship, Nationality and Migration in Europe*, London: Routledge.

Sparrow, A. and D. Vikram (2009) 'Immigrants will have to "earn" citizenship, says Phil Woolas', *Guardian*, 3 August 2009, available at www.guardian.co.uk/uk/2009/aug/03/immigrations-citizenship-points-phil-woolas (accessed 2 May 2011).

Spencer, S. (2007) 'Immigration' in A. Seldon (ed.) *Blair's Britain 1997–2007*, Cambridge: Cambridge University Press.

Strangers into Citizens (2010) *Why Regularisation?* 27 July 2010, available at www.strangersintocitizens.org.uk/?page_id=9 (accessed 2 May 2011).

UK Government (2009) Document made available to the House to illustrate the government's emerging thinking on active citizenship, available at www.parliament.uk/deposits/depositedpapers/2009/DEP2009–0898.pdf (accessed 2 May 2011).

Yuval-Davis, N., F. Anthias and E. Kofman (2005) 'Secure borders and safe havens and the gendered politics of belonging: Beyond social cohesion', *Ethnic and Racial Studies*, 28 (3): 513.

3 Ungrateful subjects?

Refugee protests and the logic of gratitude[1]

Carolina Moulin

> We understand the challenges you face, but at the same time we want to give you a sound word of caution. Be careful not to come across as sounding ungrateful.
>
> UNHCR representative's speech in a seminar for refugees in South Africa,
> June 2006, quoted by Du Plooy (2006)

> We were good enough for them when their country was at war and they needed a place where they can have peace and protection and we are not good for them when the war in their country was over ... this shows their crass ingratitude to a country that has protected them, fed them and given their children a free education.
>
> Ghana's Interior Minister responding to protesting Liberian refugee women,
> March 2008, quoted by Sullivan and Chester (2008)

> Any deviation from the image of the passive grateful invited refugee was soon met with a swift return to devaluing representations of refugees as ungrateful, aggressive, demanding, draining and different. Thus Kosovars who refused to enter an inadequately heated army barracks were 'disgruntled' and 'unreasonable' and 'thumbing their noses' at 'frustrated officials'.
>
> Sharon Pickering (2001), in a review of the representations of refugees in
> Australian media coverage

These brief passages illustrate a common response to the presence of (certain) others in foreign territories. Usually, once incorporated (even if in tenuous and, more often than not, ambiguous ways) into host societies, refugees and migrants are expected to be grateful to their hosts. How is it possible that the refusal of certain terms of the (humanitarian) protection architecture, which is usually defined by sovereign authorities, elicits the response that these groups are 'ungrateful subjects'? How do refugee and migrant communities respond to such claims? This chapter investigates some of the normative assumptions that lie behind the expectation of gratitude from refugees and migrants by hosting societies. I argue that the justification underlying the expectation of gratitude is based primarily on a supposed tension between two fundamental rights: freedom and protection. I illustrate the paradoxes that stem from this complex normative relationship through a study of the ongoing protest of resettled Palestinian refugees in Brasilia, Brazil, who have camped outside the UNHCR office since May 2008.

In this chapter, I argue that from the standpoint of the sovereign authority (in this case represented by both the nation-state and international organisations), the granting of legal status poses a choice for refugees: either they may exercise liberty, or they may be included in the protective humanitarian scaffold. This means that, in order to be protected, refugees are expected to accept severe restrictions on their freedoms; if refugees want to be free, they can no longer be protected *as* refugees. The chapter further conveys that the tension between these two fundamental political values – freedom and protection – reflects an aporia of liberal (international) political theory, related to the process of the social construction of the refugee figure in the international system. This aporia is connected to the fact that the logic of gratitude is an intrinsic part of the international discourse on human mobility. Mobility is produced and framed in terms of the production and management of difference, always and routinely articulated in relation to concepts of citizenship. The refugee becomes a mobile referent, an 'other' upon which the idea of proper citizenship depends. Without refugees and the corrective mechanisms put in motion by the international refugee regime, citizenship would not have become the 'normal' model of belonging in contemporary democratic societies (Arendt 2004). If ungrateful citizens are usually read in terms of being active, demanding participants of their political communities, ungrateful refugees are produced as undeserving, unwelcomed others who are not entitled to climb the steps toward properly authorised citizenship status. In a sense, the ungrateful refugee is represented as the hidden antinomy and distorted image of the valiant citizen; the portrait of Dorian Gray, locked up in the attic of modern democracies.

This constitutive yet convoluted link between citizenship and refugeeness is made even more truncated in the context of peripheral societies. The thrust of modern citizenship in these communities has never been fully articulated in the fabric of social relationships (Santos 2002), nor has it acquired the status of a desirable and fulfilling juridical condition. In order to unpack these (dis)connections, this chapter builds on anthropological theories about the act of gift-giving and the concept of gratitude, showing how such moral actions are themselves embedded in social systems of symbolic exchange (Mauss 1967; Van Wees 1998), and in the international framework for the management of human mobility, notably in its bio-political form (Doty 2009; Pin-Fat and Edkins 2004). With this chapter I hope to contribute to a better theoretical understanding of the assumptions involved in the granting of protection to mobile groups and its relation to the premises of modern citizenship, especially in the context of South–South circulations.

The first part of the chapter briefly describes the arrival and reception of the resettled Palestinian refugees in Brazil, establishing the context so as to understand how and why the protest took place. The second part analyses the social construction of the refugee figure at the intersection of freedom and protection,

56 *C. Moulin*

as well as its linkage to the logic of gratitude, referring to the Palestinian protest for examples. The second part also articulates this more theoretical analysis with the specificities of the Brazilian case and indicates to what extent the confluence of global and local provides the structural basis upon which the management of 'forcibly displaced populations' is made possible. The third part concludes with some reflections on the criticisms levelled by the Palestinian refugees, and on the recurrent dilemmas derived from the hard choice they have to make between receiving humanitarian protection and exercising their freedoms.

Camped at UNHCR

> Criminals! No one will tell me what I have or not to do. I know what I want and I am incisive. If they do not like what I say in the open, or whether they do not like to see that I do not bend over [for] them, it is because you are playing with my life and with the life of my friends. It is because for you humanitarian work is another perverse war game. If as a refugee I have rights, tell me what they are. If I don't have any, also tell me. Be sincere at least once and tell me whether you are responsible or not for my situation as a refugee. If not, I can keep going my own way by myself, searching for another country that will host me, since I cannot return to my free Palestine.[2]

These are the words of protest of Hamdam Mahmoud Abu-Sitta,[3] a 65-year-old Palestinian refugee who was resettled in Brazil in September 2007. Around 100 Palestinian refugees arrived in the country as part of the Solidarity Resettlement Program established by Latin American countries in November 2004. The programme emerged from a larger review of the regional and legal framework for refugee protection that culminated with the signing of the Mexico Declaration and Plan of Action. The resettlement programme (sponsored largely by the Brazilian Government and UNHCR's representatives in Brazil) was developed in response to a perceived need to better coordinate and share the burden of assistance to forcibly displaced populations, giving particular emphasis to the situation of Colombians in border areas. The Mexico Declaration and Plan of Action can be read as an attempt, on the part of UNHCR regional officials and Latin American countries, to regain an active role in the resolution of humanitarian crises, with a special focus on the vulnerabilities of refugee groups (UNHCR 2004). Brazil's acceptance of the Palestinian refugees, within this context, represents an example of the current trend in Brazilian foreign policy to achieve a leading regional position in humanitarian affairs. Although this was not Brazil's first experience with refugee resettlement (in 2001–2002, the country received Afghan refugees, but the programme was not successful), one cannot doubt that these recent initiatives come from a more coherent regional framework as well as better and more involved coordination between government, civil society movements and international organisations.[4]

The Palestinian refugees were included in a special programme designed for a two-year period, in which UNCHR, civil society organisations and government agencies would be responsible for providing the necessary means for refugees' integration to Brazilian culture and society. The Palestinians were dispersed to different cities and were entitled to housing, medical care, a monthly financial stipend, and classes to teach them the language and culture. Unlike the majority of the refugee population living in Brazil, the Palestinians that arrived had had a long and conflictive relationship with the international mechanisms of humanitarian protection. Many of them fleeing the Israeli conflicts and, later on, the two Iraq wars had been accustomed to inhabiting the non-spaces of refugee camps for years. Having acquired an in-depth knowledge of the intricacies of the international architecture of humanitarian protection and despite being aware of the difficulties inherent within it, they arrived in Brazil with expectations of change.

> I am a refugee since 1967. I became a refugee when I was 19 years old, going to Iraq, fleeing the Israel–Palestine war. Then I went to Saudi Arabia, Libya, and returned to Iraq where I lived until the invasion. I had to run away and became, once again, a refugee in the border with Jordan at Rweished [refugee camps]. The camp belonged to the military. There was no housing, nothing. Just a piece of cloth, a little tent we lived in. We stayed four-and-a-half years in this camp.[5]
>
> (*Jornal Causa Operária* 2009)

It is in this context, and with this background, that the Palestinians arrived in Brazil. The story of hope turned, in a few months' time, into a conspicuous political battle with the national and international agencies responsible for their protection. In April 2008, three Palestinian refugees travelled over 1,000 kilometres to the federal capital, Brasilia, where they organised a sit-in protest in front of UNHCR headquarters. Lodged in plastic tents and sleeping on the sidewalks, the refugees stayed there for over a year waiting for their demands to be met. Other refugees joined the group, including women and children (Fernandes 2008). They complained about the lack of assistance received from the agencies in their hosting communities and the lack of dialogue with several organisations, notably UNHCR. Because of these issues, they decided to impose their daily presence and tried to garner the attention of the media and public to show the reality of refugees' lives in the country.

Besides setting up a camp outside the UNHCR's office, the protesting refugees organised weblogs on the Internet (with the help of individuals and groups in solidarity with their cause). Local newspapers and websites also started to take notice of their mobilisation. In these ways, the refugees were able to document their perceptions and demands, the deadlocks in the negotiation, the difficulties in talking to the agencies, their revolt against what they perceived as abuse and violence, and their appreciation of help received. One of the blogs authored by the protesters calls the group 'Refugees for Dignity', and declares that they are 'refugees of various wars. We were hosted by Brazil. So love and respect its people and its government. However, the United Nations are not giving us the proper care. We have special needs and immediate being neglected [*sic*]' (RD 2008).[6]

58   *C. Moulin*

While the refugees were clear about their self-definition, how UNHCR and civil society viewed them remained unclear, in part due to the lack of dialogue concerning the protest. Hamdam feared that the protesting refugees were seen as members of a group of unwanted people; Brazil, according to the National Committee for Refugees (CONARE),[7] 'was the only country willing to receive the Palestinians living in Rwesheid ... and the government is still committed to granting them juridical protection' (D'Andrade 2009).

From the beginning of the protest, the refugees claimed that their subsidies had been suspended and that UNHCR officials had not only refused to talk to them but also called the police on them on several occasions, and taken measures to prevent their situation from being exposed on local and national television networks. One of the videos posted on their blog shows an interview given by the protesters and by some supporting activists. The viewers are informed that the UNCHR was not available for comments. At a certain point, a police car appears. In another video, the UNHCR representative alleges that several offers had been made to the group, including the provision of medical assistance in Brasilia and the relocation to alternative cities, and that all proposals had been systematically rejected by the refugees (RD 23 September 2008).

In April 2009, the refugees were forcibly removed from the UNHCR office entrance by the police. As a result of the stalemate and in an attempt to put pressure on Brazilian diplomats to encourage negotiations, in May 2009 the protesting refugees moved the sit-in to the front entrance of Itamaraty Palace, the headquarters of the Brazilian Ministry of Foreign Affairs. The move brought more media attention; the refugees were interviewed by some international press agencies, and were promised a future meeting with CONARE officials. Several college students joined the protests and some documented the march (Interprensa 2009). Unable to continue the sit-in due to restraining orders issued by local authorities, the refugees are now wandering throughout Brazil's capital. Others have returned to their original cities of resettlement. Hamdam died in October 2009.

Refugees, freedom and the gift of protection

> I apologise for not having adapted. I had the dream of staying in Brazil. But now I have only two wishes: Go back to Palestine or to the refugee camp I used to live in. I hope the Brazilian Government hears us. I hope they will discuss with us our problem and that they will let one of these options take place. We are depressed and traumatised by the psychological torture we have suffered.
>
> (*Jornal Causa Operária* 2009)

One of the central elements of the Palestinian refugee protest is the tension elicited by the search for freedom and dignity on the one hand, and the granting and reception of humanitarian protection on the other. This tension is, in important respects, consequential to the locus of refugees in the international system of humanitarian protection, situated at the intersection of liberty and security. Refugees are, as aptly described by Haddad, a paradox of the modern international order, since they find themselves 'between sovereigns' (2003). Neither a national nor a foreigner, the refugee defines herself precisely by inhabiting this 'territory of strangement', located in between the inside and outside of states (Dillon 1999: 101). This process of strangement and the conversion of refugees into an absolute negative or condition of lack (Nyers 2006) transforms them into a political inadequacy which supposedly threatens both domestic and international orders. According to the 1951 UN Convention on Refugees, a refugee is

> a person who, owing to a well-founded fear of being persecuted on account of race, religion, nationality, membership of a particular social group, or political opinion, is outside the country of their nationality, and is unable to or, owing to such fear, is unwilling to avail him/herself of the protection of that country.
>
> (United Nations 1951: Article 1A)

It is the failure of the country of origin to provide individual security (because of violence committed by the state or by non-state agents) that justifies the search for protection in a foreign territory. The juridical (and political) liability the refugee represents is temporarily suspended at the moment that the hosting country grants legal status and obliges itself to restore, even if minimally, some sense of safety to the individual. However, the concession of legal protection by another state usually involves some sort of restriction to individual liberties, since refugees are commonly denied, for example, the right to political participation, freedom of organisation, and freedom of mobility and residence. One could argue that the international system of refugee protection mirrors an underlying liberal tradition where, for one to have security, one must abdicate certain liberties. This tradition suggests that freedom and security are contradictory principles, and that the modern state (or sovereignty) is the only institution that can mediate and balance these opposing values. In the specific case of refugees, security is equated with receiving juridical protection by a third country, and liberties tend to be restricted to their negative dimensions, that is, to the absence of external obstacles or limits to individual actions. More than that, the freedom granted to refugees is, above all, the freedom to be free from the fear of persecution and its consequent physical violence. Therefore, it is assumed that refugees must, given the lack of such barriers, be self-sufficient and, at some point, promise to be obedient and respectful of the rules established by the hosting country in exchange for these minimal liberties. Security is thus equated with economic autonomy (market-oriented freedoms) and political dependency.

Critical security studies have indicated, nonetheless, that there is nothing natural or necessary in the traditional argument of a trade-off between liberty and security (Neocleous 2008; Huysmans 2006). These studies show that both principles are reciprocally immanent and that, therefore, processes of securitisation (strategies routinely advanced in issues of migration) are built into the foundation of liberal democratic theory and practice. The perception that refugees, as a result of their mobility, have to choose one of these paths, indicates a choice by their sovereign counterparts that is both moral and political. The normative aspect behind the security–liberty equilibrium rationale tends to foster an understanding of the provision of humanitarian protection as a *gift* conceded by sovereign authorities to displaced groups. The gift exchange system thus evinced has a similar structure to the one given by the principle of international reciprocity (an ordering norm of inter-state relations), but that can be more appropriately understood as a stance of the *law of gratitude*.

In one of their first (and only) public responses to the refugee protest, CONARE officials declared that the sit-in was a demonstration of ingratitude toward the hospitality granted (D'Andrade 2009). If the refugees chose protection, they were expected to be grateful for it. If they chose liberty (and the political autonomy derived from it), they would no longer be refugees. The calculation that informs these two sets of expectation can be expressed in the following terms:

> protection + gratitude = refugee (humanitarian subject)
> liberty + autonomy = not refugee (political subject)

As Nyers (2006) highlights, this happens because liberty and autonomy lead to hope, and hope is not an emotion legitimately attributed to the refugee figure according to the international protection system. Hope is something possessed only prior to one's refugee identity, and that is lost in movement because of the individual's exclusion from the space or territory of state protection. 'Refugees are courageous citizens who, because of their words, actions, or thoughts, are forced out of their political identities (citizens) and communities (state). The refugee fear is thus a product of a prior bravery or courage' (Nyers 2006: 50).

Refugees, as stated in the UN Convention, are driven by fear, particularly by the fear of violent death – a condition that indicates their placement in a time and space outside of modern political communities. Fear, as the defining trait of the refugee, is both prior and extraneous to politics, and the depoliticisation it causes can only succeed because the principle of sovereignty (and its derived subject, the citizen), is regarded as the only method to 'keep that fear at bay' (Nyers 2006: 52). After all, as most conventional accounts of international relations state, fear is a reflection of the absence of laws and institutions, and has an enduring imprint on the recurring state of nature that supposedly characterises the modern international system. Members of an anarchical international society are, like the refugee, also driven by the fear of imminent death, and are therefore conditioned to behave in a way that guarantees their survival. The fear of states is the same fear that should inform the behaviour of refugees – once order is destabilised, subjective annihilation will follow suit. The dilemma refugees represent, nevertheless, is conveyed by the fact that their mere presence is a

Ungrateful subjects? 61

constant reminder to states that this order has already been, in fundamental ways, dismantled. Such reasoning has profound consequences for refugees, as they

> signify an emptiness, an incompleteness vis-à-vis the meaningful positive presence of political subjectivity that state citizenship provides. Without citizenship, refugees are denied not only political rights but also something more fundamental – *the capacity to speak politically and the expectation that they will be heard.*
>
> (Nyers 2006: 17; emphasis added)

The dilemma is clearly exemplified in the case of the protesting Palestinian refugees. By choosing freedom and autonomy instead of fear, and by opting for a position that is eminently political, the refugees are crossing the thin, blurred line that might lead to the loss of the gift of protection.

Sovereign authorities usually portray the recognition of the mobile presence of these groups – translated into the granting of some legal status, rights, or permanence – as a gratuitous and benevolent act. Such recognition is, in certain respects, an act of inclusion within the political community, even if tenuously, and an act to minimise the needs and suffering of not-so-distant others, even if only partially. Therefore, those who are the recipients of these benevolent actions are expected to be grateful and to somehow reciprocate the gift. What is lost in the logic of gratitude, however, is the fact that 'all forms of reciprocity in political life share a key feature: they deny, in effect, that a relation of power exists' (Van Wees 1998: 47). If, from an international relations perspective, the moral exchange of the encounter with the other represented by the refugee must generate some form of reciprocity and gratitude, from the standpoint of the mobile subjects, these forms of 'generosity' are always embedded in mechanisms of exploitation and abjection and, therefore, demand the enactment of forms of resistance. Refugees attempt to denounce and resist a reading of their narratives as either one of victimhood (making them objects of protection) or one of criminality (making them sources of insecurity). Their political intervention attests to the challenges facing refugees in their fight for liberty and security, these two supposedly irreconcilable gifts. The protesting refugees attempt to precisely question the hierarchies and moral subordination effected in the logic of protection as gift exchange. Additionally, they refuse the scaffold of gratitude as the expected reciprocal attitude and identity imposed on them. First they resist by conditioning the acceptance of protection, by requiring a condition of equality that is denied in the logic of gift-giving. They subvert the structure of international protection by disturbing the conventional identities attached to them that are reproduced in the logics of gift exchange and gratitude: they are neither victims, nor beggars. Second, they pose the dilemma of living as a refugee, and the consequences that stem from it, as one that involves duties and rights. Therefore, they call for dialogue and clear rules of procedure; they ask to know what is theirs by right and what is not, so that they can establish their courses of action and regain a certain amount of control over the course of their lives.

62   *C. Moulin*

This expectation of gratitude for the gift of protection granted by the sovereign authority, a protection reduced to the granting of a certain legal status, reflects a logic of moral exchange that has always been an integral part of mechanisms of social interaction. Aristotle, for instance, 'thought of the grateful attitude as demeaning: It puts its subject in glad acceptance of the debtor position – not a position noble natures gladly accept' (Roberts 2004: 58). For Aristotle, gratitude was not a virtue, nor something to be sought by those who endeavour to lead a good life. This understanding, as Roberts aptly remarks, seems at odds with our modern intuition regarding gratitude as something that is intrinsically connected to happiness and well-being. Gratitude, in modern Western philosophy, is usually regarded as a positive feeling connected to the need to create trust and solidarity among community members. However, the logic of gratitude also depends on important power relations and social hierarchies. Thomas Hobbes, for example, declared gratitude to be a law of nature, part of a set of qualities and dispositions acquired through reason and necessary for human beings to survive in the state of nature. For Hobbes, gratitude is necessary for achieving justice, and is derived from it. The fourth law of nature thus states that 'a man which receiveth Benefit from another of meer Grace, Endeavour that he which giveth it, have no reasonable cause to repent him of his good will' (Hobbes 2004: 105). But Hobbes also remarked that, even though human beings give voluntarily, the one who gives seeks his own good and shall be 'frustrated, there will be no beginning of benevolence, or trust; nor consequently of mutual help; nor of reconciliation of one man to another; and therefore they are to remain still in a condition of war' (Hobbes 2004: 105). According to Hobbes, gratitude is needed for the purpose of justice, but more than that, for the purpose of social order in the absence of the sovereign. These natural laws are necessary, nevertheless, even under the sovereign authority, because they reflect 'the qualities that dispose men to peace, and to obedience' (Hobbes 2004: 185). Gratitude reflects social hierarchies and places the one who receives into a subordinate position, where they are expected to obey the rules, natural or civil, as a form of reciprocity. Therefore, gratitude is necessary for ensuring that individuals will follow the norms, fulfil their duties, and thus 'gratitude joins force with the sentiment of rectitude' (Gouldner 1960: 176 quoted by Van Wees 1998: 17). It is right and righteous to feel grateful for what one receives as a benefit from others.

Marcel Mauss, in his essay on *The Gift*, also highlights the inequalities intrinsic to the gift exchange logic, and defines it as:

> prestations[8] which are in theory voluntary, disinterested, and spontaneous, but are in fact obligatory and interested. The form usually taken is that of the gift generously offered; but the accompanying behaviour is formal pretense and deception, while the transaction itself is based on obligation and economic self-interest.
>
> (Mauss 1967: 1)

Such definitions that focus on the self-interested nature of gift-giving might not necessarily hold true for day-to-day experiences of exchange among certain

Ungrateful subjects? 63

groups.[9] Nonetheless, they demonstrate the normative structure of the moral altercation that is fostered through a reading of the granting of refugee protection as a gift by the nation-state and the consequent expectations of gratitude and reciprocity on the part of those who are subjected to it. First, the granting of the refugee gift reproduces a system of hierarchies in which refugees are placed in a condition of subordination and dependency. As Van Wees states,

> the one who benefits from another's generosity in reciprocal exchange is placed under an obligation until he repays, and this may entail a degree of actual subservience to the generous giver. Often, generosity is not meant to be repaid in kind at all, but to be reciprocated with long-term subordination to the benefactor.
>
> (Van Wees 1998: 41)

Second, gift-giving depends on forms of identity construction that are, in the case of political life, not only unidirectional – from the giver to the receiver – but also involve the delimitation of clear sets of expected behaviour on the part of the receiver. For example, they will accept and receive the gift unconditionally, they will submit themselves to the imposed interests of the giver, and they will be grateful for and eventually will reciprocate such benevolent action. 'It is clear that the presentation of a gift is an imposition of identity' (Schwartz 1967: 1–2). Insofar as an individual's position in society depends on how one presents oneself and how one is treated by others, the nature of gifts offered and received affects one's social status. Up to a point, 'you are what you give and what you get' (Van Wees 1998: 30).

Once these two requisites, submission and identity imposition, are upset, the logical conclusion that follows is that we are witnessing ingratitude. This seems to have happened in the case of the protesting refugees, for they disturbed the logic of the gift, by conditioning its receipt on the acceptance of their terms. The 'advantages' of the protection-gift are nevertheless routinely questioned by those subjected to it. In their interventions and interruptions, these individuals and groups subvert the international framework and contest these topologies by questioning the place of authority and by reclaiming their speaking position through demands and through a retelling of their living conditions under their own terms (and their own language modes).

Among a set of questions posed by visitors to the RD blog, one asked precisely why they did not accept what they had been offered so far. This kind of question strikes the same chord of the expectation of gratitude from refugees toward their hosts. When answering this question, a writer for the RD replied,

> We accept everything that is offered to us from the heart. If they offer us something out of interest that is not voluntary generosity, we refuse everything. If they offer us something because they want to shut us up, we yell. If they offer us something for us to be forgotten and abandoned silently, we shall move the world. Let justice be done: we respect those who respect us,

64   C. Moulin

help those who help us, our love and consideration are for those who give us love and heart. There are no differences. We are not victims, wretched, nor do we expect scraps. We have dignity. They can take our money, our clothes, our houses, our right to travel, they can even take our medical treatment. But they will never take our dignity from us.

(RD 18 October 2008)

The logic of gratitude is, in many important respects, an intrinsic part of the international discourse on human mobility, and of the international as a governmentality of difference in general. After all, both discourses attempt to establish the criteria and standards for managing difference (between citizens and non-citizens) and the terms upon which such difference is modulated, authorised, organised, received and processed by both receiving and sending countries. Even when circumstances involve policies that try to integrate mobile groups (as is the case of the Solidarity Resettlement Program), one can identify a persistent ambiguity that can only include the other on the basis of some form of exclusion or reclusion. These forms of exclusion usually impose certain restrictions to individual autonomy and liberty (for the sake of their supposed security and protection). Forms of reclusion work to contain the other's presence in spaces authorised by sovereign agents (camps, restrictions to mobility, restricted access to the city). This ambiguity results, in part, from the idea that legal protection, the granting of a territory of hospitality and the promotion of solidarity toward victimised others, must involve, to some extent, a form of gratitude. Gratitude is translated both in terms of the establishment of social hierarchies between givers and receivers and in the expectation of reciprocity.

If we have a situation of almost four thousand refugees in Brazil, we know that the majority of them is [*sic*] forsaken. They do not show themselves, they are subjected to a degrading *condition of dependence*. Even though we might have cases of success in life for some refugees, this is the condition that is demanded. *Nothing can be more exalted than an act of charity.*

(Frente Independente pela Autonomia dos Refugiados 22 November 2008;
emphasis added)

These expectations are not, however, a unique prerogative of refugees. After all, inter-state relations, especially with regards to issues of mobility and border control, have routinely been premised on the principle of reciprocity. The treatment granted to foreign nationals by one country should be reciprocated by others in relation to its own nationals.

This is the logic implied, for example, in justifications provided by the Brazilian Government regarding the current proposals for a general amnesty to non-status migrants in the country. As of February 2009, the House of Representatives approved a piece of legislation that would grant a general amnesty to all migrants who entered the country before 1 February 2009. According to President Luis Inacio Lula da Silva, the state 'can grant the right for people to

Ungrateful subjects? 65

remain in Brazil. This country here has a *lesson to give* the world about the treatment of migrants' (Folha 2009; emphasis added). Furthermore, the executive secretary of the Ministry of Justice and president of CONARE, Luiz Paulo Barreto, stated that the objective of the new amnesty was to 'legalise the situation of these people and *obtain in return the same reaction from countries that host Brazilian migrants*' (Giraldi 2008; emphasis added). The regularisation campaigns aim, on one hand, to improve Brazil's position in international forums as a model case for the management and protection of migrants' rights (despite the fact that the country has not signed the 1990 UN Convention on the Rights of Migrant Workers and their Families). On the other hand, it also limits the potential for social inclusion of migrants, as all amnesty campaigns – the most recent one took place in 1998, under Fernando Henrique Cardoso – limit themselves to the legal regularisation of migrants' permanence in the country, normally only on a temporary basis (two years with the possibility of renewal). Additionally, justifications provided by government authorities for the amnesties suggest that the legalisation of non-status migrants in the country should produce, as a result, a reciprocal attitude in relation to Brazilian nationals abroad. Gratitude, in this case, is not so much shown to the migrant community but to the political institutions and the sovereign authorities upon which their subjectivity and modes of political existence are dependent.

Mauss, when analysing the logic of gift exchange among the Maoris, highlighted the belief in the *hau*, a form of spiritual essence that belongs simultaneously to the things that are exchanged and the individuals who exchanged them. As such, the obligation of exchange and of returning the gift has to do with the fact that the *hau* granted in the gift has to somehow return to the original giver, because for the Maoris, 'to give something is to give a part of oneself ... one gives away what is in reality a part of one's nature and substance' (Mauss 1967: 10). Looking at the granting of protection, either through the concession of refugee status or through the regularisation of permanence, one can see how sovereignty prerogatives actually enact a logic of exchange as giving part of oneself. In a sense, this logic acknowledges that sovereignty moves along with the bodies of its citizens, and that to concede some form of juridical recognition to aliens, even if only partially, is in itself an act of inclusion, ascribing to that which is foreign some qualities that belong to the sovereign body, the polity. Therefore, the regulation of human mobility is perhaps the most salient example of sovereignty as bio-politics, as the control over life and over the bodies of those who incorporate the *hau* of sovereignty's essence, namely those forms of belonging usually ascribed in terms of citizenship. Therefore, the state gives, and expects in return that other sovereigns will recognise this benevolent action and reciprocate in relation to its own 'sovereign' parts. In a sense, the life of sovereignty accompanies the life of those who, no longer being territorially inscribed, live as a border and thus in their daily encounters put to the test the hold sovereign authorities have in term of fulfilling these reciprocity expectations.

66   *C. Moulin*

(Im)possible conclusions

> It is often said that security is the gift of the state; perhaps we ought to return the gift.
>
> (Neocleous 2008: 10)

This chapter has put forward some questions about the limits of democratic practice through an analysis of the abject situation lived by refugees in the context of South–South circulations. The conditions under which these groups find themselves have triggered a growing movement of political mobilisation and protest. One of the responses given by governmental and international authorities has been to add yet another label to the protesting refugees, that of 'ungrateful subjects'. More than a simply moral opinion, the claim of ingratitude, as advanced in the preceding pages, is part of a deeper grammar that connects individual rights and political order to assumed tension between freedom/autonomy and protection/security. One of the consequences of this mode of reasoning, along with fostering a subordinate position for refugees, is that it simplifies *ad absurdum* the dilemmas and difficulties faced by these groups in their daily lives by implying a reading of their narratives as either one of victimhood (and therefore of ingratitude) or one of criminality (and therefore of police and law enforcement). This simplification works to restrain the ability of these groups to convey their own understandings and narratives about the problems they face, and also hides the contextual aspects that are central to explaining how and why they came to be in such liminal conditions. These aspects involve, for example, the historical conditions that led to migration and submission to forms of exploitation, the imbalances in the relationship between countries and societies of origin and reception, and the reproduction of social, racial and cultural cleavages in the hosting community, and sometimes even within refugee/migrant groups.

Therefore, the protesting refugees' narrative has something to teach us about how these groups attempt to reposition themselves within the scaffold of (inter) national protection. They do so by contesting the priority granted to the 'authorised' voices of the state and international organisations as the sole institutions responsible for the course of their lives. They do so by reclaiming 'the right to have rights' (Arendt 2004), and by retaking the right to voice their own understanding of their living conditions. In a sense, these narratives show that there can be no protection without freedom, and that the granting of citizenship or the regularisation of juridical status is not enough to guarantee an effective implementation of these ideals. More than that, the collapse of freedom *from* fear as a prerogative for the resolution of insecurities (later on equated with the granting of protection) leaves unanswered the extent to which positive freedoms (freedoms *to*) are also inevitably a part of refugees' claim to inclusion. The dichotomous relationship between freedom and protection is disrupted when the interpretation of freedom is problematised beyond the more conventional discourse of a trade-off between forms of protection (evinced in claims of humanitarianism, solidarity and citizenship) and liberties (of choice, participation, membership and movement).[10] A conventional reading would suggest that in order to inhabit the 'inter', one has to choose between these two forms of being: either to be protected from the insecurities and violence of the international, or be free to live, in the terms of the protesting refugees, with dignity. Unpacking the resolution to this dilemma, mobile groups show that these two competing demands, freedom and protection, are always inextricably related. There is no freedom without some form of protection. And protection should not be interpreted as another technology of government, another mechanism of tutelage. In other words, there is nothing natural or obvious in the traditional claims that in order to feel safer one has to be less free, or vice versa. In fact, as Neocleous claims, the liberal project of freedom (embedded in humanitarian and human rights claims made to the international) is in itself also a project of security (2008). If this is so, we should not be surprised by refugee views that freedom and protection are two sides of the same coin, and fear and hope are hence contemporaneous emotions for most mobile groups.

But these are always ambiguous political performances. Our construction of these groups should not lead to a romanticised version of their political subjectivity (or of their fight for it). The undecidability of the foreigner (Honig 2001) is inextricably related to the undecidability of citizenship as a marker for the ability to claim access to rights and social resources, especially in the context of South–South displacement. This has to do with the context in which such claims are made, one where the translation of citizenship as status to citizenship as substance are, to say the least, an impossibility for a great part of the hosting community. The socio-economic marginality of mobile groups is not exclusive to them. One of the consequences of such contextual realities is to disturb the conventional narrative that the granting of juridical status is the central solution to the problems faced by these groups. In fact, the demand to receive 'preferential' treatment attests to the recognition of the peculiar situation of these groups, but also the latent inability of their supposed 'protectors' to transform such protection into a sustainable condition of living. In this case, a systematic refusal of citizenship should be seen as a contextual response in which alienage is used and exploited as a political tool that enables mobile groups to press for their demands not only within the local context but also within the larger framework of international and transnational relations. Caught in between the drive toward citizenship as a suitable discourse for equating freedom and protection, and the protective humanitarian one, these groups attest to the demise of both narratives as effective solutions to their demands.

Mobile subjects *qua* political subjects, refugees have their own agendas and interests, some of which are in strong disagreement with the perceptions of their own significant others (and even within their own groups). And assuming a political stance of responsibility over the course of their lives (and regaining control over their own international mobility) should also be premised on the fact that they, too, are responsible, even if partially, for their current situation. Therefore being political has nothing to do with judgements of value, whether theirs is a more benevolent, progressive or inclusive agenda. It has to do with the

68   C. Moulin

recognition that their demands and mechanisms of participation, despite being necessary and relevant, are also embedded in their own forms of discriminations and violence. To expect anything different would be to follow the modes of representation and participation, which have been at the root of their problems. In the words of Neocleous (2008), the protesting refugees are 'returning the gift' of security and protection to states and international organisations who are supposedly responsible for them.

The (im)possible solutions to these dilemmas depend, however, on our ability to listen to what these individuals and groups, under conditions of political abjection, have to say. And, because of that, I leave the concluding words to the protesting refugees:

> There isn't any advantage in being a refugee:
>
> It is extremely humiliating to be considered an 'effect of war' and to need everything.
>
> It is extremely humiliating to be helped and have people demand a reward for such beautiful humanitarian act[s] all the time (beauty found exactly when political issues are supplanted by humanitarian aspects).
>
> It is extremely humiliating not to be able to self-determination [sic] because we are seen throughout the world from the vantage point of systemic discriminatory policies.
>
> It is extremely humiliating not to be able to care for our families because they have been decimated or spread throughout the planet.
>
> It is extremely humiliating not to be able to be what we wanted to be or even to expect that one day that might occur.
>
> It is even less advantageous to be a Palestinian refugee. We do not even have the possibility to have the right to return to our land. When we came to Brazil, we did not come for tourism, we did not even come to take the house, health services or work from the Brazilian people. We came because UNHCR in Jordan fed our hopes: we watched a movie that told us that we would have here housing, work, health, that we would not suffer any persecution, as any other Brazilian. These hopes were not so that we could live with luxuries, nor to have any privileges. We do not dream to live in palaces in Europe, nor enjoy the 'American way of life', even less to make the Brazilian people our enemy, a people that has hosted us so well. We dream of a better life. If it is to misery that they want to condemn us once again, we do not accept. We do not admit being treated like rogues on the verge of death. ... To place us as the problem is to divert the focus of attention away from the truly responsible. We like the Brazilian people and government; our

problem is with the fact that we have been mistreated by some who should have dealt with us with more respect, that should have not treated us like pitied poor always thrown from one side to the other.

Why is it that always and only when some people in high official positions say something, it is considered to be true? Why don't they ask us directly? If anybody doesn't know what we want, it is simple: come to us and ask. Throughout these four months we have been in Brasília, anyone knows where to find us.

(RD 28 August 2008)

Notes

1 Many thanks to Will Coleman, Peter Nyers, Kim Rygiel and Naeem Innayatullah for their comments on earlier drafts of this chapter.

2 Quotes have been translated by the author from the original Portuguese, and were taken from the blog Refugiados em Busca da Dignidade (Refugees for Dignity, www.acampadosnoacnur.blogspot.com, hereafter referred to as RD) and the Frente Independente pela Autonomia dos Refugiados (Independent Front for the Autonomy of Refugees, www.autonomiadosrefugiados.blogspot.com). Dates are referenced according to the blog entry from which quotes were taken. The blog has been removed and transferred to a website in Arabic: http://blahdood.com/blahdod/index.php.

3 Hamdam died on 19 October 2009 of respiratory problems. He was the second of the 115 resettled Palestinian refugees to die in Brazil. This chapter is dedicated to him.

4 The Mexico Declaration and Plan of Action is the result of a series of meetings and events planned for the twentieth anniversary of the Cartagena Declaration (the regional instrument for refugee protection signed in 1984). Solidarity Resettlement is one of the pillars of the agreement, along with Solidarity Integration and Solidarity Borders. Preparatory meetings involved a large array of actors, and several sub-regional agreements were approved in the process. For a current evaluation of Latin American agreements on refugee protection see Lavanchy (2006).

5 Quotes are from an interview with the protesting refugees by *Jornal Causa Operária* published in June 2009, translated by the author. The full interview, in Portuguese, is available at www.pco.org.br/conoticias.

6 Original in English.

7 CONARE is a branch of the Ministry of Justice and is the governmental agency responsible for refugees in Brazil. Its mandate includes processing refugee cases and granting asylum, the coordination of assistance, and all legal and administrative affairs regarding refugees. It is both a decision-making and management agency in all refugee affairs.

8 The translator of Mauss's *Essai sur le don* to English, Ian Cunnison, chose to keep the word 'prestation' from the French because, according to him, 'there is no convenient English word to translate the French *prestation* so this word itself is used to mean any thing or series of things given freely or obligatorily as a gift or in exchange; and includes services, entertainments, etc., as well as material things' (Mauss 1967: xi).

9 There is an important critique of classic gift-giving approaches, especially levelled at the priority granted to exchange in their analysis. Some scholars have tried to reorient the analysis by focusing on the politics of care and on community bonds enabled by a non-individualistic understanding of the social role of gifts. Kuokkanen (2007),

70 *C. Moulin*

for example, demonstrates how some indigenous peoples' relationship with the gift is itself premised on notions of autonomy and of coexistence. The central problem with the gift-giving logic prevailing in the politics of protection and integration of mobile subjects relates also to the exchange assumption and the consequential expectation of particular modes of reciprocity and gratitude. Therefore, the challenge still requires movement away from a patriarchal and paternalist framework of exchange toward the practice of giving as 'sharing' and 'strategic partnerships' (Kuokkanen 2007: 22).

10 See Huysmans (2006) for a discussion on the linkage between liberty and security within the framework of the securitisation of migration.

Bibliography

Arendt, H. (2004 [1948]) 'The decline of the nation-state and the end of the rights of man' in H. Arendt, *The Origins of Totalitarianism*, New York: Schocken Books, 341–384.

D'Andrade, W. (2009) 'Frustrado, grupo de Palestinos quer ir embora do Brasil' [Frustrated, group of Palestinians want to leave Brazil], Agencia Estado, 16 January 2009, available at www.abril.com.br/noticias/brasil/frustrado-grupo-palestinos-quer-ir-embora-brasil-237006.shtml (accessed 9 February 2009).

Dillon, M. (1999) 'The scandal of the refugee: Some reflections on the "inter" of international relations and continental thought' in D. Campbell and M. Shapiro (eds) *Moral Spaces: Rethinking Ethics and World Politics*, Minneapolis: University of Minnesota Press.

Doty, R. (2009) *The Law Into their Own Hands: Immigration and the Politics of Exceptionalism*, Phoenix: University of Arizona Press.

Du Plooy, C. (2006) 'South Africa: Don't be ungrateful, refugees are told', *Pretoria News*, available at www.afrika.no/Detailed/12461.html (accessed 12 January 2009).

Fernandes, S. (2008) 'Refugees camped in Brasilia for ressetlement', *Folha de São Paulo*, 24 December 2008, available at www1.folha.uol.com.br/folha/mundo/ult94u482893.shtml (accessed 2 May 2010).

Folha de São Paulo (2009) 'Lula admite que governo vai apresentar projeto de anistia a imigrantes ilegais' [Lula admits that government will propose amnesty to illegal immigrants], 30 January, available at www1.folha.uol.com.br/folha/brasil/ult96u496527.shtml (accessed 8 February 2009).

Frente Independente pela Autonomia dos Refugiados [Independent Front for the Autonomy of Refugees], blog, available at http://autonomiadosrefugiados.blogspot.com/ (accessed February 2009).

Giraldi, R. (2008) 'Governo prepara anistia geral para estrangeiros ilegais que vivem no Brasil' [Government prepares general amnesty for illegal foreigners living in Brazil], available at www1.folha.uol.com.br/folha/brasil/ult96u466572.shtml (accessed 10 January 2009).

Gouldner, A.W. (1960) 'The norm of reciprocity: A preliminary statement', *American Sociological Review*, 25: 161–178.

Haddad, E. (2003) 'The refugee: The individual between sovereigns', *Global Society*, 17 (3): 297–322.

Hobbes, T. (2004 [1651]) *Leviathan*, Cambridge Texts in the History of Political Thought, ed. R. Tuck, Cambridge: Cambridge University Press.

Honig, B. (2001) *Democracy and the Foreigner*, Princeton: Princeton University Press.

Ungrateful subjects? 71

Huysmans, J. (2006) *The Politics of Insecurity: Fear, Migration and Asylum in the EU*, New York: Routledge.

Interprensa (2009) 'Refugiados Palestinos acampam no Itamaraty e recebem a solidariedade de brasileiros e turistas estrangeiros' [Palestinian Refugees camped at Itamaraty receive solidarity of Brazilians and foreign tourists], 10 June, available at http://somostodospalestinos.blogspot.com/2009/06/os-refugiados-em-brasilia.html (accessed 2 May 2011).

Jornal Causa Operária (2009) 'Palestinian refugees in Brazil' [interview], 7 June, available at www.pco.org.br/conoticias or http://somostodospalestinos.blogspot.com/2009/06/refugiados-palestinos-no-brasil-pelo.html (accessed 2 May 2011).

Kuokkanen, R. (2007) 'The politics of form and alternative autonomies: Indigenous women, subsistence economies and the gift paradigm', *Globalization Working Paper Series*, Hamilton, ON: Institute on Globalization and the Human Condition, McMaster University, available at http://globalization.mcmaster.ca/wps/Rauna.pdf (accessed March 2009).

Lavanchy, P. (2006) 'ACNUR e América Latina: Estratégias regionais e soluções aos problemas no continente' [UNHCR and Latin America: Regional strategies and solutions for problems in the continent], available at www.mj.gov.br/main.asp?Team={C728A416–5AA7–476D-B239-CC89FFB36301} (accessed 20 October 2009).

Mauss, M. (1967) *The Gift: Forms and Functions of Exchange in Archaic Societies*, transl. I. Cunnison, New York: Norton and Company.

Neocleous, M. (2008) *Critique of Security*, Edinburgh: Edinburgh University Press.

Nyers, P. (2006) *Rethinking Refugees: Beyond States of Emergency*, New York: Routledge.

Pickering, S. (2001) 'Common sense and original deviancy: News discourses and asylum seekers in Australia', *Journal of Refugee Studies*,14 (2): 169–186.

Pin-Fat, V. and J. Edkins (2004) 'Life, power, resistance' in V. Pin-Fat, J. Edkins and M. Shapiro (eds) *Sovereign Lives: Power in an Era of Globalisation*, New York: Routledge.

Refugiados em Busca da Dignidade [RD, Refugees for Dignity], blog, http://acampadosnoacnur.blogspot.com (accessed 16 December 2008).

Roberts, R.C. (2004) 'The blessings of gratitude: A conceptual analysis' in R.A. Emmons and M.E. McCullough (eds) *The Psychology of Gratitude*, 58–97, New York: Oxford University Press.

Santos, B. de S. (2002) *Towards a New Legal Common Sense: Law, Globalization, Emancipation*, London: Butterworths LexisNexis.

Schwartz, B. (1967) 'The social psychology of the gift', *The American Journal of Sociology*, 73 (1).

Silva, S. (2003) *Virgem/Mãe/Terra: Festas e tradições bolivianas na metrópole* [Virgin/Mother/Earth: Bolivian festivals and traditions in the metropolis], São Paulo: Hucitec/FAPESP.

Sullivan, M. and P. Chester (2008) 'Safeguard refugee rights in Ghana', available at www.afrikanieuws.nl/site/Safeguard_refugee_rights_in_Ghana/list_messages/16847 (accessed 22 April 2009).

UNHCR (2004) *Mexico Declaration and Plan of Action to Strengthen the International Protection of Refugees in Latin America*, November 2004, available at www.acnur.org/biblioteca/pdf/3453.pdf (accessed 6 April 2007).

United Nations (1951) *Convention Relating to the Status of Refugees*, 28 July 1951.

72 C. Moulin

United Nations, *Treaty Series*, vol. 189: 137, available at www.unhcr.org/refworld/docid/3be01b964.html (accessed 7 November 2008).

Van Wees, H. (1998) 'The law of gratitude: Reciprocity in anthropological theory' in C. Gill, N. Postlehwaite and R. Seaford (eds) *Reciprocity in Ancient Greece*, New York: Oxford University Press.

4 'We are all foreigners'

No Borders as a practical political project[1]

Bridget Anderson, Nandita Sharma and Cynthia Wright

> Only the battles which aren't even begun are lost at the start.
> Madjiguène Cissé, spokesperson for the Sans-papiers in France

Across the world national states, especially in what the *Economist* likes to call the 'rich world', are imposing ever more restrictive immigration policies. Such state efforts are being enacted at precisely the time when migration has become an increasingly important part of people's strategies for gaining access to much-needed life resources. These may be a new livelihood, closeness to significant persons in their lives, or escape from untenable, even murderous, situations, such as persecution and war, as well as the opportunity to experience new people, places and situations. The greater freedom of mobility granted to capital and commodities through neo-liberal reform that has taken place alongside this lessening of freedom of mobility for people has been analysed by many as constituting one of the great contradictions of the present era. In contrast, we argue that the simultaneous process of granting more freedom to capital and less to migrants is far from a contradiction but rather a crucial underpinning of global capitalism and the equally global system of national states.

The growing restriction on the freedom of people to move has not led to fewer people crossing nationalised borders: today more people are doing exactly this than ever before,[2] which is not to say that restrictive immigration policies have no effect. Militarised border controls have increased the costs paid for migration, be it the monetary cost of securing passage or the cost of one's own life. There are a growing number of nominally temporary camps (refugee camps, detention camps, transit camps and so on), and more and more dead bodies are being found washed up on the shore, in scorched desert valleys, on frozen mountain passes, or in any number of other dangerous crossing points through which migrants have been funnelled (Nevins 2002; Fekete 2003: 2–3). This has allowed national states to cynically claim that the greatest threat to migrants are those who assist them in their movement, thereby deflecting blame from their own border control practices and setting the stage for further criminalising 'traffickers' and 'smugglers'.

74   *B. Anderson* et al.

The greater, though less studied, effect of restrictive immigration policies has been to restrict the rights and entitlements that migrants can claim once they are *within* national states. In practice, rather than simply restricting movement, restrictive immigration policies have enabled states to shift the status they accord migrating people. Fewer people are now given a status that comes with rights (e.g. 'permanent resident' or 'refugee') and more and more are legally subordinated (e.g. through the status of 'illegal') or are forced to work in unfree employment relations (including through the status of 'temporary foreign worker').[3] Since 2005 in the US, more migrants have been given the status of illegal than all of the various legal statuses combined (Passel and Suro 2005). In Canada, more people enter as temporary foreign workers than as permanent residents (Sharma 2001: 5–15; Sharma 2006).[4] Such a situation calls into question the entire array of contemporary migration controls which are ostensibly about limiting entry into a particular national territory. Instead, we see that the totality of migration controls have worked to make many migrants more vulnerable and their lives and livelihoods more precarious both in their routes of travel as well as in what they experience once having crossed borders.

One important and underexamined response to this historical conjuncture is the emergence of calls for No Borders. These are made on the basis of interrelated ethical, political, social and economic grounds. Their challenging of nation-states' sovereign right to control people's mobility signals a new sort of liberatory project, one with new ideas of 'society' and one aimed at creating new social actors not identified with nationalist projects (projects which have been shown to be deeply racialised, gendered, sexualised and productive of class relations) (Anthias and Yuval-Davis 1993; Balibar 1991; Potts 1990). As a practical, political project develops against borders, its relevance to other political projects grows, often challenging them in profound ways. There is a mounting need, therefore, to open an intellectual and political environment in which arguments for No Borders are further debated. In this essay, we first consider migration as a human social practice, as well as what borders are and how they are constructed. We then examine some of the critical responses to borders, their possibilities and limitations. We identify some of the key problems with these approaches, in particular the assumption that migration is a problem and that the nation-state framework persists unchallenged. We then describe some of the elements of a No Borders approach and refute the claim that it is utopian. We examine the centrality of migrants to the more general liberatory project that is No Borders and go on to indicate some of the ways that it is part of a larger project for the realisation of a new global commons.

Rethinking migration as a human activity

The tales people tell all point to the fact that, far from being an aberrant behaviour, mobility is a deeply human practice. Around the world human beings have always moved, and they will continue to move. Yet state responses to migration and their often fatal consequences have contributed to an analysis that regards

'We are all foreigners' 75

(certain) people's mobility as only ever caused by crisis and as crisis producing (Sutcliffe 2001).

Importantly, while millions of people move about, not all are classified as 'migrants'. This is not simply to do with one's length of stay: a tourist may only be resident for a short period, but then, so is a temporary worker; neither is it to do with employment – how many of us attending international academic conferences write down that we are present 'for the purposes of employment' even though we are scarcely going for a holiday? Who counts as a migrant depends on who is doing the counting, and on the purpose of the counting. It is shifting and contradictory. There are multiple ways and scales by which the figure of 'the migrant' is imagined, defined and represented (both in the abstract and in the particular). The figure is generally negatively gendered, racialised and classed: US financiers, Australian backpackers and British 'expats' are not, generally, constructed as migrants. It is not just the state, but a wide range of other actors, including local government, academia, the media, NGOs, trade unions and the daily practices of individuals (both citizens and non-citizens) that work with and against each other to construct and identify who counts as a migrant.

One thing that all these constructions have in common is that the constitution of 'the migrant' is nation-state-centric. One might move thousands of miles or only a few feet, but whether one is seen to be migrating or not ultimately rests on whether one has crossed a nationalised boundary. Hence, working with the often racialised and gendered understanding of who constitutes a national subject, the legal meaning of migrant rests on the idea of the 'foreigner'.[5]

The 'foreigner' is a very special figure in the global systems of capitalism and national states. Today, the foreigner is someone who can be legally (and often socially) denied most, if not all, of the rights associated with membership in a state (and the associated ideological understanding of membership in a nation). Mobility controls are largely directed at 'managing' the movement of foreigners. However, in the initial period when regulations on people's mobilities were put into place in the emergent global system, it was people's movement *out* of the realms of rulers that was the main concern. Yet, like today, early controls on mobility were very much related to the creation and maintenance of a proletariat, that is, a commodified workforce for (at the time, nascent) capitalists.

For example, the original Poor Laws in England were designed both to control the mobility of peasants fleeing their now-privatised commons and to coerce those classified as 'vagabonds' into working.[6] As states developed, controls governing the movement of those who were ruled were pushed to nationalised borders (Torpey 2002; see also Viyas Mongia 2003). Historically (and currently) coerced *immobility* acted to discipline the unruliness of the expropriated in order to make them productive workers whose labour power could be exploited. Indeed, capturing and containing a potential workforce by compelling them into not moving was a key element in making nascent capitalist ventures possible. It is in part for this reason that early passports were designed to control people's *exits from*, not their arrivals into, the territories controlled by various ruling groups (Torpey 2002). Mobility out of a particular space was defined as a major problem by and for those who needed reliable access to a workforce. Thus, as Papadopoulos, Stephenson and Tsianos note, 'It is no coincidence that the word mobility refers not only to movement but also to the common people, the working classes, the mob' (2008: 55). It was this mob and their attempts to flee expropriation and exploitation that posed one of the greatest threats to the success of capitalism. And it was, in part, their sedentarisation that helped to ensure its success. The word 'state' derives from 'stasis' or immobility.

Relatedly, criminalising people's mobility, and denying access to resources, services and rights to those deemed to be illegally migrating and residing in a place, was an important part of how the modern proletariat was formed. As today, it also served as a method for the creation of 'cheap labour'. 'Above all', as Sucheta Mazumdar notes, 'new states and institutions marking borders and passports developed only after the slave trade ended' and in a context in which migrants and migrations continued to be shaped by the continuing legacy of slavery, apartheid and diverse forms of unfree labour (2007: 128). In the context of the formerly colonized world, immigration controls and the expelling of 'non-indigenous' workers, as well as other forms of state-sponsored xenophobia, were a feature of many newly independent states (Adepoju 2007: 163).

These processes have been both masked and promoted by nationalism which is, as Benedict Anderson notes, 'the most universally legitimate value in the political life of our time' (1991: 3). According to nationalist narratives 'the people' are seen as attached to particular lands in ways that are either primordial (they themselves are portrayed as 'rooted' to the land) or providential (they were 'destined' to be on certain lands).[7] These narratives, together with restrictions on mobility and the subordination of those who have moved without permission, have worked to *territorialise* people's relationship to space, to their labour, to their ability to maintain themselves and to one another. One's wage rates, access to employment, to rights, to welfare benefits, to land etc. were all bound to one's recognised legal residence in particular spaces. Thus, through attempts at rendering people immobile, '[b]odies become territorialized; people become subjects of a specific territory, of a sovereign power' (Papadopoulos *et al.* 2008: 48). As rights and livelihoods were territorialised, so were people's subjectivities.

Borders, then, are thoroughly ideological. They are productive and generative of placing people in new types of power relations with others. Moreover, they are not fixed, even though their work is all about fixing, categorising, and setting people in relations of power. Importantly they are not only territorially drawn: they inevitably are inscribed 'inside' as well as 'outside' of any given national state (Ngai 2004; see also Nyers 2008). Borders follow people and surround them as they try to access paid labour, welfare benefits, health, labour protections, education, civil associations and justice (Balibar 2004: 109). Michael Walzer's fear of 'a thousand petty fortresses' that he predicted would attend a borderless world is already being realised, though the barriers pass largely unnoticed by citizens, who take access across them for granted (Walzer 1981).

Nevertheless, despite their assumption of free passage, citizens are not exempt from the power of borders, and their impact is both direct and indirect. In the

UK, fear of 'foreign national terrorists' has resulted in the development of Control Orders. These originally provided the state with the legal authority to indefinitely detain non-citizens without trial if a trial put secret intelligence at risk. When this was found to be discriminatory, instead of ending the practice, the UK simply extended the state's powers to citizens. The loss of civil liberties for citizens thus is often foretold by the treatment of non-citizens. More indirectly, there continue to be claims by employers that 'local workers' (of whatever nationality) are 'lazy' and that migrants have a 'good work ethic'. However, it is immigration controls that give employers greater power over migrants, particularly new arrivals or those who are dependent on them for their visa status, a power they do not always have over citizens. While these divisions are often naturalised and expressed in terms of culture and national stereotypes, they are directly produced, and have the additional merit of serving a disciplinary function over citizen-workers, fostering resentment and competition rather than solidarity.

It is not only 'hard workers' who are produced at the border. 'Good wives' who do not challenge patriarchal families, 'straight guys and gals' who adhere to correct sexual scripts, 'good parents' whose parenting accords with the requirements to produce 'good children' are policed through immigration requirements. Such requirements rest on ideological, even fantastical, re-presentations of the 'nation' that states nominally 'represent'.[8]

Temporal aspects of migration and their consequences can also structure people's experiences of borders and, increasingly, state responses to migration. Being able to imagine a future with oneself in it (even if, at the time of imagining, a person is content with living in the moment), feeling that one can anticipate and take risks, and have a sense of possibility, these are important aspects of human experience and subjectivity. Immigration controls and the relationships that they generate undermine these and can force people to live in an eternal present. Studies of those working without state endorsement, for example, find that the extreme insecurity of their situation results in the intensification of their working time and effort – with increased profitability for their employer.

The temporality of borders means that migrants on renewable working permits, spousal visa holders, children, and students live in a state of dependency on others for their continued legally recognised residence in a state. Those who are on temporary visas, like those who are going through the years of legal wrangling of immigration and asylum challenges, find themselves suspended in time with devastating consequences. Time, however, does not stop: relatives may die without being visited, children become too old to be granted the right to be with parents and carers, opportunities are missed. Such consequences have intensified as states have fortified their territorial borders and curtailed the ability of people to move out of national states in which they live their lives as 'illegals'. There has been an important and largely unrecognised shift by states to exert greater control over these temporal aspects of mobililty, in particular through the encouragement of temporary worker programmes and the ever increasing obstacles to citizenship.

78   *B. Anderson* et al.

Rethinking protest: beyond citizenship and human rights

The contradictions and injustices within the production of borders have not passed unnoticed, and in recent years there has been considerable debate about the intrinsic tension within the liberal project between imagined national belonging on the one hand and universal human rights on the other. There have been myriad attempts to make ideas of citizenship compatible with human rights, both theoretically and in practice, and to make immigration controls more 'humanitarian'.

Among the most globally influential – and deeply problematic – are purported attempts (whether by states and policing bodies, NGOs, or religious or women's groups) to end 'human trafficking'. Indeed, it is the Victim of Trafficking – often figured as a woman in the sex industry – who has now become the symbol of concern for non-citizens (until the last decade it was the 'refugee') (Sharma 2003; Kempadoo 2005, 2007; Anderson 2010; Brace 2010). Under the discursive practice of 'anti-trafficking', immigration controls and enforcement are argued as necessary for the protection of migrants themselves, particularly since those who are illegal can be 'vulnerable and often desperate people' (United Kingdom Home Office 2007). The language of harm prevention and protection that has slipped into immigration enforcement at a now global scale is extremely powerful. While the scope of positive duties may be controversial, the prohibition of harm is something that people with very different political opinions find relatively easy to agree upon. This has meant that borders are increasingly presented as points of humanitarian intervention where states can protect the local labour force and businesses from unfair competition, *and* protect migrants from abuse and exploitation.

However, the problem with the language of humanitarianism and 'human rights' is that it leaves no room for migrants' subjectivities, engagements and actions. They are constructed as objects of control, rescue and redemption rather than as full human beings (Kempadoo 2007: 81). As Brace has written in her exploration of the politics of abolitionism:

> Once you value powerlessness, then you are buying into a politics that cannot be transformative because it cannot explore capacities, contingency and multiplicity, or engage in the affairs of the world. Part of the problem of focusing on the victimhood of slaves, is that their labour disappears, making it harder to see how they are engaged with the world and part of our own moral economies and global markets.
>
> (Brace 2010)

But migrants are not naturally vulnerable; rather *the state* is deeply implicated in constructing vulnerability through immigration controls and practices. As has been argued above, immigration controls are not neutral but *productive*: they produce and reinforce relations of dependency and power. The problem with the language of human rights is that it inscribes the state as an appropriate protector for vulnerable migrants. Concern with trafficking focuses on borders and immigration controls while missing the crucial point that immigration controls *create* the relations of domination and subordination that they are then said to relieve. This, handily, leaves the work that national states do to produce illegality and (im)migrants' vulnerabilities completely out of the picture.

Human rights, and the disjuncture between human rights and citizenship rights, can be important in highlighting the gaps and contradictions between liberal claims, and liberal practice. In the US and Canada, for example, demands for regularisation of undocumented and precarious-status workers have featured prominently even as the possibilities for such a policy option have receded rapidly, thereby opening up the ground for more radical alternatives (Wright 2006; Nyers 2003). Human rights claims can be a first step in expressing demands for justice and for equality, for opening a space for politics by those otherwise excluded (Rancière 2004), and we are not arguing, for instance, that anti-deportation campaigns are not crucial arenas of struggle; rather, it is important to acknowledge they are only a first step, one whose potential can only be realised once it moves beyond the legitimisation of national states as 'neutral' bodies seeking the 'common good'. The risk of reinforcing both state power and territorialised subjectivities ('we' do not allow slavery on 'our soil') must be countered, and opportunities to develop new politics must be seized.

Anti-racist and transnational feminist accounts (Alexander and Mohanty 1997; Mohanty 2003; Boyce Davies 1994) – themselves informed by migration histories and by activist confrontations with 'the citizenship machinery' (Burton 2003) – have begun an inquiry into the production of non-citizen Others. This theoretical legacy, along with labour internationalism, can be renewed – and greatly extended – through an engagement with an anti-capitalist No Borders politics.

Rather than construct an abstract rights-bearing human through human rights discourses, it makes more sense to start from a theoretical standpoint that rethinks – and fundamentally relinks – labour and spatial practices (De Genova 2010; Mezzadra and Neilson n.d.). The struggle and power relations that can be obfuscated by the language of human rights are more visible in the language of workers' rights, which also signify a call to collective action and organising. Many in the mainstream of US labour unions, to take one nationalised context, have since the mid-1970s begun to realise the importance of showing solidarity with (im)migrant workers, including, at times, the illegalised and those on temporary labour contracts. Undocumented workers wield strategic power in a number of sectors of the US economy in key cities such as Los Angeles, as a substantial labour scholarship and impressive organising history has made clear. Indeed the solidarity of some trade unions is often a result of migrants having taken a leading role in important trade union organising (Bacon 2008; Delgado 1993; Moody 2007; Milkman 2000, 2006; Gordon 2005; Ness 2005; Poo and Tang 2004). This marks a real step forward in practical politics. It is particularly important because, while immigration controls promise to protect a nationalised labour force from competition by foreigners, in practice – rather than keeping

80   B. *Anderson* et al.

non-citizen workers out – they help create a group of workers that can be more preferable to employers because employers have additional mechanisms of control over them, including the threat of deportation. This may be through illegalising their labour, or it may be by tying them to particular employers. Organising migrant workers, whatever their legal status, needs to be centralised rather than an 'optional extra'.

However, in expanding their organising efforts to include the paperless, most US unions (and many unions globally, especially in the 'rich world') have not given up on their nation-state-centrism and their advocacy of restrictive border controls. They have not challenged borders and the institution of national citizenship itself. Their focus, at best, continues to be on achieving better immigration laws even while arguing for the further securing of the border and even, at times, for the placement of migrants into subordinated categories of 'guest workers'. Thus, while organising those (im)migrants currently within the national state, unions continue to demand that future migrants be shut out (Gordon 2007).[9] In this sense, the borders surrounding labour solidarity are both spatial and temporal: current (im)migrants are included within the expanded line drawn by contemporary unions and are seen as fit for union membership, but future migrants continue to be seen as a threat to labour solidarity (LaBotz and Avendano 2008).

The limitations of many contemporary mainstream trade union approaches are not accidental, but written deeply into the history of nationalised labour movements. Many of these approaches arose precisely to restrict or exclude particular forms of subordinated labour including migrant labour and the labour of women. This was typically constructed as 'unfree' and consequently racialised, above all if workers came from currently or formerly colonised places. As historian Donna Gabaccia argues, 'Indeed, it sometimes seems that nineteenth-century observers *had* to label migrants as unfree *in order to* exclude them as racially undesirable' (1997: 186). In the process, vast differences in labour practices and levels of coercion were collapsed. Of course, there was also an alternative internationalism to be found in this period in such radical proletarian formations as the International Workers of the World, and the global syndicalist tradition – a tradition that largely went down to defeat. As Gabaccia concludes, 'To defend free labor, labor activists had curtailed free migration. Immigration restrictions in turn helped to replicate under capitalism some of the inequalities of colonialism' (ibid.: 195).

Importantly, not everyone counts as a worker, and not everyone *wants* to count as a worker. The gendered history of the institution of wage labour means that the regularisation demand cannot adequately encompass, for example, gendered unpaid reproductive and domestic labour, not to speak of paid sexual labour (Federici 2004). Thus, at the same time as acknowledging the importance of labour organising within a migrant justice context, we must not forget the production of gender, sexualities, families and households, as well as the production of labour relations, that is a function and consequence of borders. Moreover, we must keep in mind another border, that between the 'public' and the 'private', a

'We are all foreigners' 81

central divide within the institution of citizenship (Lowe 2006). That divide simultaneously devalues and genders labour, and means that only certain types of work are regarded as work, as much rich feminist scholarship on social reproduction, the welfare state, the institution of wage labour, and citizenship and immigration has elucidated (see Benhabib and Resnik 2009).

The position of migrants demonstrates the limitations of theoretical scholarship and practical-political projects that assume, explicitly or implicitly, national citizenship as the ground on which political mobilisations, claims and rights ought to be organised (Baines and Sharma 2003; Bosniak 2002: 339–40; Nyamnjoh 2006). The fact is that citizenship-rights-based NGO approaches, whether at the national or transnational level, are very limited in practice (Gordon 2007). For a start, none of the current citizenship-rights-based frameworks are ultimately prepared to challenge frontally the rights of states to control their borders and territories, or the rights of states to exclude and deport; rather, they have often attempted to reinforce unsustainable divisions among various categories of migrants ('refugees', 'illegals', 'economic migrants' and so on). Even regularisation programmes, while they do bring practical improvements to the lives of some individuals, ultimately produce national subjects and reproduce ideas of the nation. Migrants must prove themselves 'deserving' of regularisation. While there may be protest at the deportation of 'hard workers', 'good neighbours' and 'lovely parents', this often rests on communitarian ideals of belonging. On the other hand, the 'foreign national prisoner' is an important (spectacular) figure in the justification of enforcement policy and practice, a rallying point whose deportation can be universally agreed on. This group has become an important figure in liberal democracies' enforcement as the acceptable face of deportation (see Bhabha 1998). There are few anti-deportation campaigns fought in solidarity with foreign national prisoners.

Additionally, citizenship-rights-based approaches often reinforce a rather passive politics in which, as has been argued, claims are made through judicial processes and NGO approaches that can take organising and political contestation – politics, in short – out of the hands of people (Neocosmos 2010). This passivity has been challenged by the burgeoning literature, drawing on more republican versions of citizenship, which claims citizenship is 'not an institution or a statute but a collective practice', as Étienne Balibar contends (2000). Here, citizenship is understood as constructed by action, as the building of relations of belonging and inclusion and the claiming of politics. Similarly, Engin Isin has elaborated the concept of 'acts of citizenship' to theorise these moments of politics (Isin 2008). However, as William Walters (2008) has argued in a recent critique, such an analytical framework, while valuable in certain respects, is unable to take on board forms of politics that involve the *refusal* of citizenship, including for example by colonised people. Additionally, attempts to move beyond the citizenship designated by border controls and capitalist social relations, relationships borne of – and still dependent on – practices of expropriation and exploitation, do not tackle the problem of *exclusion*. Exclusion inevitably accompanies inclusion, however broadly the boundaries of inclusion are drawn and whoever

82 *B. Anderson* et al.

draws the boundaries. There is a need to move beyond the rehearsing of the arguments about de facto and de jure citizenship, to think about new forms of relating each to one another, other than the model of citizenship and subjecthood.

Elements of a No Borders approach

Since the creation of the very first illegalised person, whenever and wherever controls have been placed on people's movements, they have been rejected. As William Walters comments, 'In certain respects the power of autonomous movement has been the hidden secret of the history of class struggle' (Walters 2008: 189; see also Rodriguez 1996). Some have offered a philosophical rejection of the limits to the human activity of migration. Others have rejected the territorialisation of their subjectivity and their relationships. Still others have rejected attempts to make them live a life that has become untenable due to acts of expropriation, terror and/or impoverishment. No set of border controls has ever worked to fully contain people's desire and need to move. In this sense, it can be argued that an *everyday practice* of refusing the border has existed as long as borders have.

A contemporary politics for No Borders can, nonetheless, be said to have emerged in the mid-1990s. It is marked by the repoliticisation of the very legitimacy of (im)migration restrictions and the distinctions made between 'national' or even 'regional' or 'continental' (e.g. 'European') subjects and their foreigners. What distinguishes a No Borders politics from other immigrant-rights approaches is its refusal to settle for 'fairer' immigration laws (higher numbers, legal statuses and so on). Within a No Borders politics, it is understood that the border-control practices of national states not only *reflect* people's unequal rights (e.g. whose movements are deemed to be legitimate and whose are not) but also *produce* this inequality. Thus, the signal demand of No Borders is for every person to have the freedom to move *and*, in this era of massive dispossession and displacement, the concomitant freedom to not be moved (i.e. to stay).

In this, a No Borders politics, far from reaffirming the significance of citizenship, calls into question the legitimacy of the global system of national states itself and the related global system of capitalism. In making these demands, a No Borders politics clarifies the centrality of border controls to capitalist social relations, relationships born of – and still dependent on – practices of expropriation and exploitation.

Social justice movements must not only 'confront' the question of the border, they must *reject* borders that work to multiply both control devices and differentiated labour regimes (Mezzadra and Neilson n.d.). In so doing, a No Borders project distinguishes itself from calls for open borders made by the Right, calls that centre on the availability of persons made mobile largely because of prior instances of dispossession and displacement (*Wall Street Journal* 1984; Riley 2008). The Right's call for open borders can thus be seen as a continuation, in new form, of the strategy of 'accumulation by dispossession' (Harvey 2003).

'We are all foreigners' 83

While most associated with events in Western Europe, a current No Borders politics also has its immediate predecessors in North America and is linked to prior movements for free mobility there. For instance, the popular No Borders cry that 'No One Is Illegal' first arose against Operation Wetback, a 1954 US government programme which resulted in over one million people being forced to leave the US for Mexico. The Sans Papiers in France, widely credited with first articulating a contemporary No Borders politics, gave new life to this slogan. Largely made up of migrants from Africa who found themselves categorised as 'illegals', the Sans Papiers began in 1996 by refusing to accept the right of the French state to control their lives through rendering them 'paperless'.[10] Part of the French state's efforts to lessen the impact of this uprising was to begin deporting activists categorised as (im)migrants. An important response to these deportations was captured in the slogan, 'We are all foreigners'. That the slogan was not 'We are all French' is significant and signals a kind of nascent No Borders rejection of having one's subjectivity aligned with the national state by which one is governed.

The rejection of borders and of the differences they make among people (as labourers and lovers, as comrades and classmates, etc.) comes from a shift in standpoint from one centred on citizens and 'their' organisations or 'their' state to one that begins from the standpoint of migrants themselves. The initial organisations of a movement for No Borders were led by migrants who insisted that migrants were legitimate political actors within national polities and did not want or need citizens' groups to act as a cover for their activities. Such acts of autonomy brought back to people's attention that, in the struggle for liberty, freedom, democracy, livelihoods and more, one needed to act with, and not against, those defined as (im)migrants and foreigners. That is, interests between people in these two categorical groups were shared rather than conflicting.

The recognition and naming of people's refusals to accept borders is of crucial importance in the light of the typical response to calls for No Borders: that it is utopian and impractical. This is often accompanied by what Phillip Cole (2000) calls the 'catastrophe prediction'. This argues that No Borders would undermine equality and welfare protections within liberal democratic states and that this would have an impact on the most marginalised and disadvantaged. It is also said that a lack of borders would erode national identities and commitments to liberal democratic values. It is this dystopic vision that allows for either the consequent Hobbesian response (that states must be given sovereignty and the power to enforce compliance in the interests of citizens) (ibid.) or the related communitarian response (in which national state formations are defended on the grounds that democracy itself can flourish only if bounded with strong insides and outsides) (Walzer 1981, 1983; Freeman 1986). In both scenarios, national sovereignty, although potentially unjust, is cast as a necessary evil.

This vision must be challenged. It has been countered by some through claims that a world without borders would not be altogether that different: not many people would move, migration would have a very limited impact on labour markets, and non-migrants as well as citizens would continue to be able to enjoy

84   *B. Anderson* et al.

the privileges of citizenship, even if they are somewhat diminished (Hayter 2004). We reject the politics of these sorts of arguments.

A radical No Borders politics acknowledges that it *is* part of revolutionary change. If successful, it will have a very profound effect on all of our lives, for it is part of a global reshaping of economies and societies in a way that is not compatible with capitalism, nationalism, or the mode of state-controlled belonging that is citizenship. It is ambitious and requires exciting and imaginative explorations, but it is not utopian. It is in fact eminently practical and is being carried out daily.

Under a general rubric of No Borders (if not always explicitly) are a wide variety of individuals and groups. They include groups of self-conscious activists directly confronting the state's imposition of barriers to people's mobilities (be they migrant detention camps, deportation schemes, harassment by various arms of state, or ejection by landlords). Examples of such groups are the Sans Papiers in France mentioned above and groups inspired by their actions, such as the Sin Papeles in Spain. In Europe, there is also the broader No Border network, a loose affiliation of individuals, sometimes in organisations, who unambiguously reject any controls on people's migration and stage demonstrations and solidarity events with detained migrants. In South Africa, the recent wave of terrible attacks on migrants, resulting in dozens of murders, led to important organising among shack-dwellers who issued a powerful manifesto against such killings, against xenophobia and for common rights for all ('Statement on the Xenophobic Attacks in Johannesburg' 2008).

Informed by a No Borders politics there also exist campaigns that attempt to eliminate the use of (im)migration status as a tool for the control of migrants. These include Don't Ask Don't Tell campaigners in the US and in Canada calling for an end to citizenship and immigration status distinctions among people in the provision of social services and in the receipt of protection (against patriarchal violence, substandard employment conditions, etc.). Elsewhere, there exist groups such as Doctors of the World who provide needed medical assistance without applying status or residence restrictions on the receipt of aid. Such groups often call for legalisation (or regularisation) of illegalised migrants as a means for them to gain rights and entitlements currently restricted to citizens and some permanent residents.

Under the rubric of No Borders there are also groups who may not be entirely committed to the abolition of borders, nation-states and capitalism but who, in their everyday activities, provide much-needed support, be it in the form of information, shelter, water and food to travelling migrants, or when trade unions purposely ignore a person's (im)migration status in their organising drives or even specifically address the vulnerabilities faced by persons because of their Illegal or temporary status. Also active are other individuals and groups who argue for the abolition of the multiple borders that national states impose, such as borders created by laws regarding 'official languages' and other 'banal nationalisms' (Billig 1995). These include groups such as 'No More Deaths', which works at the US/Mexico border, and labour unions such as Justice for Janitors in

'We are all foreigners' 85

the US and Canada and the United Food and Commercial Workers Union in Canada. These unions have crossed the ideological divide created by the state between nationals and foreigners in order to secure higher wages, better working conditions, and health care for any worker in the occupational sectors they organise. Indeed such a rejection is what, in part, links disparate campaigns, groups, and individuals together within a broader No Borders politics.

These efforts raise the question of what sorts of political communities are desirable within a world without borders, and we would suggest that one way of framing our responses to this could be by considering the struggle for the commons. The No Borders demand for the right to move or stay is not framed within a liberal (capitalist) praxis as are the rights of states, citizens, private property owners, or even the ambiguous and largely symbolic arena of human rights. Instead, the rights to move and to stay are understood as a necessary part of a contemporary system of *common rights*. Thus, while focused on realising their demand for freedom of movement (which includes the freedom to not be moved), a No Borders politics can be seen as part of a broader, reinvigorated struggle for the commons.

Peter Linebaugh, in his *Magna Carta Manifesto*, has identified four key principles historically evident in the practice of commoning and in the rights held by commoners, rights that differ substantially from the modern regime of citizens or human rights (2007: 45). First, common rights are 'embedded in a particular ecology', one that is reliant on knowledge of sustainable practices (ibid.). In this sense common rights are neither abstract nor essentialist but are based on one's actions. Second, 'commoning is embedded in a labor process' and is 'entered into by labor' (ibid.). Hence commoning, by definition, rejects parasitic class relationships centred on the dialectic of exploiters and producers. It also recognises as inherent the rights of producers to belong. Third, 'commoning is collective' (ibid.). That is, it is a social practice. Fourth, commoning is 'independent of the state' and the law (ibid.). There are no sovereigns in the commons. In sum, commoning is the realisation of not only political rights but also social and economic rights of the commoners. Indeed, commoning, as a practice, resolves the capitalist separation of falsely divided spheres. Common rights have historically included the principles of: neighbourhood; subsistence; travel; anti-enclosure; and reparations (ibid.). Commoning rejects notions of property and property relations, recognising that they are based on force and serve to separate human beings and create inequality. It acknowledges, even celebrates, mutuality and Winstanley's 'evenness' between fellow commoners (Brace 2004).

The rights held by commoners are the rights of persons. In contrast to the rights of property (of which national citizenship can be seen as a subset), consisting of the right to exclude others from enjoying that which has been privatised, the right of persons consists of the right to not be excluded (Dye 2009). Thus, the right of persons is not something that is granted. Instead, it is an entitlement that each person carries in her/himself. To have the right of persons entitles one to the resources of society. It includes the right to not be distinguished from others who also carry the right of persons. We contend that it is this right

86   *B. Anderson* et al.

of persons in the commons that alone can build the foundation by which to construct a society of equals. Indeed, we argue that the political, No Borders demand for the right to move and to stay ought to be seen as a necessary part of a contemporary common right of persons.

Today's commons is operational only at a global scale and can only exist against the nation (e.g. citizenship), the region or the continent (e.g. the European Union). From an ecological perspective, we have long known that destructive (or helpful) practices in one part of the globe have effects, sometimes immediate, on all others. From a social perspective, creating restrictions on the movement of people, plants, animals, food, fuel, medicines, ideas and more in a world that has long come to be shaped by such movements is tantamount to accepting the imposition of inequalities of one sort or another.

Many taking a No Borders political position, therefore, move from challenging national forms of belonging to trying to activate new subjectivities, ones that correspond with the global level at which human society is actually organised, in order to affirm a conception of freedom based on the collective political action of *equals*. The call for the commons requires the nurturing of the subjectivities that are not the autonomous sovereign individuals of the liberal imagination, whose self-ownership is premised on exclusion and mastery, or a fixed boundary between self and other that arises from a territorial understanding of the self. It requires a profound re-imagining of our relation to the world, a relation that is created even as it is imagined. A No Borders politics thus redefines equality by positing it as a relationship among co-members of a global society and not one among national citizens.

What a No Borders politics demonstrates is that borders and their institutional relation, citizenship, like states and nations, are highly volatile and unstable. While this means that borders are adaptable it also means that their authority can be challenged, indeed it *is* challenged on a daily basis. Awakening ourselves to the political potential of these challenges is an important aspect of No Borders struggles.

It is clear that there is a great deal of discussion and debate within the emergent politics of No Borders. There are many new opportunities for praxis which require listening to the theorising of those who reject borders and the entire apparatus of nation-states, global capitalism, and bounded imaginations which give them support. We must seize a 'line of flight' away from the struggle of differentiated rights and towards the recognition of a common right of movement, livelihood, and full and equal societal membership for all.

Notes

1 This essay began its life as the authors' introduction to a special issue of *Refuge* on 'No Borders as a Practical Political Project' (B. Anderson *et al.* 2009, 'Editorial: Why No Borders?', *Refuge*, 26:2).

2 From 1980 to now, there has also been an increase in the overall global population of humans. Taking this into account allows us to understand that international migration has remained more stable than the sheer numbers would indicate. Nonetheless, it is important to note that a large proportion of the world's people continue to see

'We are all foreigners' 87

migration as an important part of their life strategies. Unlike in 1980, however, their ability to secure rights following migration has become severely restricted. See the Global Commission on International Migration (GCIM), 'Migration in an Interconnected World: New Directions for Action,' report (2005) 1: 5–6, GCIM, available at www.unhcr.org/refworld/docid/435f81814.html (accessed 20 July 2010).

3 We initially place state categories of citizenship and immigration within quotation marks to problematise them and highlight their socially constructed character. We don't continue with this practice for the sake of easier reading.

4 The latest statistics on 'temporary foreign workers' in Canada show that there has recently been a significant increase in the number of people brought to Canada under this subordinated status since 2005. As per Citizenship and Immigration Canada's 'Facts and Figures 2009,' on 1 December 2009, there were 282,771 temporary foreign workers in Canada; see www.cic.gc.ca/english/resources/statistics/facts2009/temporary/02.asp (accessed 29 July 2010). For comparative Canadian statistics, see also Nakache and Kinoshita (2010).

5 For some reflections on understanding 'internal' and 'international' migrations together, see D. Feldman, 'Global Movements, Internal Migration, and the Importance of Institutions,' *International Review of Social History* 52 (2007): 105–109.

6 On vagabonds in European context, see Lucassen (1997).

7 For some remarks on challenging 'nationalist historiographies' in the Asian context, see Mazumdar (2007).

8 This is reflected in a new Citizenship Guide released by the Canadian state in 2009. Meant as a study tool for new applicants for citizenship, it not only defines Canadianness in starkly neo-liberal terms – one must be the citizen-worker who is part of a self-reliant family – it also reproduces old racist, colonial scripts. Along with '[g]etting a job, taking care of one's family, and working hard in keeping with one's abilities', the guide tells immigrants that Canada is a place where 'men and women are equal under the law' and warns them that 'Canada's openness and generosity do not extend to barbaric cultural practices that tolerate spousal abuse, 'honour killings', female genital mutilation, or other gender-based violence' (see Citizenship and Immigration Canada: 2009). While male violence against women, significant pay differentials between men and women, sexual abuse of children and other heinous activities are not uncommon features of life in Canada, 'immigrants' are ideologically set apart from 'Canadians' so as to imply the latter's superiority.

9 For an interesting exchange within the US labour context on the politics of open borders, see LaBotz and Avendano (2008).

10 Their radical stance, and the outpouring of solidarity for them from people across the spectrum of state statuses, stood in marked contrast to the wide legitimacy given to Operation Wetback in the US and can be seen as part of the legacy of the Paris Uprising of 1968 (see K. Ross, *May 68 and its Afterlives*, Chicago: University of Chicago Press, 2002).

Bibliography

Adepoju, A. (2007) 'Creating a Borderless West Africa: Constraints and Prospects for Intra-Regional Migration' in A. Pecoud and P. de Guchteneire (eds) *Migration without Borders: Essays on the Free Movement of People*, New York: Berghahn Books and UNESCO.

Alexander, M.J. and C.T. Mohanty (1997) *Feminist Genealogies, Colonial Legacies, Democratic Futures*, New York: Routledge.

Anderson, B.R. (1991) *Imagined Communities: Reflections on the Origin and Spread of Nationalism*, London: Verso.

88   *B. Anderson* et al.

Anderson, B. (2010) 'Where's the Harm in That? Immigration Enforcement, Trafficking and Migrants' Rights,' paper presented at workshop Human Rights, Victimhood and Consent, University of Bergen, 10–12 June 2010.

Anthias, F. and N. Yuval-Davis (1993) *Racialized Boundaries: Race, Nation, Gender, Colour and Class and the Anti-Racist Struggle*, London and New York: Routledge.

Bacon, B. (2008) *Illegal People: How Globalization Creates Migration and Criminalizes Immigrants*, Boston: Beacon Press.

Baines, D. and N. Sharma (2003) 'Is Citizenship a Useful Concept in Social Policy Work? Non-Citizens: The Case of Migrant Workers in Canada,' *Studies in Political Economy* 69 (Autumn): 75–107.

Balibar, E. (1991) 'The Nation Form: History and Ideology' in E. Balibar and I. Wallerstein (eds) *Race, Nation, Class: Ambiguous Identities*, London: Verso.

Balibar, E. (2000) 'What We Owe to the Sans-Papiers' in I. Guenther and C. Heesters (eds) *Social Insecurity*, Toronto: Anansi.

Balibar, E. (2004) *We, the People of Europe? Reflections on Transnational Citizenship*, Princeton and Oxford: Princeton University Press.

Benhabib, S. and J. Resnik (eds) (2009) *Migrations and Mobilities: Citizenship, Borders, and Gender*, New York: New York University Press.

Bhabha, J. (1998) ' "Get Back to Where You Once Belonged": Identity, Citizenship, and Exclusion in Europe,' *Human Rights Quarterly* 20 (3): 592–627.

Billig, M. (1995) *Banal Nationalism*, London: Sage.

Bosniak, L. (2002) 'Critical Reflections on "Citizenship" as a Progressive Aspiration' in J. Conaghan, R.M. Fischl and K. Klare (eds) *Labour Law in an Era of Globalization: Transformative Practices and Possibilities*, Oxford: Oxford University Press.

Boyce Davies, C. (1994) *Black Women, Writing and Identity: Migrations of the Subject*, London: Routledge.

Brace, L. (2004) *The Politics of Property: Labour, Freedom and Belonging*, Edinburgh: Edinburgh University Press.

Brace, L. (2010) 'The Opposites of Slavery: Contract, Freedom and Labour,' paper presented at workshop Human Rights, Victimhood and Consent, University of Bergen, 10–12 June 2010.

Burton, A. (2003) 'Introduction: On the Inadequacy and the Indispensability of the Nation' in A. Burton (ed.) *After the Imperial Turn: Thinking With and Through the Nation*, Durham, NC: Duke University Press.

Citizenship and Immigration Canada (2009) *Study Guide – Discover Canada: The Rights and Responsibilities of Citizenship*, available at www.cic.gc.ca/english/resources/publications/discover/index.asp (accessed 13 July 2010).

Cole, P. (2000) *Philosophies of Exclusion: Liberal Political Theory and Immigration*, Edinburgh: Edinburgh University Press.

De Genova, N. (2010) 'The Deportation Regime: Sovereignty, Space, and the Freedom of Movement' in N. de Genova and N. Peutz (eds) *Deported: Removal and the Regulation of Human Mobility*, Durham, NC: Duke University Press.

Delgado, H.L. (1993) *New Immigrants, Old Unions: Organizing Undocumented Workers in Los Angeles*, Philadelphia: Temple University Press.

Dye, T. (2009) *The Maka'ainana Transformation in Hawaii: Archaeological Expectations Based on the Social Effects of Parliamentary Enclosure in England*, Honolulu: T.S. Dye and Colleagues, Archaeologists, Inc.

Federici, S. (2004) *Caliban and the Witch: Women, the Body and Primitive Accumulation*, Brooklyn, NY: Autonomedia.

'We are all foreigners' 89

Fekete, L. (2003) 'Death at the Border – Who Is to Blame?' *European Race Bulletin* 44.

Freeman, G. (1986) 'Migration and the Political Economy of the Welfare State,' *Annals of the American Academy of Political and Social Science* 485 (1): 51–63.

Gabaccia, D. (1997) 'The "Yellow Peril" and the "Chinese of Europe": Global Perspectives on Race and Labor, 1815–1930' in J. Lucassen and L. Lucassen (eds) *Migration, Migration History, History: Old Paradigms and New Perspectives*, Bern: Peter Lang.

Gordon, J. (2005) *Suburban Sweatshops: The Fight for Immigrant Rights*, Cambridge, MA: Belknap Press of Harvard University Press.

Gordon, J. (2007) 'Transnational Labor Citizenship,' *Southern California Law Review* 80 (3): 503–588.

Harvey, D. (2003) *The New Imperialism*, Oxford: Oxford University Press.

Hayter, T. (2004) *Open Borders: The Case against Immigration Controls*, London: Pluto Press.

Isin, Engin F. (2008) 'Theorizing Acts of Citizenship' in E.F. Isin and G.M. Nielsen (eds) *Acts of Citizenship*, New York: Palgrave Macmillan, 15–43.

Kempadoo, K. (2005) 'Victims and Agents of Crime: The New Crusade against Trafficking' in J. Sudbury (ed.) *Global Lockdown: Race, Gender, and the Prison-Industrial Complex*, New York and London: Routledge, 35–55.

Kempadoo, K. (2007) 'The War on Human Trafficking in the Caribbean,' *Race and Class* 49 (2): 79–85.

LaBotz, D. and A. Avendano (2008) 'Open Borders? A Debate,' *New Labor Forum* 17 (1): 9–24.

Linebaugh, P. (2007) *The Magna Carta Manifesto: Liberties and Commons for All*, Berkeley: University of California Press.

Lowe, L. (2006) 'The Intimacies of Four Continents' in A.L. Stoler (ed.) *Haunted by Empire: Geographies of Intimacy in North American History*, Durham, NC: Duke University Press.

Lucassen, L. (1997) 'Eternal Vagrants? State Formation, Migration, and Travelling Groups in Western-Europe, 1350–1914' in J. Lucassen and L. Lucassen (eds) *Migration, Migration History, History: Old Paradigms and New Perspectives*, Bern: Peter Lang.

Mazumdar, S. (2007) 'Localities of the Global: Asian Migrations between Slavery and Citizenship,' *International Review of Social History*, 52.

Mezzadra, S. and B. Neilson (n.d.) 'Border as Method, or, the Multiplication of Labor,' European Institute for Progressive Cultural Policies, available at http://eipcp.net/transversal/0608/mezzadraneilson/en (accessed 21 July 2010).

Milkman, R. (ed.) (2000) *Organizing Immigrants: The Challenge for Unions in Contemporary California*, Ithaca: Cornell University Press.

Milkman, R. (2006) *L.A. Story: Immigrant Workers and the Future of the U.S. Labor Movement*, New York: Russell Sage.

Mohanty, C.T. (2003) *Feminism Without Borders: Decolonizing Theory, Practicing Solidarity*, Durham, NC: Duke University Press.

Moody, K. (2007) 'Harvest of Empire: Immigrant Workers' Struggles in the USA' in L. Panitch and C. Leys (eds) *Socialist Register 2008 (Global Flashpoints: Reactions to Imperialism and Neoliberalism)*, London, Merlin Press.

Nakache, D. and P.J. Kinoshita (2010) 'The Canadian Temporary Foreign Worker Program: Do Short-Term Economic Needs Prevail over Human Rights Concerns?' Study no. 5, Institute for Research on Public Policy, available at www.irpp.org/pubs/IRPPstudy/IRPP_Study_no5.pdf (accessed 29 July 2010).

Neocosmos, M. (2010) *From 'Foreign Natives' to 'Native Foreigners': Explaining*

90 *B. Anderson* et al.

Xenophobia in Post-apartheid South Africa, Citizenship and Nationalism, Identity and Politics, Dakar: CODESRIA.

Ness, I. (2005) *Immigrants, Unions, and the U.S. Labor Market*, Philadelphia: Temple University Press.

Nevins, J. (2002) *Operation Gatekeeper: The Rise of the 'Illegal Alien' and the Making of the U.S.-Mexico Boundary*, New York and London: Routledge.

Ngai, M. (2004) *Impossible Subjects: Illegal Aliens and the Making of Modern America*, Princeton: Princeton University Press.

Nyamnjoh, F.B. (2006) *Insiders and Outsiders: Citizenship and Xenophobia in Contemporary Southern Africa*, London: Zed.

Nyers, P. (2003) 'Abject Cosmopolitanism: The Politics of Protection in the Anti-Deportation Movement,' *Third World Quarterly* 24 (6): 1069–1093.

Nyers, P. (2008) 'No One Is Illegal between City and Nation' in E. Isin and G. Nielson (eds) *Acts of Citizenship*, London: Zed.

Papadopoulos, D., N. Stephenson and V. Tsianos (2008) *Escape Routes: Control and Subversion in the Twenty-First Century*, London and Ann Arbor, MI: Pluro Press.

Passel, J.S. and R. Suro (2005) 'Rise, Peak, and Decline: Trends in U.S. Immigration 1992–2004,' Washington, DC: Pew Hispanic Center, available at http://pewhispanic.org/reports/report.php?Report ID=53 (accessed 12 July 2010).

Poo, A. and E. Tang (2004) 'Domestic Workers Organize in the Global City' in V. Labaton and D. Lundy Martin (eds) *The Fire This Time: Young Activists and the New Feminism*, New York: Anchor.

Potts, L. (1990) *The World Market For Labour Power: A History of Migration*, London: Zed Books.

Rancière, J. (2004) 'Who is the Subject of the Rights of Man?' *South Atlantic Quarterly*, 103 (2–3): 297–310.

Riley, J. (2008) *The Case for Open Borders: Six Common Arguments Against Immigration and Why They are Wrong*, New York: Gotham Books.

Rodriguez, N. (1996) 'The Battle for the Border: Notes on Autonomous Migration, Transnational Communities, and the State,' *Social Justice* 23 (3): 21–37.

Sharma, N. (2001) '"Race", Class and Gender and the Making of "Difference": The Social Organization of "Migrant Workers" in Canada,' *Atlantis: A Women's Studies Journal* 24 (2).

Sharma, N. (2003) 'Travel Agency: A Critique of Anti-Trafficking Campaigns,' *Refuge*, 21 (3): 53–65.

Sharma, N. (2006) *Home Economics: Nationalism and the Making of 'Migrant Workers' in Canada*, Toronto: University of Toronto Press.

'Statement on the Xenophobic Attacks in Johannesburg' (May 2008), available at www.abahlali.org/node/3582 (accessed 25 July 2010).

Sutcliffe, B. (2001) 'Migration and Citizenship: Why Can Birds, Whales, Butterflies and Ants Cross International Frontiers More Easily than Cows, Dogs and Human Beings?' in S. Ghatak and A. Showstack Sassoon (eds) *Migration and Mobility: The European Context*, New York: Palgrave.

Torpey, J. (2002) *The Invention of the Passport: Surveillance, Citizenship, and the State*, Cambridge and New York: Cambridge University Press.

United Kingdom Home Office (2007) *Enforcing the Rules: A Strategy to Ensure and Enforce Compliance with Our Immigration Laws*, London: Home Office.

Viyas Mongia, R. (2003) 'Race, Nationality, Mobility: A History of the Passport' in A.

Burton (ed.) *After the Imperial Turn: Thinking With and Through the Nation*, Durham, NC: Duke University Press.

Wall Street Journal editorial (3 July 1984).

Walters, W. (2008) 'Acts of Demonstration: Mapping the Territory of (Non-)Citizenship' in E. Isin and G. Nielson (eds) *Acts of Citizenship*, London: Zed, 182–206.

Walzer, M. (1981) 'The Distribution of Membership' in P. Brown and H. Shue (eds) *Boundaries: National Autonomy and Its Limits*, Lanham, MD: Rowman and Littlefield.

Walzer, M. (1983) *Spheres of Justice: A Defense of Pluralism and Equality*, New York: Basic Books.

Wright, C. (2006) 'Against Illegality: New Directions in Organizing By and With Non-Status People in Canada' in C. Frampton, G. Kinsman, A. Thompson and K. Tilleczek (eds) *Sociology for Changing the World: Social Movements/Social Research*, Halifax: Fernwood.

5 Ethnography and human rights

The experience of APDHA with Nigerian sex workers in Andalusia[1]

Estefanía Acién González

The Asociación Pro Derechos Humanos de Andalucía (APDHA – Association for Human Rights in Andalusia) works to encourage fulfilment of the United Nations Universal Declaration of Human Rights (1948), centring its work on supporting individuals who are socially or otherwise 'excluded'. Our work in the field of migration has developed out of direct contact with the migrant population already living in Andalusia and with those who are still in transit, for example, in Morocco. We particularly work for the rights of those who are employed in the sex industry, the majority of whom are migrant women residing in Spain without legal status. APDHA approaches its work in both areas – migration and sex work – by applying a methodology of research and action. We use an ethnographic perspective[2] to try and improve our understanding of migration, while on the one hand, asking ourselves how we can be useful to individuals in their migratory processes, and on the other, denouncing the human rights violations to which they are subjected. In this chapter, I will describe how our organisation carries out investigative research and social action in our work with Nigerian women who have travelled through Morocco to Andalusia in Spain.[3]

APDHA is a private non-profit organisation with a mandate to uphold the United Nations Universal Declaration of Human Rights of 1948. Although the area in which APDHA works directly is the territory of Andalusia, the most populous and second-largest of Spain's 17 autonomous communities (see Map 5.1), the organisation's territory of activity can in fact be regarded as global, since we have contacts in several other countries and human rights are universal.

APDHA works in the following five areas: (1) prison and civil liberties, (2) education for peace, (3) social exclusion and marginalisation, (4) international solidarity and (5) immigration. We have extended our work in the last two areas into other countries, such as Palestine and Africa. In addition, we have permanent working groups researching more specific issues, such as minors and prostitution. As the Coordinator of the Working Group on Prostitution, APDHA, I belong to this latter working group, and it is from this standpoint that I present this chapter.

Our aim, as an organisation, is to demand the full implementation of the UN Universal Declaration of Human Rights, raise the awareness of Spanish citizens,

Map 5.1 APDHA's working area (Andalusia).

and ultimately transform society. In order to achieve this, APDHA denounces with all the means at our disposal the failures of countries, organisations and individuals to comply with the declaration. We also offer as much support as we can to individuals whose rights have been violated, and work to increase general awareness about human rights in Andalusian society.

Members of APDHA do not limit themselves to an abstract or theoretical defence of human rights. We enter at the grass-roots level and conduct fieldwork to try and better understand the populations we serve. We believe this work is vital if the social interventions we design are to be useful for the people involved. For this reason, using an ethnographic approach in our research is crucial in order to collect information first-hand that takes into account the complexity of the realities we are studying. In order to denounce the injustice of a situation, APDHA produces reports to raise awareness, organises campaigns and public demonstrations, and sets up programmes of social support and intervention where we believe they are necessary.

In total, APDHA has 11 local offices spread throughout Andalusia, in Seville, Sierra Sur, Huelva, Bahia de Cadiz, Algeciras, Jerez de la Frontera, Cordoba,

94   *E. Acién González*

Malaga, Granada, Almería and Ronda. Our organisation aims to influence public policy in the region by applying political pressure and lobbying local government. We regard many of the current public policies as being directly related to the causes of social exclusion for the most disadvantaged sectors of society.

For the purposes of this chapter, the most relevant aspects of APDHA's work are the description of the activities we carry out in the field of immigration, on the one hand, and the experiences of our working group on prostitution, on the other. The convergence of these two aspects has resulted in the strategy that we have applied to the Nigerian women working in Almería, which I will now describe.

Work on immigration and prostitution

Immigration

At APDHA, we strive to undo some of the out-dated, stereotypical notions about illegal immigration and immigrants, and campaign for migration to be recognised widely as the legal right that it is, according to article 13 of the Universal Declaration of Human Rights. We have been working with migrants in all of APDHA's local offices, as well as in various African countries. In Andalusia, we have established centres where migrants can seek legal advice, particularly about their immigration status in Spain. Currently, most of the work being carried out in these centres concerns the reforms to Immigration Law (LOEX 8/2000)[4] which the Spanish government is trying to put into place, and which introduce an even greater restriction of immigrants' rights, in line with recent European directives.

To note just three of the most negative aspects of this proposed legal reform, these are: (1) an insistence on distinguishing between legal and illegal immigrants when granting rights which should be universal, with the result of criminalising and rendering the latter group invisible, (2) restricting the right to family 'regroupment', and (3) allowing unaccompanied foreign minors to be forcibly repatriated.

In Africa we work with immigrants who are still in transit, and we attempt to maintain a watchful presence on the ground to defend human rights at the Spanish and African borders, particularly since the latter are increasingly becoming externalised frontiers of the European 'Schengen space'[5] (Walters 2002). With the implementation of this policy, many African countries are now being pressured into taking over a large part of the responsibility for policing their borders with Europe, and preventing migrants from reaching its shores. National police forces in these countries are therefore taking over the job of the Spanish police, and this tends to put migrants at even greater risk of experiencing human rights violations while in transit.

APDHA's goal is to carry out ethnographic research in such contexts, collaborating wherever possible with humanitarian organisations in Morocco (specifically Tangiers), Mali and Mauritania, among other states.

Ethnography and human rights 95

Working group on prostitution

The APDHA Working Group on Prostitution is concerned with fighting for the rights of sex workers. In Spain, as in the rest of the world, there is fierce debate between those who consider prostitution a form of sexual exploitation of women – and consequently an evil that should be eradicated – and those who believe that it is a job carried out by people whose rights must be protected. The former position, that of the abolitionist, is the dominant one at the institutional and political level. The practical implementation of policies upheld by its adherents requires both 'rescue' operations (so that these women abandon sex work and *reinsert* themselves into society), and measures of 'control'. In Spain, this latter position has adherents who tend to forbid prostitution in the street and to focus on detaining and expelling immigrant sex workers who do not have papers, under the pretext of cracking down on supposed human trafficking rings.

According to the results of our research, such measures – although they may indeed be useful for some sex workers – do not address the needs and demands of the majority, and tend to make life more difficult for them. We firmly believe that it is not prostitution per se that is truly unacceptable, but rather the injustices to which sex workers are subjected because they cannot count on legislation or the justice system to effectively protect them against abuse from clients, pimps, members of organised crime gangs and the security forces of the state itself.

This is a reality for all sex workers, even though it is now commonly accepted that there is a need to conduct research from an objective standpoint before the state intervenes. If the participation of those who will be the beneficiaries of such intervention is actually sought and heeded, we would be better able to ensure that the measures implemented are of real use. For example, one common prejudice in society is that all women who work in the sex industry must want to leave it. Consequently, many social intervention policies are focused almost exclusively on 'rescuing' these women. Another example of public policy being shaped by preconceived notions – even if this is done unconsciously – is the fact that most HIV/AIDS programmes are aimed at prostitutes, based on the assumption that all prostitutes have HIV/AIDS.

APDHA began its research with the Working Group on Prostitution in 2001, when colleagues from other NGOs alerted us to the precarious situation of a group of Nigerian women working in Almería. We thought it was vital to research the situation and gain first-hand experience to try and understand their particular realities, rather than jumping in with ready-made solutions that might not be appropriate to their needs.

Thus, we began trying different methods of research, and carried out in-depth interviews with various members of the group, interviewing Nigerian women working as prostitutes in private houses in remote rural areas of the Poniente Almeriense. Among other problems with this method, we found that they generally distrusted us, and the limitations of the formal interview format, along with the significant bias in their answers, made it impossible for us to investigate the issues we were really interested in. These early difficulties proved to be extremely valuable to us later on, as they caused us to abandon the formal interview format and limit ourselves to listening, observing, and chatting casually with these women.

We realised that the failure of our first methodology had been due largely to our own assumptions. We found that, even on a subconscious level, many of our questions in the formal interviews had sprung from stereotypical or preconceived notions, and that they already suggested or contained the 'correct' answer within them. As a result, we were only able to accumulate lies and misinformation that was of little use to anyone. We now recognise that attempting to apply the same questions and interview criteria in all cases was a mistake, and this taught us to adapt our methodology to each individual. The ethnographic approach of observation and informal social interaction has allowed us to do this much more effectively.

We therefore had to begin our research again from scratch, going to see the women at their venues merely as visitors, accepting the stereotypes they also held about us, and venturing into a whole new and treacherous terrain: the fluidity and dynamism of personal relations. We spent almost a year and a half working like this before managing to play any real role in the Nigerian community in the Poniente Almeriense, and this time was (and continues to be) a period of intense learning. However, we decided that it was important to be flexible and not to rush this process, so that the women themselves could eventually reveal to us, in their day-to-day lives, what their needs were and what actions they believed should be taken.

This process has culminated in the provisional design of what we call a 'Program of Social and Sanitary Mediation with Women in Contexts of Prostitution'. We have tried to maintain a kind of continuous self-evaluation throughout, centring around two main concerns: (1) measuring how useful our work is to these women and (2) deepening our understanding of their difficulties, in order to be able to draw up concrete proposals for action.

We share Esteban Ruiz's view that the planning of intervention measures requires a form of social thinking, and that it is intimately related to the key element of determining which social needs are the ones that must be dealt with (Ruiz 2005: 12). These needs are of a dynamic and relative nature (Collectivo Ioé 1995), and it is always problematic to attempt to identify them from a position of power or privilege. For us, the most important question is the following: What is the best way to create the objective conditions necessary for these people, and all others in similar situations, to be able to freely manage their own lives on an equal footing with the rest of society?

The programme of social and sanitary care that we designed continues to operate, and since we have been working closely with this group of Nigerian women, we have come to know them very well. They have shared with us a great deal about their individual migratory projects, from their initial decision to leave their country of origin up until their arrival in Spain. This sharing and recounting of subjective experiences has (perhaps paradoxically) allowed us, over time, to gain a much more objective and balanced perspective of their real

Ethnography and human rights   97

situation because it is informed by a much broader and situated view of their situations. It has also enabled us to establish a more equal relationship of trust with them.

Nigerian women in sex work

Transit and arrival

The geographic location of Nigerian sex workers in Almería is centred in the triangular area formed by the municipalities of Roquetas de Mar, La Mojonera, and Vícar, in the region of the Poniente Almeriense (Acién and Majuelos 2003). This location is significant for a number of reasons. The first is that this is an area of intense greenhouse agricultural production, and is rather like its own self-contained world, since it functions largely outside of and parallel to the mainstream legal and economic structures of Spanish society. Most of the people who work in these greenhouses are illegal immigrants, and the police tend not to encroach too much on this area, preferring to turn a blind eye because this industry provides the principal source of income and wealth for the region.

There is a significant Nigerian community already present in this area, which attracts other Nigerian migrants through a network of established contacts as a result. In addition, the lack of police presence in the greenhouse mini-economy gives more or less free rein to those who wish to set up or operate illicit businesses, such as the 'house-bars' where Nigerian sex workers work, which are tailored to the needs of the immigrant community. Finally, Andalusia is also in the southernmost part of Spain, the community closest to Africa. This means that the house-bars in Almería are, in many cases, an immigrant's first point of entry into the European labour market, and are often considered by migrants as being places of transit.

Currently in this part of Almería, about 25 per cent of the total population consists of foreign-born residents, and the great majority of them are from Africa and Eastern Europe. Many of these immigrants live in fairly poor housing located on the paths between the greenhouses, or along regional roads in very isolated areas (see Figure 5.1.) Many of the houses throughout this area are set far apart from one another; Spanish residents previously inhabited these houses and now rent them out to immigrant workers, a population predominantly made up of Moroccans and Sub-Saharan Africans.[6]

In some of these houses, certain women have decided to establish businesses where they offer a wide range of services to a local immigrant client base. These include accommodation, hot meals, use of a bathroom and shower, clean clothes, access to the Internet and international phone calls, musical performances and other entertainment, clothes made to measure, the sale of clothing and shoes, traditional African cloth, imported African food and drink products, alcohol, and above all, sex services. These venues are also used for parties such as, for example, one to celebrate a birth in the community.

Figure 5.1 Examples of housing (and house-bars) where Nigerian women set up their businesses in this area.

Figure 5.1 continued.

100   E. Acién González

However, these places are also the homes of the people who work there, or at least of the person who manages the business. Therefore, such establishments tend to be referred to by the women who own or run them as their house-bar or their bar. By way of explanation, they frequently say, 'My house is in the bar', or 'I live in the bar'. We use the term house-bar since this is what the women themselves call it, and the term usefully encompasses the double function of the space.

The space is divided into public and private rooms. The central area is the salon or living room, which is the main space for social interaction. All kinds of people pass through this area, ranging from family members to friends, clients, ambulant vendors and so forth. This constant flow of people through the space guarantees a minimum daily income to the women in charge. For this reason, not everyone who visits the house-bar is seen or treated as a client solely interested in sex services.

Indeed, these house-bars have become one of the very few places where undocumented immigrant workers can freely go in their leisure time to socialise, relax, have a drink or buy something. This is partly due to their precarious legal situation – which prevents them from going into town, frequenting Spanish bars or mixing with the local population – and partly due to the geographical isolation of their housing, which means that there is nowhere else nearby for them to go. Such places also offer immigrant workers the opportunity to be in a familiar, intra-ethnic environment with other people who share, at least in part, the same origin, background, and language.

The way these businesses operate is highly diverse. Often, the owners of the house-bar have signed the tenancy agreement for the building in their own name and then sublet rooms to other women, who use them for their work. The bar owners or managers are usually Nigerian women who have previously worked as prostitutes, have lived in Spain for several years, and have acquired residency and work permits. As Acién and Majuelos (2003: 15) explain,

> Once they have obtained 'papers', [these women] decide to rent out their house, thus leaving their work but continuing to share their living space with other women who still practice it. In this way, they maintain an activity that is related to prostitution, but without working in prostitution directly: [for example] sub-letting housing, selling drinks, etc. In other cases, they set up a new and independent line of business such as an internet café, telephone cabins, a shop with imported African products, hairdress[ing], etc.

The physical appearance and decoration of these venues varies widely. It is common to see coloured lights or Christmas decorations in the living room, with sofas, low tables and one or more televisions. Only in a few cases did we find an actual bar. The way that sex workers make contact with their clients also differs from place to place; they may wait in the living room for clients to enter the house-bar, or go out into the street to find them. They normally keep the profit from their work in its entirety, paying the amount due for the daily rate of their rooms from their earnings. In exchange, the house-bar owner deals with clients and keeps the profits from drinks sales. How much business is done at any time depends on a number of factors that vary, such as the location of the house-bar, the day of the week, the time of day, and the spending power of its client base, which in turn depends on seasonal agricultural production.

The vast majority of these women are from Nigeria (94 per cent), of which 80 per cent are from Edo State, with many coming from the same place, Benin City. Consequently, almost 85 per cent belong to the Edo ethnic group. Very few of these women speak Spanish, either because they have not been in the country for very long or because their opportunities for interaction with Spanish speakers are scarce. Even if immigrants from other countries do frequent a house-bar, they tend to be Moroccan or Senegalese, and they also do not have a very high level of fluency in Spanish.

According to our research, these women are between 20 and 39 years of age and almost 80 per cent are single. Those that are married do not generally include their husbands in their migratory projects. Nevertheless, they do have dependents, either in their country of origin or at their destination, such as parents or younger siblings for whom they provide financial support. Some 38 per cent affirm that they have children (two, on average) either back in their country of origin or with them. These are often the result of unprotected sex or sexual abuse during their journey. More than 73 per cent of these women have completed secondary education.

The migratory process

From our fieldwork carried out through informal conversations, we determined that almost all of the women in this group made the decision to migrate for economic reasons, except in a few cases, where certain individuals alluded to fleeing violent conflicts, forced marriages, or threats. Most affirmed that their parents had previously been farmers or merchants, but that these activities no longer generated enough income to guarantee the welfare of the whole family, so they were obliged to emigrate in order to help provide monetary support. Some of the women also mentioned an element of 'social' motivation in their decision to leave Nigeria, referring to the greater freedoms that they expected to enjoy in Europe.

The decision to migrate is usually made in post-adolescence, when the individual recognises that the family cannot pay for further education after they have completed high school, and alternative options for the future are scarce or entirely absent.

It is, however, difficult to provide a general description of the journey itself, since individual experiences seem to vary greatly. In addition, there is widespread confusion among academics concerning the survival and migration strategies employed by female immigrant sex workers on the one hand, and situations of slavery, forced migration, or trafficking of women for sexual exploitation on the other. In Spain, as in many other countries, we have a genuine problem with

102   *E. Acién González*

confusing terminology, and many leaders allow stereotypes to intrude into political and academic debate. It is common, for example, to hear influential intellectuals and politicians affirming that all immigrant women who have travelled alone (without a family or partner) to Spain, and who work in the sex industry, are victims of human trafficking for sexual exploitation.

At APDHA, we have found it necessary to introduce a number of clarifications in the terminology we use, and above all to insist on differentiating between situations of human trafficking – where people are forced to migrate involuntarily, and are usually at the complete mercy of their traffickers – and illegal immigration. The terms 'network' and 'mafia', as well as 'facilitating' and 'trafficking', are frequently used interchangeably. Perhaps, at its root, these errors stem from the dominant, patriarchal view of women, especially poor women, as beings who are dependent, and therefore vulnerable. As Juliano writes, 'the social imagination tends to see women as relatively immobile spatially ... a social model is maintained in which men are allowed the possibility of voluntary displacement while women are given the attribute of permanence' (2002: 117).

According to Garaizábal, 'the term *mafia* refers to those organised structures that use extortion through blackmail, coercion and violence to make people do something against their will' (2003: 45). In contrast, the concept of *network*, when it refers to the facilitation of illegal immigration, describes the group of people who organise a migrant's journey. We believe this distinction is crucial, since presupposing that all female migrants are victims of human trafficking actually denies their potential agency and ability to make a deliberate choice to travel.

Moreover, although all illegal immigration mafias are also networks, not all immigration networks are mafias. Some are merely tools used by economic migrants who are travelling voluntarily. Similarly, human *traffickers* will always use *facilitators* at different stages along the journey, but not all *facilitators* – very few, in fact – can accurately be described as *traffickers*. In addition, most female migrants use several different kinds of networks during the course of their journey, of which only very few may turn out to be mafia-based. And lastly, it is important to understand that even those networks that are run by mafias are often not perceived as such by the women involved, even in the cases where they were victims of trafficking.

In a report for the NGO ACSUR-Las Segovias, Bonelli and Ulloa (2001), who researched the journeys of Ecuadorian and Colombian sex workers in Galicia and Madrid, developed a descriptive typology of the different methods these women used to access Spain. These methods fall into the following categories:

- independent migration – an autonomous process carried out with the disinterested help of friends and family;
- migration with the profit-motivated participation of individuals and entities in the country of origin – these can include creditors, travel agencies, etc., that charge a high rate of interest, but organise just about every aspect of the journey;

Ethnography and human rights   103

- migration with the profit-motivated participation of individuals and contacts in Spain, who may or may not be linked with their country of origin – these can include providers of forged papers, people who find contacts in the country of destination and give advice, and people who receive migrants upon arrival and take them to safe houses or their workplace;
- human trafficking – organised networks or mafias that are involved in the trafficking of women for the illegal sex trade (Bonelli and Ulloa 2001: 69–74).

The observations of these researchers led them to establish a gradation in the links to third parties and in the various strategies employed by female migrants. Juliano (2001) makes an interesting point when he comments that the authorities tend to view all facilitating and support structures in the migratory process – even those offered by NGOs – as criminal networks or organisations, while immigrants tend to see them as necessary intermediaries, even in some of the most coercive and exploitative cases. He continues,

> the way in which migrants are treated [during the migratory process] depends on the type of network with which they are involved, and can range from a reasonable debt held with friends or relatives who are willing to wait for repayment if necessary, to enormous debts which carry an extortionate rate of interest and are difficult to cancel. In the latter case, the debt is often taken on under duress by means of coercion, violence or deceit.
>
> (Juliano 2001)

APDHA rejects and denounces such treatment, and any similar situations where women are put in a position of non-consenting dependence. However, we strongly believe than any social intervention measures that are developed to fight human trafficking mafias, or illegal immigration networks that work in a particularly exploitative or predatory way, must give top priority to the well-being and best interests of the women involved. Policies that fail to recognise the diversity of the migratory experience will be of little use, since they make it almost impossible to adopt a response that is appropriate to the needs of each individual.

In our experience, most of the attempts by authorities to 'crack down' on human trafficking mafias are limited to police raids in which the majority of people detained are the women who are working. They are then pressured, under threat of expulsion, to inform on the people who helped them get to Spain. It is our view that this method does not produce tangible results in the fight against human trafficking, other than to criminalise immigrant sex workers, thereby creating an atmosphere of fear and secrecy among them and their immediate social circle.

Using the Nigerian women with whom we work in the Poniente Almeriense as an example, we have found it is most common for the immigration networks that have facilitated their journey to be complex and diverse. There are those that practise human trafficking, are of a mafia-like nature, and are 'compact' – that is

104 *E. Acién González*

to say, they control the journey from beginning to end, and at every stage along the way. For example, a house-bar owner may 'order' a 15-year-old girl from Nigeria through one of these networks, knowing that by the time she arrives in Spain, she will be over 18 and able to work. These compact organisations tend to exercise enormous pressure on migrants, use violent strategies of control during the voyage, and, once it is completed, continue to use violence in order to ensure repayment of the debt.

However, we have also come across many women who used multiple networks at different stages in their journey. For example, a woman may contact one group of people to travel from Nigeria to Morocco, another to obtain resources in the countries of transit, another to access Spain, and yet another to get work at her destination. These heterogeneous circumstances, which seem to be the norm, make it impossible to generalise about the survival and migration strategies of Nigerian women who immigrate to Spain. Often, these networks charge inflated prices for their services, use unfair or very strict measures to ensure repayment, and maintain overly unbalanced power relations with the migrants (in some cases even relations of domination or slavery). Notwithstanding, in many other cases it is merely a question of a mutually accepted and voluntary pact that is entered into between customer and provider, and the migrant is capable of fulfilling the terms on time without any major disruptions.

Within this wide range of different situations, we have identified three frequently used routes and methods of transportation for the journey: (a) Nigeria–Morocco–Spain by motor vehicle, foot and zodiac boat; (b) Nigeria–Libya–Italy–Spain by similar means; and (c) Nigeria–Spain by plane with a fake visa. Until recently, the most common route taken was the first one. The second route only started becoming more popular two years ago when FRONTEX (the European border policing agency) significantly stepped up its presence in northern Morocco, and the third route is the most expensive and least frequently used.

If the first route is taken, the migrant group departs from Benin City in Nigeria, passes through Niger and Mali, stops initially at Tamanrasset in Algeria, and stops again at Tangiers or Oujda in Morocco. The group then waits in Tangiers for an opportunity to catch a zodiac that will take them to the coast of Andalusia (they are dropped at Algeciras, Tarifa, or somewhere along the coast of Granada or Almería). There are also groups in Rabat and Casablanca, at the southern border, that wait to try and gain refugee status instead.

Most of the journey to Morocco is carried out by bus, by car (especially those with four-wheel drives, such as jeeps) and on foot, so in fact the whole journey to Spain can take months, or even years. Men and women travel together in the convoys, starting out by car or jeep, though later there are long distances that have to be crossed on foot, especially through the Sahara desert. These are usually the hardest parts of the journey, where some of the most dramatic and tragic events occur. Several journalists have documented these sections of the route with audio-visual and written testimonies in recent years, and they reveal a terrifying reality.

Ethnography and human rights 105

Often, the most dangerous situations occur at the border, where European pressure to protect the Schengen area is increasing all the time, and is being translated into increasingly repressive measures adopted by the police of each country involved in detecting and detaining migrants.

During the course of our informal conversations with Nigerian women already in Spain, we were able to collect several testimonies highlighting this reality. For example, Blessing (a 21-year-old woman) told us about how at one border point – she did not specify which – she had to dodge the bullets of the police in the middle of the desert after a long walk. 'I was lying on the ground with two girlfriends and one guy friend', she said, explaining that they had thrown themselves down because the police had started shooting at a group of people that was walking in front of them. She continued, 'When I got up again, I did not see the face of one of my girlfriends, she had died of exhaustion.' (Interview with Blessing, 2006.)

In addition, if they are going on foot, it is not unusual for 'guides' – or drivers, if they are travelling by jeep or mini-bus – to abandon a group of migrants in the middle of the desert if they believe that they have only been paid to take them up to a certain point. If this happens, the travellers will have to try and find a new guide or another convoy to join, and must pay another sum of money in order to continue their journey. This tends not to happen with those networks or organised mafias that are 'compact' and that manage every step of the journey, but there is never a complete guarantee. For all central African migrants, this is an extremely stressful stage of the migratory process and a time of great vulnerability, especially for women. Incidents of sexual abuse, pregnancy and birth are common during the journey.

Since FRONTEX stepped up its operations along the Moroccan–Spanish border and coastline two years ago, it has become extremely difficult to enter Spain by zodiac, as people did before. Because of this, the number of migrants choosing the Nigeria–Libya–Italy–Spain route is constantly increasing. The travelling conditions on this itinerary are very much the same as those on the first. Moreover, Maccanico writes,

> the hardship of the journey can last several months and have various stages. It is worth highlighting the fact that at each one of these stages the migrants are at the mercy of a number of different agents ... whether they be traffickers, police or military officials, security guards in detention centres or even ordinary people who sometimes rob them or threaten to call the police if they do not give them money.
>
> (Macciano 2009: 85)

These migrants do not have legal rights in any of the countries through which they pass because they lack papers. Therefore they cannot stay in regular hotels, use public transport, work, or move around freely. Conditions in Libya are just as difficult as they are in Tangiers, and detention centres in Libya are frequently denounced for power abuses and repression. Libya is used as the transit point for

106   E. Acién González

entering Italy due to historical and infrastructure links between the two countries dating from colonial times. It is also used because the stretch of sea that separates the two nations is far larger than that between Spain and Morocco, and is therefore more difficult to police, though its size also makes it more dangerous for boat crossings.

When they finally arrived in Europe, whether in Andalusia or southern Italy, all the Nigerian women told us they felt immensely relieved that the ordeal was over. However, each woman then faced other kinds of difficulties that also form part of the same European system that places pressure on illegal immigrants. These are no longer the result of international repatriation agreements between countries and the externalisation of frontiers, but of immigration laws that are translated into measures ranging from expulsion orders to imprisonment in immigration detention centres (which in practice act as prisons for a crime that is merely administrative).

The price of a migrant's journey varies enormously from case to case, since it depends on the number of intermediaries involved in the process. The price that ends up being paid by the migrant is, of course, far higher than the real cost of the journey, and it is far more expensive for women to travel than it is for men. Some of our contacts in Tangiers told us that the reason for this is 'women have children, they need more help, the journey is more difficult for them' (interview with Evelyn, 2006). Consequently, the price of the journey for a Nigerian woman can be as high as €50,000. The price of the third route, travelling by plane from Nigeria to Spain with a fake visa, is even higher, and can reach €80,000.

Upon arrival in Spain, the work options available to the undocumented migrants in order to pay back their debt from the journey are extremely limited, and only exist within the shadow economy. Often the women are taken immediately, or soon after their arrival, to Madrid, and spend some time living there and in other cities in Spain (some 56 per cent of our respondents). We have also met women who passed through other European countries, such as France, where they waited for a flight to take them to Madrid (especially those who travelled with a fake visa), Italy (where they also worked in prostitution), or Austria.

Exactly how these women have ended up working as prostitutes in our part of Almería is a complex topic. We know that sometimes they arrive at the homes of friends or acquaintances they have met through compatriots. In other cases, they have been given the telephone number of one of the house-bar owners in the area by a contact. In still other cases, they are working for the person who is the last link in the chain of their network, and therefore the one to whom they must repay their debt.

According to our latest calculations, around 460 Nigerian women are working as prostitutes in this area. This number is increasing all the time, and the rate of arrival is also accelerating. Generally, all the women share a desire to stay and live in Spain, but they also want to legalise their immigration status (82 per cent lack residency and/or work permits) in order to be able to change jobs. As can be expected, none of them feel satisfied with their current work situation, citing

Ethnography and human rights 107

dissatisfaction with their work status, the impossibility of finding another job, and their lack of papers or money as reasons. Most of them believe that the difficulty of their situation is due largely to their lack of legal status, so they hope that it will improve when they obtain residency or work permits.

In this region, the women who work in prostitution offer sexual services almost exclusively to the immigrant population and therefore at a very low price, oscillating between €10 and €20. The economic position of Nigerian sex workers differs greatly from that of other women who work in prostitution in the region who are of Romanian, Russian, Lithuanian or Latin American origin. Since the client base of the latter group is made up of Spanish men who generally have greater spending power, these immigrant women can charge a higher price for their services.

Conclusions

This brief description of a fragment of the migratory experience of Nigerian sex workers in Almería makes sense if we place it in the context of APDHA's action and research work. It is not necessary to apply dogmatic ideology to understand the situation of social injustice that surrounds us. The migratory process of these women demonstrates the failure of most of the governments of the countries through which they pass to fulfil the majority of the articles contained in the United Nations Universal Declaration of Human Rights of 1948.

An ethnographic research methodology can help us to gain a greater understanding of the reality these women face, at the same time allowing us to come into close contact with those people who are at serious risk of social exclusion. The results of the research that we have carried out are, in themselves, a denunciation of unsustainable social conditions. This is the foundation and aim of our organisation: to research in order to understand, and to understand in order to intervene, support and denounce.

Notes

1 This chapter has been translated from Spanish into English by Sara Louise Roberts.
2 I take Malinowski's definition of the term here. He states that in ethnography, 'the goal is, in short, to manage to understand the other's point of view, his or her view of life, their vision of their world'. In order to do this, he adds, it is important not only to immerse oneself in their institutions, customs, codes, or to study their behaviour and mentality but also to 'become aware of why the man lives and in what resides his happiness' (1922: 42).
3 Andalusia is an autonomous community situated in the south of Spain.
4 LOEX 8/2000 stands for Ley Orgánica 8/2000, de 22 de diciembre, de reforma de la Ley Orgánica 4/2000, de 11 de enero, sobre derechos y libertades de los extranjeros en España y su integración social [legislation on the rights and freedoms of foreigners in Spain and on their social integration].
5 The Schengen cooperation space is based on the European Treaty of 1985 signed in Schengen and represents a 'free movement of persons' area. States that have signed the Treaty abolished all internal borders and instead have set up a single external border.

108   *E. Acién González*

Within this, common standards and procedures apply regarding short stay visas, applications for asylum and border controls. At the same time, there is increased cooperation and coordination between law enforcement and judicial authorities to ensure safety. The Schengen cooperation was incorporated into the law of the European Union by the Treaty of Amsterdam in 1997. The states including in the Schengen space are: Germany, Austria, Belgium, Cyprus, Denmark, Slovenia, Slovakia, Spain, Estonia, Finland, France, Greece, Holland, Hungary, Ireland, Italy, Latvia, Lithuania, Luxembourg, Malta, Poland, Portugal, United Kingdom, Czech Republic, Sweden, Iceland, Liechtenstein, Norway and Switzerland.

6 Checa (2007) analyses the process of invasion and succession that has occurred in these areas of rural housing in the Poniente Almeriense.

Bibliography

Acién, E. and F. Majuelos (2003) *De la exclusión al estigma: Mujeres inmigrantes africanas en contextos de prostitución en el Poniente Almeriense. Una aproximación,* APDHA, available at www.giemic.uclm.es/index.php?option=com_docman&task=doc_view&gid=1113&Itemid=60 (accessed 5 May 2011).

Bonelli, E. and M. Ulloa (eds) (2001) *Tráfico e inmigración de mujeres en España: colombianas y ecuatorianas en los servicios domésticos y sexuales,* Madrid: ACSUR-Las Segovias, available at www.ucm.es/info/IUDC/img/biblioteca/Informetraficoacsur. pdf (accessed 5 May 2011).

Checa, J.C. (2007) *Viviendo juntos aparte,* Barcelona: Icaria.

Collectivo Ioé (1995) 'Desigualdad e integración social: Dispositivos de regulación y "determinación política" de las necesidades,' *Desigualdad y pobreza hoy,* Madrid: Talasa.

Garaizábal, C. (2003) 'Derechos laborales para las trabajadoras del sexo,' *Mugak,* no. 23, available at www.pensamientocritico.org/crigar0703.htm (accessed 5 May 2011).

Juliano, D. (2001) 'La telaraña de las redes migratorias,' *Ciudadanía Sexual,* Boletín 11, available at www.ciudadaniasexual.org/publicaciones/Doc_La%20_Telarana_de%20_las_Rede_Migratorias.pdf (accessed 5 May 2011).

Juliano, D. (2002) *La prostitución, el espejo oscuro,* Icaria: Barcelona.

Maccanico, Y. (2009) 'Relaciones peligrosas: El acercamiento italo-líbio y sus efectos para los migrantes,' *Informe Derechos Humanos en la Frontera Sur, 2008,* Seville: APDHA, 80–90.

Malinowsky, B. (1922) *Argonauts of the Western Pacific,* New York: E.P. Dutton & Co. Inc.

Ruiz, E. (2005) *Intervención social: Cultura discurso y poder,* Madrid: Talasa.

Walters, W. (2002) 'Mapping Schengenland: Denaturalizing the border,' *Environment and Planning D: Society & Space,* 20 (5): 561–580.

Interviews

Blessing, 3 August 2006 (interview with Estefanía Acién González at Roquetas de Mar, Almería, Spain).

Evelyn, 24 August 2006 (interview with Estefanía Acién González, Tangiers, Morocco).

6 Moments of solidarity, migrant activism and (non)citizens at global borders

Political agency at Tanzanian refugee camps, Australian detention centres and European borders

Heather Johnson[1]

This chapter emerges from chance encounters that took place during my field work in 2007–2008 in Tanzania, Spain and Australia. The use of qualitative methods embedded in the field leaves the researcher open to interactions and relationships outside of the central focus of a study, and in each field site I found myself interacting with migrants for seemingly unique, disconnected moments that were nevertheless profoundly revealing about the divide between citizen and non-citizen and the practice of legitimate politics. Refugees who, in defiance of prohibitive laws, chose to work outside the camp in Kibondo, Tanzania, 'illegal migrant' children who demanded that the Spanish authorities hear their complaints about their living conditions in Melilla, Spain, and detainees and ex-detainees who participated in a public protest outside of the immigration courts in Sydney, Australia were each transgressing expected behaviour for individuals caught within the webs of global migration control. My encounters with each were fleeting, momentary and elusive. Nevertheless, they reveal glimpses of a deeper political activity that operates at the level of the everyday and the local; they reflect political decisions being made quietly that have the potential to profoundly reshape our understandings of the ways in which migrants enact agency, and how those decisions intersect with political action and agency. In their 'rewriting of the script' these moments can be understood as non-citizen activism that is both momentary and powerful.

In this chapter I ask what moments of solidarity between citizens and migrants – be they refugees, asylum seekers, or those understood as 'illegal' or 'irregular' – can add to our understandings of political activism. I ask what implications are suggested if we begin from the migrant perspective rather than that of the citizen, and particularly what may be contributed to how we theorise and understand political change. The global politics of asylum are complex and constantly shifting, and increasingly represent a similarity of policy and practice at diverse global borders. As such, they create a similarity of political experience for those who are crossing global borders without the prior sanction of the state.

110 *H. Johnson*

I begin by providing a brief account of each 'moment' in the field, connecting migrant narratives to the policies of encampment and detention and to broader understandings of the political agency of non-citizens. I then assess our contemporary understandings of activism, and assess how this changes in shifting from the perspective of the migrant citizen to that of the migrant. Finally, I introduce the concept of 'moments' to reshape understandings of activism, and argue that 'momentary activism' is better placed to capture the political actions and agency of highly vulnerable populations, particularly in their everyday resistances to the systems of exclusion that operate at global border spaces.

Moments in the field

The agency of non-citizens, and of irregular migrants and asylum seekers particularly, is shaped profoundly by their position within the power relations of a global society of sovereign nation-states. As non-citizens, they are not a part of the broader social contract that underpins the territorial sovereign power of the nation-state. They are thus outside of the complex of rights and obligations upon which the state is based and so are unable to make 'legitimate' claims to either citizenship rights or to political participation. As migrants, their crossing of the border represents a rupture in the capacity of the state to control the border, and thus territorial membership of the citizen community. The consequence of this both marginalising and potentially threatening position is that non-citizens as migrants are subject to tight control and to increasingly restrictive and exclusionary policies as practices. The extremes of these are those policies of encampment and detention within global border spaces that exert control over non-citizens by making the boundary between citizen and non-citizen not only political but spatial.

For Agamben (2000), sovereign power is founded upon the ability to decide upon the state of exception, and the camp is the space in which this is permanently realised. He understands 'the camp' as a spatial arrangement of the permanent state of exception that remains outside of the normal state of law (ibid.: 39). It is a space of containment that operates not only to exclude individuals from the normal operations of society, but also to keep them outside and to prevent any possibility of bridging this gap. Agamben writes that 'we will … have to admit to be facing a camp virtually every time that such a structure is created, regardless of the nature of the crimes committed in it and regardless of the denomination and specific topography it might have' (ibid.: 41). In this, he is gesturing to the existence of the space of a camp even outside of our traditional imagination of such a place. He describes a soccer stadium used to house illegals and airport zones as possibilities. Each of the following 'moments' in the field reflects the ongoing interactions between the practices of 'the camp' and non-citizens as they challenge and resist its/their exclusions and exceptionality. In the refugee camp of Kibondo, reception centre of Melilla, and detention centre of Sydney non-citizens are bridging the gap in moments of activism and solidarity.

Moments in Tanzania

By government count, commonly held to be under-estimation, Tanzania was hosting 630,000 refugees in the April of 2004. At the time, only Pakistan, Iran, Jordan and Palestine were hosting more refugees individually (Kamanga 2005: 100). Tanzania has historically been, and continues to be, the largest refugee-hosting state in Africa. This is largely due to its highly porous land borders, and also to a high degree of cultural affinity within the Great Lakes region which makes migration within the region an easier prospect. These conditions have led to near incapacity for border control and describe a border regime that is highly vulnerable to irregular migration of asylum seekers.

The 1990s ushered in a sea change in Tanzania's approach to refugee migration and began what has been called a 'temporary protection' emphasis, which replaced the old focus on integration (Ministry of Home Affairs 1999). The 1998 Refugee Control Act repealed the 1966 Refugee (Control) Act that had governed an 'Open Door' policy (Kamanga 2005: 102–103). Khoti Kamanga (2005) argues that the 1998 Act signals both a deterrence message and a disenchantment with the insufficient support provided through the international humanitarian assistance system. It is directed at reassuring the Tanzania population, wary of large refugee flows, by creating legal means to deal with the problem of migration (104–105). The Act rejects local integration as a solution, and shifts back to individual determination of full refugee status in place of group determination and en masse regularisation (108–109). These shifts parallel shifts that are perceptible in the global regime. Deterrence is now a key part of border control in most places; it is a stated goal for the European border security agency of FRONTEX and for the Australian government. The individual determination of refugee status is an even more important reflection of the globality of increasingly rigid regimes. It marks a moment whereby to become a refugee, to achieve full Convention status with all associated rights and freedoms including those to employment and movement, is a rare and difficult thing.

The 1998 Act makes residence in a 'Designated Area' (DA) mandatory (Kamanga 2005: 110). A DA is a refugee camp, and anyone in Tanzania claiming refugee status either by individual application or via *prima facie* status must live in a camp. The confinement of refugees to camps is directly linked to the control of migration. A Ministry official stated that the limits on refugee mobility are designed to reduce the number of refugees accessing residency permits or permits for further migration. He went on to explain that the camps are kept close to the border to facilitate repatriation (interview: Ministry of Home Affairs, Dar es Salaam, 2007). Such limitations are also supported by both local and international non-governmental organisations. Given the experience of the refugees, and 'because some of them are criminals', the limitation of movement is seen as a necessary evil (interview: Norwegian People's Aid worker, Dar es Salaam, 2008). Tanzania's policy change is 'not so much about border control as it is about migration control' (interview: European Commission humanitarian aid worker, Dar es Salaam, 2008). The border cannot be controlled, but there is

112 H. Johnson

within those borders significant capacity to control migrants. Law can be enforced in the villages, even if it cannot be enforced at the border (interview: European Commission humanitarian aid worker, Dar es Salaam, 2008).

In the DAs, the rights of refugees are tightly circumscribed. By policy and through the management of the international community, basic education and health care (including necessary drugs) are provided. Participation in the local economy via employment, however, is forbidden, and the only income refugees can earn beyond basic provisions and the food aid provided by the camp management is through 'income generating programmes' that include raising cattle and handicrafts. Participation in the broader society is prohibited. Refugees cannot go more than four kilometres outside the boundaries of the camp, and must be within its borders by five in the afternoon, by which point all non-refugees, including international staff, must have departed for the day. A strict division between the citizens and non-citizens – refugees – is maintained.

In December of 2007 Nduta was hosting approximately 50,000 refugees, the majority of whom were from Burundi. At the time, Tanzania was undertaking a repatriation programme for the Burundian refugees according to the tripartite agreement that had been signed with both the United Nations High Commissioner for Refugees (UNHCR) and the government of Burundi. It had been decided that with the tentative peace accord signed in the summer of 2007 in Burundi the violence between the government and the FLN (Forces for National Liberation) had ceased, rendering the country safe for return for refugees living abroad. As part of the repatriation efforts, refugee camps in Western Tanzania were being consolidated as people returned 'home'. As a result, the two refugee camps remaining were suffering from overcrowding and several thousand refugees were living in makeshift shelters while they awaited for their long term assignments.

It was evening, and I was walking close to one of the local villages with one of the aid workers at Nduta. We ran into a boy about 17 years old, who recognised her from the camp. He was sitting on a rock when we approached, and initially he ran off, but he returned. He had recognised Rosa[2] as from the camp, and had initially run because he feared we would report him for being well outside of the boundary. He asked us whether we could help him get a visa to go to the United States, or to Australia. The answer, as it always was when we were asked, was no. Rosa challenged him, then, on why he was out of bounds. He initially panicked, but then explained that he had found work on a local farm, and was getting paid the same as the Tanzanians. He seemed to know that it was against the rules, but explained that it was fine because the local people were happy to have him and he was pretending to be Tanzanian. His account correlated with several accounts from local Tanzanians about illegal workers from the camp: they saw no difference between the Burundians who crossed the state border daily for work and refugees who had left the camp. They knew of several refugees who had 'escaped' the camp and were living in local villages. The work was not necessarily sustained over time, but was instead day labour, one-time tasks and solitary encounters. Sustaining the relationship over time, if the status of the worker as a refugee was known, was too dangerous.

Moments in Spain

The border regime of Europe has become notorious in the past decade as representing 'Fortress Europe'; as internal borders have become less regulated, the external frontier has been further restricted rendering any border crossing – whether for asylum or otherwise – a challenging endeavour. This is particularly visible in the south of Spain, and in the Spanish enclave of Melilla, located across the Mediterranean Sea and in Moroccan territory. Calavita (1998: 543) writes that the evolution of Spain's immigration laws has been 'hand in hand' with the process of European integration. During the 1970s and 1980s, Spanish regularisation programmes and perceived lack of attention to its Southern frontier led to the perception among the Northern members of the European Union of Spain as the 'soft underbelly of Europe' (see Geddes 2003). Spain was seen to be the weak point in the external border control of Europe, and changes since the early 1990s in Spanish policy are largely perceived as being at the behest of the European Union (interview: government worker, Madrid; NGO, Almería, UNHCR 2008; interview: government worker, Rabat, 2008). As a result, the focus is on border control, and the Spanish responsibility is to 'Stop! Stop! Stop!' (interview: NGO, Almería, 2008).

As European integration has developed, the gap between Spanish policy and European interests has closed. According to a federal government worker, when Spain joined the European Community there was intense pressure on the Ministry of the Interior to 'step up' in its control of the border. Now, however, they are very much on the same page as Germany, France and other Northern European member states. It is important, he argues, to have a sense of effectively dealing with migration because it gives the population a sense of control – although, he acknowledged, this may not be good for the migrants in Spain (interview: government worker, Madrid, 2008). In recent years, Spain has been one of the staunchest proponents for tougher border controls, signing several readmission agreements that allow irregular migrants to be returned, if not to their country of origin, then to a transit country outside of Europe (Andreas 2003; Lindstrøm 2005; Geddes 2005). The readmission agreement that Spain has with Morocco enables migrants to be sent to Morocco if there is no agreement with their country of origin (Geddes 2005: 165).

Lavenex (2006: 337) argues that the goal of the European migration regime is to curtail unwanted flows before they reach the common territory. Melilla is before the common territory. It is, however, within the auspices of European policy, and so migrants find themselves caught in stasis, unable to more either forward or back. The arrival of irregular migrants by boat on the Spanish coast has engendered public panic, and provided further justification for restrictive measures and increased surveillance of the border. Within this rubric the enclaves of Ceuta and Melilla have a unique role. They are simultaneously part of Europe, and outside of the 'Fortress'. In this, they have become a kind of migratory 'non-place' within the border control regime. In the space of the autonomous city, migration to Europe has an exceptional character. Far from

114 H. Johnson

being included in the migration zone of Europe, within the enclaves, the violence and repressive elements of the securitised migration regime loses whatever thin veil of humanitarian motives might remains present on the continent.

Melilla is an area of 12 square kilometres that has a 10-kilometre border with the Moroccan province of Nador. This border is marked by a double barbed wire fence, patrolled on each side by both Spanish and Moroccan authorities. The only break in the fence is a gate across the main road, heavily guarded and with two check points for entry, and two check points for exit. The road is lined by a high fence, with a walkway for pedestrians that is similarly surrounded. Those crossing the border must present identification and all necessary visas and documentation. Reflecting an agreement between Spain and Morocco, residents of Nador are able to cross the border freely, primarily to work, and each day thousands who live in Morocco but work in Melilla do so (Carling 2007: 23). This border crossing is part of their daily commute, and it is this kind of mobility that characterises 'regular' migration to Melilla. Strict regulations about residence and work establish the rules by which Moroccan citizens find employment in the Spanish territory. Crossing the Mediterranean to the mainland of Spain, however, is entirely different and requires accessing the regular Spanish immigration regime of visas and permissions. When crossing the Mediterranean, migrants cross another border. The border of sovereign Spain may be the fence in Nador; the border of Fortress Europe is the sea.

Upon arrival in Melilla most migrants register with the police immediately (Carling 2007: 24; interview: government worker, Madrid, 2008). Their assumption and hope is that registration, which frequently coincides with the filing of an asylum application, will effectively time-stamp their arrival. A lack of documents combined with the asylum claim protects them from immediate removal. The belief is that after a certain fixed time period they will be transferred to the mainland. While it is the case that a three-year period in the mainland will entitle a person to residence regardless of how s/he achieved entry to Spain, such a policy does not exist in practice in Melilla (interview: NGO, Melilla, 2008). The city's autonomy has meant that Spanish state policies are only selectively applied, and the 'waiting time' for migrants not only regularly exceeds three years but also frequently ends not in residence in Spain, but in deportation to the country of origin. As a Melilla asylum lawyer and claims assessor says, 'only the Spanish government knows when people will be able to move' (interview: NGO, Melilla, 2008) – and in what direction.

While they wait, those few who successfully cross the border are housed in 'immigration reception centres', sometimes for years, as they await determinations on their asylum applications to Spain. While the centres are 'open' in that individuals can come and go, migrants are prohibited from working or earning an income, and are required to eat and sleep in the centres.

In Melilla, where I conducted research in the spring of 2008, there is a Centre for Unaccompanied Minors where several children who have crossed the borders on their own are housed while they are processed by the state. Most of the children, aged six to 15 years old, are Moroccans who claim to have come to work.

Formally, they are required to attend one of the local schools. Their actual attendance, however, is poorly monitored and of the 12 children I met personally, at least two (aged 12 and 13) were working for a local café and being paid under the table.

Towards the end of my first trip to Melilla, another researcher and I were approached by a group of about 10 boys who were looking for Miguel, an advocate for human and child rights that we were both working with. They had 'escaped' from the centre, and wanted his assistance. They had been beaten several times and denied food and showers, but had finally left (by climbing the wall) because they had been told that they were no longer allowed to go outside. They wanted Miguel to help them file a complaint with the local police station about their living conditions and treatment in the centre. While we waited for Miguel, their spirits were high as they laughed, talked and joked. They told us about their families back home, talked about their hopes for 'when they grew up' – which included being a doctor, a mechanic and an astronaut. Often, they broke into a chant in Spanish: 'We are children! We have rights!' Miguel initially tried to dissuade them from going to the police themselves, offering to file the complaint on their behalf, which, he felt, would reduce their vulnerability to any repercussions. They refused, and insisted upon going to the station themselves. Once there, it took four hours, but they filed a complaint like any other citizen. The police officers took them back to the Centre where the complaint was followed up, and formal reprimands were administered.

Insisting upon making a police complaint did not challenge the overarching Spanish border policy; it was far more localised and everyday in its challenge. It did, however, establish the children as rights-bearing subjects despite their non-citizenship, and brought to bear their change even on those conditions of exception determined and shaped by the state.

Moments in Australia

Partially due to its unique geography as an island nation, Australia has one of the most heavily regulated, defended and restricted border regimes in the world. Government policies actively differentiate between different categories of migrants with approximately 62 visa categories. The emphasis is on both mode of arrival, and whether a migrant has government permission to arrive. This applies to asylum seekers as much as it applies to any other migrant. Onshore claimants are those asylum seekers who arrive in Australia without referral, sponsorship or state permission. They are often undocumented, and have been dubbed in Australian discourse as 'illegal arrivals'. Generally, they are representative of the 'boat people' that began arriving in the early 1970s. For Australia, the issue of border control is not rooted in a challenge to the concept of asylum itself – a stance that would likely be unpopular both domestically and internationally. Rather, the issue is in choice and sovereignty: the Australian state is fiercely protective of its right to determine precisely who is able to claim and receive asylum within its territory. By arriving in Australian territory

116 H. Johnson

without prior permission, onshore claimants are represented as attempting to circumvent and undermine Australian sovereignty by breaching its borders. In this they are a threat that must be – and is being – managed and controlled. In 2001 Prime Minister John Howard ran with the election slogan: 'We will decide who comes into this country and the circumstances in which they come here' (Moran 2005: 181). He was re-elected for a third term.

In a 1992 amendment to the *Migration Act*, mandatory detention was put into place for all unauthorised arrivals, and Australia became the only developed state to implement detention as a universal policy. Detention is required for these individuals from the time of their arrival to the time of either their departure or their acquisition of an Australian visa (Brennan 2003: 86). The policy of mandatory detention gained international notoriety as a result of both the extreme conditions of its six detention centres and a policy of interception and offshore encampment that became known as the 'Pacific Solution'. The detention centres on mainland Australia gained condemnation from both domestic and international human rights activists for extreme conditions and became the sites of significant detainee protests which included acts of self-harm such as lip sewing, self-burial and hunger strikes.

In the Pacific Solution, Australia's outlying islands, such as Christmas Island, were excised from the 'migration zone'. This move prevented those who arrive on those territories from making an asylum claim in Australia. Instead, they were transferred to processing centres and detention in either Papua New Guinea or Nauru, where they were assessed by the UNHCR. In exchange for this access, Australia provided these states with financial compensation (Curran and Kneebone 2003: 3). Between 2001 and 2005 all but two of Australia's onshore detention centres were closed as the Pacific Solution was preferred by the Howard government for housing migrants. A change of government in late 2007 to Rudd's Labour Party led to the official cancellation of the Pacific Solution. However, a new and isolated high security centre on Christmas Island was opened, and it remains the only perceptible replacement. While Villawood detention centre in Sydney and Marybong in Melbourne remain open, Christmas Island is the preferred detention centre for 'unauthorised migrants'.

During my research in the summer of 2008 I worked with members of the Refugee Action Coalition, an activist group with chapters in most Australian communities, and through the RAC I had met two former detainees and one current detainee. In August of 2008 there was a great deal of advocacy taking place on behalf of the individual remaining in detention, whose asylum claim had been denied. He was due to be deported at the end of the month. He had lived in Australia for eight years before being detained, and had been in detention at Villawood Detention Centre in Sydney for seven years. As a part of the effort, a rally was held in front of the department of immigration in Sydney. Inside, the final appeal against his deportation order was being heard. He was on a hunger strike, and had made several legal claims to the highest levels of the refugee and immigration system. The small crowd that gathered listened to several speeches made about his case, including a statement he had prepared and

Moments of solidarity 117

provided to one of the activists, each advocating his release from detention and the regularisation of his status in Australia. One of the leader and organiser of the protest was a former detainee who had known the appellant in detention, and who was using existing networks of citizen activism to gather support. Afterwards, another organiser confided to me that he was sincerely worried because very few detainees were being held on the mainland any longer. Asylum seekers were no longer held in Melbourne, he said, because the activism was too strong (interview: migrant, Sydney, 2008). There were very few left in Sydney, and the Christmas Island centre (very remote, and very hard to get to) was ready to open, and that is where people were being sent: out of the reach of citizens.

Moments

Each of these 'moments' represents contexts that are dramatically different from one another, in different states, subject to different border regulations, with different conditions determining the choices being made. The policy context of each, however, has established a space of exclusion which (irregular) migrants inhabit. Refugee camps in Tanzania, the reception centres of Spain and the detention centres of Australia are each spatial representations of broader practices that control both the mobility and the agency of the non-citizen. In each case, however, the migrants were involved in a contestation of their right to remain in their states of asylum: the boy who wished to remain in Tanzania despite the repatriation programme; the children who wished to remain in Melilla to work; the detainee who wished to become a status refugee and remain in Australia. In each case, migrants were transgressing 'expected' behaviours: the refugee was working in the community; the children were making conscious, political demands of the police; the detainee and former detainee were openly challenging the legal system of Australia. Finally, in each case, the migrants involved engaged with citizens in their activities, and their activisms represented, if only temporarily, the establishment of a relationship of solidarity between non-citizens and citizens within the politics of asylum. In these moments, the 'activism' that takes place is easily understood as activism when we begin from the citizen position, as part of a long-term challenge to the established state order. Can these moments be understood as activism when we begin from the position of the migrants? I argue that they can, and that the implications of this understanding contain possibilities for a reshaping of our understanding of activism and agency. The importance of each arises from the solidarity that is expressed and experienced across the citizen and non-citizen divide.

Political activism

The implications of these moments for non-citizens living in spaces of exception as characterised by the refugee camp in Tanzania, the reception centres of Melilla, and the detention centres of Australia are profound for our understanding of their political agency, and recognition of their actions as 'political

118   *H. Johnson*

activism'. Writing of the study of global social movements, traditional 'activist' communities, Nyers (2006) argues that scholars typically ask whether they are part of a global civil society, whether they have transnational connections, or whether they have created a cosmopolitical public sphere. They rarely ask who can speak, who can act, or who possesses transformative agency (50). These questions are rarely posed for activism more generally. This is at least partially because, for many, the answer is already given: it is the citizen. This assumption of what is normal maintains the boundary between non-citizen and citizen, and thus constructs the citizen as the legitimate agent, the possible activist.

A traditional citizen-centred understanding of legitimate political agency is deeply rooted in nation-state theory and practices of sovereignty. In this framework the citizen is the archetypical political agent who is endowed with the capacity to act and so to engage in politics. Within the structure of the nation-state system, political agency is enabled, but it is also managed and controlled, concretising a rigid separation between the citizen and the non-citizen. The non-citizen is divested of this capacity to participate and thus of recognition as a political agent. The question is not one of potential agency within this discourse. Rather, it is one of whether political participation is legitimate. The impact of living in a camp space is to be rendered as, in Agamben's terms, 'bare life'. Agamben (2000) argues that state power is founded upon the ability of the state to keep bare life safe and protected to the degree that it submits itself to the sovereign's right to decide life and death. A state of exception exists when this life is put into question, and revoked as the foundation of political power (ibid.: 4–8). As such, bare life *no longer matters*; it does not justify or support power, and so is ultimately vulnerable to power. It 'cannot be inscribed into the order' (Agamben 2000: 43). As Agamben writes, such a state means that literally anything can happen within the camp as the exercise of sovereign power is arbitrary (ibid.: 42). The lived consequence of this state of being is that migrants caught within the space of a camp are denied the capacity for political agency, and are instead laid bare to the will of the state not simply to exclude them, but also to remove them entirely.

The framework of citizen as political agent for understandings of political activism – both in academic analysis and in strategy for activists themselves – has serious implications for what is seen as effective in making change. This is not to denigrate or dismiss action by non-citizens, but instead to observe that within this traditional framework for understanding agency the citizen forms the crucial bridge between the activists and the state/power structures. The citizen becomes a necessary partner – indeed, a central partner – for change to be effective, for action to be seen as 'activist'. Without the citizen to sustain and interpret the discourse, non-citizen activism is not 'political' in its mobilisation of agency and voice. Huysmans (2002) argues that migrant protest in bodily acts such as lip-sewing, which has been dramatically prevalent in global detention centres, only has political significance if mediated by public media, mobilisations on behalf of asylum questions, contestations of human rights in the courts, etc.[3] They require the intervention of the citizen.

Political activism can be understood as resistance to particular structures of power; it is about building relationships among people that foster change (Martin, Hanson and Fontaine 2007: 3). In more traditional analysis, it is found in social movement organisation, collective action and public protest. Studies suggest that at the centre of the activism discourse is a commitment to change and a methodology relying on public protest. The notion, be it implicit or explicit, is that activism requires organised, collective action and social protest (Sowards and Renegar 2006: 57–58). It is most easily recognizable in what Zolberg (1972: 183) refers to as 'moments of madness' where people believe that 'all is possible'. He argues that Paris of 1968 was such a moment, where those participating in the streets challenged the structures of their society, demanding change: 'The moment of immense joy, when daily cares are transcended, when emotions are freely expressed, when the spirit moves men to talk and to write, when the carefully erected walls which compartmentalise society collapse' (ibid.: 186).

These moments are how political activisms are imagined – rallies, marches, letter writing campaigns, alternative newsletters. In all, however, it is those who are 'members of society' who are talking and writing, or who are enabling others to do so. Without the citizen, the movement collapses. Activism, in this understanding, is directed at the society (the state, the world) as a whole, and at resisting social norms and pressures (Sowards and Renegar 2006: 65, 59). It is public and collective, sustained and outspoken, and explicitly directed at broad power structures.

What Isin (2008) terms 'acts of citizenship' are central to an understanding of activism as distinct from simple civic participation. Isin argues that an 'act' is distinct from 'action' in that it represents a challenge to 'habitus' – the ways of thought and conduct internalised by members of society over the long term (ibid.: 15). For Isin, it is momentous acts that are required to break with habitus (ibid.: 18). Such a notion corresponds closely with Zolberg's conception of moments of madness. Such a focus allows our understanding of political activism to call into question the traditional focus of social and political thought on orders and routinised practices, and to instead enact the unexpected, unpredictable and unknown (Isin 2008: 20, 27), making a rupture in the given (ibid.: 25). An activist, Isin argues, is engaged in writing, not following, scripts. Activists are creative, answerable and responsible; they actualise ways of being political in that they break with habitus, and thus challenge the normal of society. They create and effect change. And, most crucially for Isin, acts produce actors; they produce activist citizens (ibid.: 38). An 'activist' citizen is thus differentiated from the 'active' citizen in that while an active citizen may participate, there is not necessarily fundamental systemic challenge in their action. An 'activist' citizen, however, is understood in this conceptualisation as an individual who mounts just such a foundational challenge.

But activists here remain cast in the mode of the citizen, and thus activism remains the privilege of the citizen. Too often, the world of the legitimate political act is accepted as being that of the citizen, while the non-citizen – the refugee, asylum seeker, irregular migrant etc. – is understood as being excluded from such an arena. The citizen, then, can advocate on behalf of the non-citizen, and solidarity thus becomes a clientelist relationship rather than one of equally powerful political voices. In order to be effective in expressing demands or giving voice to concerns, non-citizen activism as understood within this frame requires the citizen to 'deliver' the message. Without the involvement of the citizen, no voice is possible and the demands or concerns go unheard.

Nyers (2006: 97) argues that conventional representations of refugeeness cast the refugee as the mirror image of the citizen. He also writes that '[refugee] voices are emptied of political content, reduced to a pitiful cry vis-à-vis the articulate speech of the citizen' (2006: 50). For Edkins and Pin-Fat (2004: 4, 9), the issue is that migrants and non-citizens within spaces of exception are caught not in true relations of power, in which resistance is not only possible but always present, but in relations of violence. They argue that the controlling spaces in which non-citizens are captured by sovereign power operate as exceptional spaces that not only marginalise non-citizens, but exclude them entirely. For them, '[f]reedom is the condition for the existence of power relations' (ibid.: 5). This draws striking parallels with Arendt's famous assertion (1951) that 'human rights' are not possible outside of the structures of citizenship in that any rights require a state to protect and enact them. She writes that the true denial of human rights is the denial of 'a place in the world which makes opinions significant and actions effective' (1951: 176). Caught within structures of border control and management that deny such a place, migrants are not free. The distinction that is made by Edkins and Pin-Fat is telling. They argue that a relationship of violence acts 'immediately and directly upon others', while a relationship of power 'acts upon ... actions' (2004: 10). To be engaged in relations of power, then, individuals must have a recognised capacity to act. What is in question is not their political being, but instead their capacity to challenge the established order. Non-citizens do not have a recognised capacity to act.

The operation of such relations of violence is apparent in all three of our moments. In Tanzania, an official understanding of refugees as potentially dangerous and threatening to the national community has enforced a physical removal of refugee bodies from Tanzanian society as they are compelled by law to live in a camp. Their actions are not a challenge; their presence is. Similar relations exist in Spain, where migrants are required to live in the immigration reception centres and are constantly subject to the threat of deportation which, in most cases, is understood as imminent. Again, in Australia, the practice of mandatory detention is about the presence of the non-citizen and their existence in society.

Within this frame, starting from the position of the citizen, each of our moments from the field is easily coded as being 'about' citizen action 'on behalf of' non-citizen migrants. In Tanzania, those national Tanzanians who facilitate work for the refugees by hiring them and paying them wages in spite of the law, and who protect refugees who are outside of the camp from detection and arrest, are not necessarily engaged in large-scale, organised protest. By their decisions and actions, however, they are resisting the frameworks proposed and enforced by the state. It is the citizens' actions, their agency, which enables the refugees to challenge the structures and regulations that control their lives. In Spain, it is the assistance of Miguel, the human rights activist who is a citizen, that enables the children to gain access to the police. It is his ongoing advocacy and action that has created (or, at least, largely created) the context within which they are able to make claims and demand a change to their condition. Finally, in Australia, it is the citizen presence at the rally that enabled the safe presence of non-citizens and that mobilised both political and moral leverage against the government by enacting citizen rights of free-speech. Further it was a citizen who delivered the message from the detainee about to be deported, without which his voice would not have been present.

In each case the impetus for action did not necessarily begin with the citizen. In each, non-citizens were present and it was their 'world' and condition that was the object of the demands being made. But in each case, it is possible to assume or understand the citizen as the translator of non-citizen demands into legitimate political voice, who enabled the claims, and who made the actions effective. Within a traditional framework and by beginning from the citizen position, the picture that emerges is one of citizen action as political activism. Clearly, controlling the presence of migrants/non-citizens also impacts their capacity to act. The practical implications of such policies are that where removal is imminent, and exclusion into defined spaces removed from general society is mandated by law, actions are also controlled. The object of the policy, however, is not non-citizen action but non-citizens themselves. Non-citizen protest, therefore, is 'a demand for a return to properly political power relations' (Edkins and Pin-Fat 2004: 12). It is a demand that the actions of non-citizens be, in Isin's terms, 'acts'.

Beginning from the non-citizen

Recent scholarship within migration and refugee studies has argued convincingly in favour of the capacity of non-citizens to exert agency and thus participate in transforming the relationship of violence in which they are embroiled into relations of power. Nyers (2006: 49) writes, 'By challenging the state's prerogative to distinguish between insiders and outsiders, political movements by and in support of undocumented migrants and "non-status" refugees force the matter of sovereignty to the forefront of their political strategy'. In challenging the drawing of lines between citizens and non-citizens on the basis of the capacity for political action and voice, such movements attempt to dispense with the categorical definition of refugee identity as non-political (Nyers: 128).

Isin's definition of 'acts of citizenship' enables such a reconceptualisation. In focusing on the act rather than the actor, the identity category is displaced from being the defining concern. Indeed, inasmuch as refugee political action is 'unexpected, unpredictable and unknown', it represents a more profound rupture in habitus than many acts by citizens. In its challenge to 'normal' understandings

122   *H. Johnson*

of who can act, non-citizen/migrant activism is extremely productive of claim-making subjects. If understood as practices and acts carried out by the refugee, such activism and advocacy becomes acts from an exceptional space, speaking from outside and the margins which, while powerful in its challenge, is more easily dismissed from official or legitimate discourse. I propose that we regard such moments as moments of solidarity that reflect 'acts of citizenship' in that they reflect practices that produce a particular, active subject. Scholars such as Soguk (2007: 300) argue that 'of all the insurrectionary struggles, migrants' struggles, especially the movements of illegal migrants, asylum seekers and refugees, exemplify insurrectional politics most instructively'. For Soguk, they epitomise the challenge to territorial and national orders (ibid.: 300). Mezzadra and Neilson (2003) similarly highlight this challenge, and connect it to the logic of domination that Agamben speaks of. They argue that this logic is diffused throughout society. To effectively challenge it, we must escape the paternalistic vision of this categorisation and see migrants as central protagonists (Mezzadra and Neilson 2003).

Moulin and Nyers (2007), in their examination of the Sudanese refugee protests in Cairo, have established an extremely strong case for understanding political action by non-citizens as activism. They argue that in order to articulate a political voice, migrants must take the strategy of interruption (Moulin and Nyers 2007: 361). Although they describe the protest as a 'tragedy of failures and false expectations' – taken from the title of the report produced by the Forced Migration Studies Centre at the American University in Cairo – they assert the fundamentally political nature of the protest, and argue that it was productive of claim-making subjects that, despite 'normal' structures of society, emerge as 'alternative and contested political subjectivities that speak "out of place"' (ibid.: 310).

These understandings allow us to shift the frame for understanding political activism from one that centres on and begins with the citizen to one that begins with the non-citizen. This makes possible a reconceptualisation of the engagement of citizens as simply one part of the overall event rather than the enabling factor. Rather than working or speaking 'on behalf of' migrants, citizens are thus working and speaking 'with'. Further, as demonstrated by Moulin and Nyers, citizens are themselves not entirely necessary to understanding an event or act as political. Such an understanding shifts events and decisions within the politics of asylum from moments where the citizen enables the non-citizen to moments of solidarity between citizen and non-citizen. 'Solidarity' implies here not one legitimate voice speaking for another illegitimate/vulnerable/less outspoken voice, but a multitude of voices speaking together in the same message, demand or refusal.

What remains, however, is the question of what 'counts' as activism. Isin argues that activism involves 'momentous acts', evoking images of public and risky acts. Moulin and Nyers, Soguk, and Mezzadra all retain a focus on public protest or broad movements. In each of the moments in the field that provoked this study, however, such loud, public assertions are either absent or not central

Moments of solidarity 123

to the larger claims. It remains true that, even if we are able to understand action and voice on behalf of non-citizens and migrants as political, their subject positions within larger societal frameworks are vulnerable. Even as they demand participation in power relations, the relationship of violence identified by Edkins and Pin-Fat (2004) are still in operation. Often, a loud, demanding and outspoken politics is possible for less time than a quiet moment as the risk represented by such an engagement is very real. In Tanzania, individuals caught working or living in the local community face jail time or deportation, and so maintain as much invisibility as possible, even to the extent of denying their nationality, as a survival strategy. In Spain, the actual consequence of making the police complaint for ten of the twelve children was deportation to an unknown location. In Australia, the detainee engaged in the appeal was unsuccessful, and was deported the day following the rally. For the ex-detainee who participated on his friend's behalf, state surveillance increased and his partner's status in Australia – already precarious as she held only a bridging visa until final determination of her status was reached – was more closely scrutinised. The real life impacts of political action for non-citizens can be devastating – more devastating, it should be recognised, than those for citizens. As a result, it is easy to assume that non-citizen activism is rare. In fact, attention to heightened risk can enable a return to centralising the role of the citizen as the citizen becomes not only an enabler but, in some ways, a 'protector' as citizen engagement can buffer some of the profoundly negative effects of activism for non-citizens. Solidarity slips away in this framework.

Building on feminist theories of everyday activism, however, and accepting that 'acts' can be both individual and collective with short and long term durations, a different analysis is possible as incidents of 'momentary activism' are revealed that capture eruptions of non-citizen political agency in ways that profoundly challenge and shape societal structures – even if for only a moment.

Moments

The contribution of feminist theory to understandings of activism is to bring it to the level of the personal and the everyday. Sowards and Renegar (2006) argue that activism might also include grass-roots models of leadership, using strategic humour, building feminist identity at the personal level, sharing stories, and resisting stereotypes and pressures in everyday life. Feminist activism may operate in private settings, they argue, and as such may go unnoticed (ibid.: 61). Activism is thus present in everyday life and in the small contributions individuals make (ibid.: 62). Tarrow (1993: 282) asks, in reference to Zolberg, '[if] moments of madness produce as rich a tapestry of collective action as we think, why has the repertoire developed as slowly as it has?' In this, he is observing that as much as mass movements and protests are inspiring in their objectives and the political messages and meanings they carry, their ambitions are seldom realised at the scale at which they are expressed. He answers his own question by arguing that social transformation as brought about by activist politics is

124 *H. Johnson*

evolutionary and long term – change does not happen all at once, but in cycles of mobilisation (ibid.: 283). Such notions of longer-term change are important in understanding classic political activism and historical change. They also gesture, however, to the possibility of broader notions of activism that need not be captured only by the mass, momentous movement but can instead be found in smaller 'acts' at the individual or local level. Edkins and Pin-Fat quote Foucault on resistance to the same ends:

> [There are] a plurality of resistances, each of them a special case: resistances that are possible, necessary, improbable; others that are spontaneous, savage, solitary, concerted, rampant or violent; still others that are quick to compromise, interested or sacrificial; by definition they can only exist in the strategic field of power relations. But this does not mean that they are only a reaction or a rebound, forming with respect to the basic domination an underside that is in the end always passive, doomed to perpetual defeat.
>
> (Edkins and Pin-Fat 2004: 5)

Martin *et al.* (2007: 2) similarly work to open up the conception of activism 'to consider actions and activities that, because of their limited geographic reach, normally are considered too insignificant to count as activism and yet do create progressive change in the lives of women, their families and their communities'.

In such arguments, theorists are shaping an understanding of activism that does not necessarily operate in the public view and that aims not to transform the 'entire' world, but rather the life-world of the activist herself (Sowards and Renegar 2006: 65). Martin *et al.* write: '[o]ur intention is not to identify every daily act as activist, but to theorise how small acts transform social relations in ways that have the potential to foster social change' (ibid.: 2). The criterion set out, therefore, is one of political meaning. When viewed in light of Isin's work on 'acts of citizenship', this can be operationalised as acts that produce a rupture and a 'newness' in the 'script' of society. Such ruptures can be embedded in everyday life as much as they can be 'moments of madness' or 'momentous' acts that are collective; they can be small, quiet and individual as much as they can be grand, outspoken and collective. Indeed, from the perspective of the irregular migrant and non-citizen, they often are. Zolberg observes that beneath the macro-events of protest and mass mobilisation lies 'a multitude of micro-events' (1972: 207). For Soguk, a new view of being in society is both created and carried out in the day-to-day reality of migrants (2007: 307). Understood by Maxey (2004: 160) as 'attempting to do as much as we can from where we are at', activism 'always involves creating change, but creating change can mean simply intervening when and where one happens to be' (Martin *et al.* 2007: 8). This includes intervening from the subject position, status and political identity one happens to have within the 'normal' of society, in an effort to change what that normal is. For Sowards and Renegar, '[p]owerful forms of activism can be individual and private. This individual activism may or may not inspire public protest' (2006: 69).

Moments of solidarity   125

It is this kind of everyday activism that characterises the activism of the marginalised, the irregular migrant and the non-citizen. It is both ongoing in struggles of resistance and survival in their daily lives, and momentary in that it becomes visible in moments of solidarity between citizen and non-citizen. Within a dominant nation-state structure shaped by sovereign power that is in a relation of violence with the non-citizen, citizens make the activism visible. They do not, however, enable the acts themselves, nor do they make the challenges audible. The challenges are there; the demands are spoken. What is needed is recognition not in speaking on behalf of, but in speaking with so the volume can be turned up.

Rancière (1999: 11) writes: 'Politics exists when the natural order of domination is interrupted by the institution of a part of those who have no part.' Those who have no part are those who cannot be incorporated into the order of society, and made a partner in its processes. They are, in Agamben's terms, the bare life that is captured and controlled within the state of exception (2000). What we traditionally think of as politics – the procedures and systems of legitimation by which the societal contract is achieved – is, for Rancière, not politics at all, but the end of such. Such a process is, instead, a disciplining exercise for the purpose of governing bodies; it is policing (Rancière 1999: 2–29). Politics is not achieving agreement, thus indicating acceptance and the end of contestation. For Rancière, it is the disagreement, the defiance and the breaking down of such an agreement; it is the challenging of consensus by those who are not part of the normal order. Politics is ongoing, but not omnipresent in this understanding. As Rancière makes note, it actually happens 'very little' or 'very rarely' (ibid.: 16). Politics is momentary, and appears in glimpses and moments of disagreement. It is shut down, only to reappear in moments of insurrection and challenge. In Rancière's terms, by ascribing these individuals the 'status' of irregular migrants, asylum seekers or refugees and by confining them to a camp space, the state is attempting to make them 'a part' – to incorporate them into the state-controlled consensus framework of the border that is the end of politics. With Rancière's understanding of politics, however, the fleeting interruptions and flashes of resistance create politics itself within this state of exception. Within such moments, these migrants find a voice and demand an equality of place.

Locally, moments have profound impacts. Citizens who believe in a benign state are jolted out of placidity by the relations of violence revealed by the sudden absence of individuals. In Tanzania, local villagers who identify with refugees in both language and ethnicity come to see them as neighbours and workers rather than as 'dangerous', 'criminal' or 'foreign'. In Melilla, customers of the local café notice the absence of children, and question the nature of the border control apparatus governing their territory. In Australia, non-citizens take a leadership role in activist movements, and remind citizens that the struggle is ongoing despite a change in government. The absence of the non-citizen, after a moment of solidarity, leaves a mark in the local politics of borders and asylum and, while they may push the state to greater extremes, they also alert individual citizens to the politics of their own space. In this way, a bridge is created

126   *H. Johnson*

between the non-place of the camp, or the reception centre, or the detention centre, and the community in which the citizen resides.

Moments such as these carry limited political meaning without the production of longer-term struggles and patterns, a succession of encounters where the moment is revealed to not be unique, but instead to be an eruption of ongoing political struggle. Studied in isolation, they can be seen as isolated and exceptional. Read together, across multiple contexts, they become something else as an ongoing story of which we have only had a glimpse. Drawing on an emerging field of critical citizenship studies, Isin argues that citizenship is increasingly understood as practices of becoming claim-making subjects (2008: 16). He writes:

> We define acts of citizenship as those acts that transform forms (orientations, strategies, technologies) and modes (citizens, strangers, outsiders, aliens) of being political by bringing into being new actors as activist citizens (claimants of rights and responsibilities) through creating new sites and scales of struggle.
>
> (Isin 2008: 39)

The migrants themselves must tell the story. In each case they do, in the terms of citizenship from a place of non-citizenship: the right to work and to reside, the right to claim the protection of the state, and the right to remain and to raise a voice for change. It is in these transgressive solidarities, therefore, that the citizen may be able to re-found the practices that define 'acts of citizenship' and re-enable citizenship as a practice rather than a state of being. Edward Said (quoted in Rushdie 1991: 178) declares: 'there seems to be nothing in this world which sustains the story; unless you go on telling it, it will just drop and disappear'. Within the global politics of asylum, new and crucial understandings of both agency and activism are possible only if we allow the migrants to sustain the/their story.

Notes

1 I would like to gratefully acknowledge the financial support of the Institute for Globalization and the Human Condition at McMaster University, the Canadian Consortium of Human Security, and the Social Sciences and Humanities Research Council for the field research supporting this chapter. Thank you, also, to Peter Nyers, Kim Rygiel, Amanda Coles and Mark Busser for very helpful comments on earlier drafts.
2 All names of participants used in this chapter are false.
3 This stands in contrast to important analysis presented by Isin and Rygiel (2007) and Ziarek (2008), among others, that asserts the biopolitical power of using the body as a way of accessing political voice when other possibilities are otherwise denied.

Bibliography

Agamben, G. (2000) *Means without End: Notes on Politics*, Minneapolis: University of Minnesota Press.

Andreas, P. (2003) 'Redrawing the Line: Borders and Security in the Twenty-First Century,' *International Security* 28 (2): 78–111.

Arendt, H. (1951) *The Origins of Totalitarianism*, New York: Harvest.

Brennan, F. (2003) *Tampering with Asylum: A Universal Humanitarian Problem*, Queensland: University of Queensland Press.

Calavita, K. (1998) 'Immigration, Law and Marginalization in a Global Economy: Notes from Spain,' *Law and Society Review*, 32 (3): 529–566.

Carling, J. (2007) 'Unauthorized Migration from Africa to Spain,' *International Migration* 45 (4): 3–37.

Curran, L. and S. Kneebone (2003) 'Overview' in S. Kneebone (ed.) *The Refugees Convention 50 Years On: Globalization and International Law*, Aldershot: Ashgate.

Edkins, J. and V. Pin-Fat (2004) 'Introduction: Life, Power, Resistance' in J. Edkins, V. Pin-Fat and M.J. Shapiro (eds) *Sovereign Lives: Power in Global Politics*, New York: Routledge.

Geddes, A. (2003) *The Politics of Migration and Immigration in Europe*, London: SAGE Publications.

Geddes, A. (2005) 'Europe's Border Relationships and International Migration Relations,' *Journal of Common Market Studies* 43 (4): 787–806.

Huysmans, J. (2002) 'Defining Social Constructivism in Security Studies: The Normative Dilemma of Writing Security,' *Alternatives* 27: 41–62.

Isin, E. (2008) 'Theorizing Acts of Citizenship' in E.F. Isin and G. Nielson (eds) *Acts of Citizenship*, London: Zed Books.

Isin, E.F. and K. Rygiel (2007) 'Abject Extrality: Frontiers, Zones and Camps' in E. Dauphinee and C. Masters (eds) *The Logics of Biopower: Living, Dying, Surviving*, Basingstoke: Palgrave MacMillan.

Kamanga, K. (2005) 'The (Tanzania) Refugees Act of 1998: Some Legal and Policy Implications,' *Journal of Refugee Studies* 18 (1): 100–117.

Lavenex, S. (2006) 'Shifting Up and Out: The Foreign Policy of European Immigration Control,' *West European Politics* 29 (2): 329–350.

Lindstrøm, C. (2005) 'European Union Policy on Asylum and Immigration: Addressing the Root Causes of Forced Migration: A Justice and Home Affairs Policy of Freedom, Security and Justice?' *Social Policy and Administration* 39 (6): 587–605.

Martin, D.G., S. Hanson and D. Fontaine (2007) 'What Counts as Activism? The Role of Individuals in Creating Change,' *Women's Studies Quarterly* 35 (3/4): 78–95.

Maxey, L.J. (2004) 'Moving Beyond from Within: Reflexive Activism and Critical Geographies' in D. Fuller and R. Kitchin (eds) *Radical Theory/Critical Praxis: Making a Difference Beyond the Academy?*, Victoria: Praxis Press.

Mezzadra, S. and B. Neilson (2003) 'Border as Method, or, the Multiplication of Labor,' *Transversal* [EIPCP multilingual webjournal], available at eipcp.net/transversal/0608/mezzadraneilson/en (accessed 14 May 2011).

Ministry of Home Affairs (1999) *Refugees Act 1998* (Dar es Salaam, United Republic of Tanzania), available at www.unhcr.org/cgi/bin/texis/vtx/refworld/rwmain?docid=3ae6b 50bf (accessed 14 May 2011).

Moran, A. (2005) *Australia: Nation, Belonging and Globalization*, New York: Routledge.

Moulin, C. and P. Nyers (2007) ' "We Live in a Country of UNHCR": Refugee Protests and Global Political Society,' *International Political Sociology* 1: 356–372.

Nyers, P. (2006) *Rethinking Refugees: Beyond States of Emergency*, New York: Routledge.

Nyers, P. (2009) 'The Accidental Citizen: Acts of Sovereignty and (Un)Making Citizenship' in P. Nyers (ed.) *Securitizations of Citizenship*, New York: Routledge.

128 *H. Johnson*

Rancière, J. (1999) *Dis-agreement: Politics and Philosophy*, Minneapolis: University of Minnesota Press.

Rushdie, S. (1991) 'On Palestinian Identity: A Conversation with Edward Said' in S. Rushdie, *Imaginary Homelands*, London: Penguin.

Soguk, N. (2007) 'Border's Capture: Insurrectional Politics, Border-Crossing Humans, and the New Political' in P.K. Rajaram and C. Grundy-Warr (eds), *Borderscapes: Hidden Geographies and Politics at Territory's Edge*, Minneapolis: University of Minnesota Press.

Sowards, S.K. and V.R. Renegar (2006) 'Reconceptualizing Rhetorical Activism in Contemporary Feminist Contexts,' *The Howard Journal of Communications* 17: 57–74.

Tarrow, S. (1993) 'Cycles of Collective Action: Between Moments of Madness and the Repertoire of Contention,' *Social Science History* 17 (2): 281–307.

Ziarek, E.P. (2008) 'Bare Life on Strike: Notes on the Biopolitics of Race and Gender,' *South Atlantic Quarterly* 107 (1): 89–105.

Zolberg, A.R. (1972) 'Moments of Madness,' *Politics and Society* 2: 183–207.

7 Building a sanctuary city
Municipal migrant rights in the city of Toronto

Jean McDonald

Scholars of citizenship have identified the city as a strategic location for an emergent and active citizenship, a space in which formal notions of citizenship have been challenged and where social, economic and political rights typically associated with formal citizenship have been substantively demanded, acquired and enacted by non-citizen actors (Isin 2002, Sassen 1998, Holston and Appadurai 1999, Holston 1998). Similarly, the migrant justice organisation No One Is Illegal–Toronto – largely through the Sanctuary City movement and the complementary Don't Ask Don't Tell (DADT) campaign – has developed a strong, consistent and strategic focus upon *the city* as a space in which to focus political activism.

The city is a social and political space that is productive of active forms of citizenship. Policies at local, municipal levels that create accessible social rights and community services for all residents, regardless of immigration status, pose a challenge to state-defined 'migrant illegality'. I look specifically at the realm of service provision in Toronto, and the governmentalised, internal borders enacted within these spaces of social inclusion and exclusion. I argue that when services are made accessible to people with precarious status, these governmentalised, internal borders can be circumvented, and migrant illegality can be 'unmade'. I explore the idea of 'regularisation from below', a term coined by members of Toronto's Sanctuary City movement, which seeks to allow access to social rights and community services without fear of detention or deportation.

The city and citizenship

Why this focus upon the city? Clearly migrant justice issues emerge from a global system, and within the Canadian context, immigration policy tends to remain firmly the domain of the federal ministry, Citizenship and Immigration Canada (CIC), with few exceptions. As James Holston and Arjun Appadurai have asked, 'Why cities?' (1999: 1). They argue that cities have been and remain a key strategic arena for the development of active citizenship, pointing out that with 'concentrations of the nonlocal, the strange, the mixed, and the public, cities engage most palpably the tumult of citizenship' (ibid.: 2). In his critique of modernist urban planning, Holston argues that the state is not the only source of legitimate citizenship, and that instead, the city is a potential space in which 'insurgent citizenship' can become manifest and legitimate (1998: 39). For Holston, 'insurgency', in terms of citizenship, is understood as new and non-state sources of citizenship and its legitimation (ibid.: 39). While many studies of globalisation and transnationalism have neutralised the importance of place, Holston and Appadurai argue that this dematerialisation of space is mistaken (1999: 2–3). Indeed, cities have become a primary and important location for the study of contemporary negotiations of citizenship (ibid.: 3).

In a sense, active citizenship is a process, one that is engaged and enabled through assemblages of various components including (but not limited to) formal legal status, access to social services, right to use to public spaces, social and political obligations and the ability to make claims on society and state. Despite the fact that people living with precarious immigration status are denied the ability to make claims to social, economic and political rights, many people reject this reality. As Étienne Balibar notes in reference to Sans-papiers within France, *droit de cité* and citizenship are not primarily 'granted or conceded from above but are, in an essential respect, constructed from below' (2004: 48). Saskia Sassen points out that the city has emerged as a space in which new claims are being formulated and made (1998: xx).

Cities are also a key site and strategic terrain for a number of conflicts and contradictions, including that of the internationalisation of capital (Sassen 1998: xxv). As well, linkages between identity and spatial location – 'unmoored' from their 'traditional' strongholds of village and nation – are opening up new notions of community, membership and entitlement (ibid.: xxxii). Indeed, the existence and visibility of people living with precarious immigration status in Canada, as Joe Painter and Chris Philo have argued, shows that there is no straightforward connection between space (e.g. the territorial limits of the nation-state) and inclusionary citizenship (1995: 112).

Holston and Appadurai argue that formal citizenship is becoming less necessary for access to substantive rights and emphasise a decreased necessity for formal citizenship (1999: 4). Yasmin Soysal makes a similar point: 'Access to a formal nationality status is not the main indicator for inclusion or exclusion in today's Europe. Rights, membership and participation are increasingly matters beyond the vocabulary of national citizenship' (1994: 12). Soysal's point is largely in reference to member states of the European Union, yet she extrapolates her point to include North America. Verena Stolcke, on the other hand, argues that as intra-European borders are becoming more porous, external borders are becoming more fortified and impermeable (1995: 2). Such assertions make an important argument for understanding citizenship beyond a formal, statist definition as a legal status and as something that is also practised through daily experience. Yet the fundamental flaw in the arguments of Holston and Appadurai, and Soysal, is that they homogenise the category of 'immigrant'. They fail to recognise the multiple ways in which exclusion and inclusion work – through gendered, racialised, able-ist and classist ways. (Im)migrants, unfortunately, are not equally received and accepted by the nation-states to which they migrate. The notion of 'sanctuary cities' in some ways bolsters Holston and Appadurai's argument. Yet it is clear that without formal legal status, people living with precarious immigration status face insecurities that make active citizenship extremely difficult. As Vicki Squire and Jennifer Bagelman note in their discussion (Chapter 8 of this volume) of 'mobile enclaves of sanctuary' in the UK, sanctuary city movements do not 'effectively guard against the violences of state practices of forced (im)mobility, such as detention, deportation and dispersal'. Similarly in Toronto, the creation of a sanctuary city would not necessarily bar federal authorities from enforcing federal immigration laws – arresting, incarcerating and deporting those persons not deemed acceptable within the national body politic.

Scholars have identified Sanctuary City measures as a form of 'municipal foreign policy', whereby cities become de facto immigration policy makers (Hobbs 1994, Magnusson 1996). Yet by theorising that Sanctuary City movements are a type of 'foreign policy', Heidi Hobbs (1994) takes for granted and reaffirms the common understanding that (im)migrant communities are 'outsiders' who do not belong and do not hold a stake in the communities in which they are living. Instead, the approach that the Sanctuary City movement takes in Toronto is to consider all community members, regardless of immigration status, as stakeholders and meaningful residents of their communities.

Cities across the United States have adopted various resolutions that in many ways challenge federal immigration laws; indeed, some have referred to themselves as 'sanctuary cities' or 'safety zones' (National Immigration Law Center, 27 February 2004). Over 50 cities have passed legislation that forbids the use of municipal funds, resources and workers for the enforcement of federal immigration laws. Others, such as Los Angeles, Chicago, Portland, Seattle, New York City and Minneapolis, have taken more proactive roles, whereby specific legislation bars city workers from inquiring into and/or disseminating immigration information regarding persons using city services (ibid.). Resolutions passed in Baltimore, Austin, Cambridge and several other cities affirm that no city service will be denied on the basis of formal citizenship status (ibid.). These changes in municipal policy were not simply 'granted' by municipalities; rather, these transformations were hard-won by (im)migrants, refugees and their allies through research, networking, advocacy and political action.

Municipal policies that affirm access to city services, regardless of formal legal status and without fear of information-sharing with federal immigration enforcement, enable a double reconfiguration. First, the potential of cities as spaces that enable substantive citizenship is re-affirmed. Second, active citizenship itself is reconfigured. The social space of migrant illegality, while certainly not abolished, is re-made through the establishment of (porous) city boundaries. Municipal policies affirming the right to public services for all members of the metropolis pose an important challenge to state definitions of migrant illegality.

132   J. McDonald

Producing migrant illegality within the realm of service provision

Understanding migrant illegality as a process ('illegalisation') rather than a fixed identity or state is crucial to a study of the practices that make and unmake migrant illegality, as it allows for an examination of the complexities and fluidity of immigration status within the context of service provision. Governmentality, a concept first developed by Michel Foucault (1991), makes possible an in-depth analysis of government as 'the conduct of conduct' and allows scholars to examine how governmental subjects are self-making as well as being made and unmade through processes of migrant illegalisation. Governmentality focuses on the detailed workings of power – how it seeps into the cracks of everyday life. The realm of service provision is an interesting site for the examination of governmentality because it is a space in which the minutiae of life are governed in the Foucauldian sense. A governmentality approach allows us to address the detailed workings of power, as migrant illegality is made and unmade within the daily operations of service provision.

Foucault outlines three dimensions that characterise the concept of governmentality. First, he points to the assemblage of institutions, procedures, reflections and analyses that take population as their principal object of knowledge and the tactics and strategies that allow for the exercise of this complex form of power (Foucault 1991: 102). The realm of service provision is comprised of various assemblages of institutions, through which a variety of procedures, policies and practices operate to govern particular populations. The second dimension of governmentality is the trend in 'the West' that has led to the ascendancy of this form of power, in which a series of governmental apparatuses have been formed on the one hand, while on the other, a whole set of knowledges have been developed (ibid.: 102–3). Service-providing organisations, in this sense, can be understood as governmental apparatuses, ones that often become intricately connected with the subjects, whom they have taken to be their central objects of knowledge.

The last dimension outlined by Foucault is the process, or result of the process, in which the state becomes 'governmentalised' (ibid.: 103). The governmentalisation of the state is the process whereby governance becomes inculcated into the practices of everyday life. In this sense, borders can be understood as 'governmentalised' when they emerge locally within spaces of service provision and municipal institutions. Foucault defines governmentality as the relation 'between the technologies of domination of others and those of the self' (Foucault 1988: 19). Governmentality provides a framework for thinking through the links between 'questions of government, authority and politics, and questions of identity, self and person' (Dean 1999: 13). This is integral for the study of migrant illegalisation, as it allows for an examination of how practices of governance over immigration status connect with the ways in which people experience, identify and self-govern in relation or in opposition to 'government, authority and politics'.

Building a sanctuary city   133

My research on the production of migrant illegality within service provision demonstrates that governmentalised borders arise, emerging as widespread and ever-present, when people try to access social services such as heath centres, social housing cooperatives, schools, food banks, welfare offices and police stations. In examining access to services, it becomes clear that the nation-state border is not just a physical geographic territorial marker that excludes or denies access. Instead, we can begin to understand the ways in which nation-state borders are also internal, used to *include* non-citizens through exclusionary practices that maintain conditions of exploitability and marginalisation. In other words, borders do not work to 'keep people out'; instead, they function to subordinate people living within the territorial borders of the nation-state. In this sense, governmentalised borders exist whenever and wherever people living with precarious immigration status come into contact or confrontation with institutional settings such as schools, hospitals, social housing offices, food banks and emergency services, all of which require some form of identification. Indeed, if one examines the internal borders which arise through service provision, a challenge to these governmentalised borders can also pose a challenge to processes of migrant illegalisation, and thus to the production of migrant illegality itself.

Migrant illegalisation is a process by which practices of subjection (self-making) are intertwined with practices that produce common-sense understandings of migrant illegality. The many intersecting identities of the people I interviewed – as migrants, racialised people, women, queer, homeless, 'illegal' – are formed through processes of subject formation. Arguing that the racial state is instrumental in subject formation, David Theo Goldberg notes that as the racial state becomes further implicated in subject formation, the more it becomes embedded within everyday social life. In this way, race becomes embedded within the conceivable; how social practices are managed, defined and regulated (2002: 115). He writes, 'In Foucauldian terms, the state not only invades the body of subjects. It goes a long way in making bodies what they are, and by extension who they are. It is thus instrumental in subject formation' (ibid.: 115). Biopower in the Foucauldian sense sees the operation of state power not only as a 'top-down' formation, but also as permeating the bodies and helping to construct these bodies in particular kinds of ways. Following Foucault, Goldberg notes that subject formation is also an internalised process, in the sense that persons are not only made (externally – politically, socially, economically, historically, etc.) but also self-making and self-regulating (2002: 117). In the context of immigration status, we can examine the ways in which varying levels of precariousness, characterised by fluidity – from temporary work permits, visitors visas and refugee claims to rejected applications and denied visa renewals or, on the other hand, permanent residency and formal citizenship – impact the making and unmaking of the 'illegal' subject.

These varying levels of status impact the mobility of subjects in multiple ways. Through the examination of processes of migrant illegalisation, we can begin to outline differential mobility rights, not only across the physical borders of the nation-state but also across governmentalised borders within the

134   *J. McDonald*

nation-state. As Mekonnen Tesfahuney argues, 'not all mobile subjects enjoy the same freedoms of movement and access to space'; these differential mobility rights are structured by such aspects as race, age, gender and class which reflect hierarchies of power and positionality (1998: 501).

Immigration policy, due to the need to sort and classify populations of migrants, is a process of migrant illegalisation. The current governmental organisation of the immigration system, then, is in itself productive of migrant illegality. Nicholas De Genova writes, 'The social space of "illegality" is an erasure of legal personhood – a space of forced invisibility, exclusion, subjugation and repression' (2002: 427). Migrant illegality, then, is a spatialised condition in which the physical borders of the nation-state are reproduced in the everyday lives of racialised (im)migrants in countless locations within the national territory. Processes of migrant illegalisation are manifest in policies, codes, regulations and practices in which governmentalised borders are revealed within the territorial borders of the nation-state. Governmentalised borders function within and beyond the scope of citizenship to make the whole of a person, in effect, illegal. As Nandita Sharma (2001) has pointed out in her discussion of ideological borders, the border is not just a physical geographic territorial marker. As such, borders (both physical and governmentalised) not only affect one's legal and political rights, but also are implicated in notions of who belongs and who does not.

In Canada, people become 'illegal' through the classist, gendered and racist processes of selection and exclusion put into practice within the Immigrant and Refugee Protection Act (IRPA). The majority of people living with precarious immigration status in Canada are people who do not meet the strict requirements of the 'points system', which emphasises particular work skills and economic status, and privileges education from white-dominated countries such as Australia, the US and the UK. The vast majority of people enter Canada through legal channels, whether on visitor, work or student visas, or as refugee claimants. However, there are very few legal channels for people to access *permanent* status. Thus it is the system itself that creates and produces migrant illegality – to the benefit, in fact, of the Canadian economy, as this system produces a pool of low-waged, highly exploitable and disposable labour.

While the federal immigration system plays a central role in determining formal citizenship status, the realm of service provision is a location in which migrant illegality can be reproduced and/or circumvented. This system produces an erasure of legal personhood and incarcerates people with precarious kinds of immigration status within the social and political space of migrant illegality. For example, a person whose visitor, work or student visa has expired, or whose refugee claim and Pre-Removal Risk Assessment (PRRA) has been rejected, has no right to obtain a Social Insurance Number (SIN) and no access to Ontario Works (OW) or Ontario Disability Support Program (ODSP) unless they have an application for permanent residency on Humanitarian and Compassionate (H & C) grounds in process. If they are working without authorisation, they do not have access to workers' compensation or Employment Insurance (EI). People whose visas have expired must pay for medical care or private insurance, and will be billed for any hospitalisation. Some people may be able to access primary, non-emergency health care through their local community health centre (CHC), although CHCs tend to be over-booked, under-funded and under-staffed. Many will only see patients within a certain catchment area, others have a very long waiting list, and some may only take on particular high-need clientele (e.g. pregnant women with precarious status). Technically, all children should have access to public education under Ontario's Education Act (s. 49.1), but many parents continue to experience difficulties enrolling children in school without government-issued identification (Sidhu 2008). Post-secondary education is available only to those able and willing to pay international student fees. Persons whose visitor visa is still valid cannot enroll children in school, obtain a SIN, or access OW or ODSP.

Refugee claimants have a separate set of social rights from those whose visas have expired. They can obtain a SIN, access OW or ODSP, and have the right to workers' compensation, Employment Insurance (EI) and employment standards. They cannot access medical care through the Ontario Health Insurance Program (OHIP), but do have Interim Federal Health (IFH) coverage. Like those with expired visas, children have the right to public education, but post-secondary is only available to those who can pay international fees. People whose refugee claims have been rejected but who have a judicial review pending in Federal Court can maintain their SIN but must pay $150 for a work permit. They also have the right to OW and ODSP, and children can continue to attend public school. If their judicial review has been dismissed, and they have no Pre-Removal Risk Assessment (PRRA) or if their PRRA is refused but they cannot be removed because their country of origin is a 'moratorium country',[1] they continue to have the same rights. When a refugee claim is accepted, a person can maintain their SIN and does not have to pay fees for work or study permits. They have the right to OHIP (although non-refugee dependents do not), can attend post-secondary education with permanent resident's fees, and access Ontario Student Assistance Program (OSAP). They must apply for permanent resident status within six months, but no longer have to pay the Right of Landing Fee, which was imposed in February 1995 and abolished in February 2000. People in this position may not be ordered deported except in cases of serious criminality or security risk, which is also true for permanent residents. People with permanent residency have these same rights, but if they have been sponsored and their sponsorship undertaking is still in force, their sponsor will be sued for the repayment of all OW or ODSP. They can also become sponsors of family class members if they earn enough income, and may lose their status if they are out of the country for more than three years in a five-year period.

As these examples illustrate, the physical borders of the state are reproduced in countless scenarios within the territory of the nation-state. Many of these situations wherein borders are frequently reproduced – attending school, going to the hospital, applying for social housing, accessing emergency shelter services and calling for police assistance – would be circumvented to a great extent

136   *J. McDonald*

through provincial, municipal and organisational policies that rescind discrimination based on immigration status. In many instances, migrant illegality surfaces when the lack of state-issued documentation produces a person's identity as an 'outsider' and bars them from necessary services. Consequently, everyday forms of marginalisation, exploitation, surveillance and repression have a significant impact on the daily lives of people with precarious forms of immigration status in Canada.

As Luciana, who is living with precarious status in Toronto, said, 'It's very hard. It's hard. It's very, very tough out there for people without status. It's not easy. We just feel, as I say, locked out. Seriously locked out.' Policies at municipal and community levels, such as those advocated by the Don't Ask Don't Tell campaign in Toronto, also challenge the subordination experienced by people with precarious status as a result of governmentalised borders functioning *within* the nation-state.

Governmentalised borders operate on a number of fronts, including child protection services. According to Renée Walsh, who works for the Catholic Children's Aid Society (CCAS) and spoke on their behalf at a panel discussion organised by the Rights of Non-Status Women Network (RNSWN) on the topic of 'Non-Status Children and the Child Protection System' in April 2009, there are approximately 600 children currently held as crown wards. Of those, at least 15 percent are dealing with issues around immigration status. For parents living with precarious status, she notes, the experience of dealing with police and children's aid societies is very different from those parents who have citizenship or even permanent residency. Parents with precarious status experience a 'double punishment'. CCAS will not contact the Canada Border Services Agency (CBSA) regarding clients with precarious status; however, they are legally obligated to inform police in cases of violence or abuse against children.

When police become involved, Walsh notes that parents quickly become criminalised and often face deportation. Even in cases where parents are charged but not convicted (or charges are dropped, as in Agnes' case below), parents may still face deportation. This means that parents will be deported without their children, which Walsh considers to be 'a whole other level of punishment and discrimination'. Jane Walsh (no relation to Renée), an intake worker with the Toronto Children's Aid Society (CAS) also speaking on the RNSWN panel, pointed out that CAS has developed an 'Ask, but Don't Tell' policy in regards to immigration status. She pointed out that CAS has no legal right to contact immigration enforcement, and that status information should also not be disclosed to police. However, in cases where police become involved, there is no guarantee that status information regarding CAS clients will not be disclosed by police to CBSA.

For Agnes, a woman originally from Greece whom I briefly supported while she was a client at the community outreach location of the shelter where I volunteered, this governmentalised border surfaced when her adult daughter (from her first marriage) reported her to Toronto Police and CAS, citing mental health concerns. Agnes had been living with her adult daughter for several months, cooking

Building a sanctuary city 137

and cleaning and doing the majority of the work around the household. Her adult daughter has formal citizenship in Canada and, after a dispute with her mother, called the police in retaliation. Her daughter withdrew the initial charges that were laid but Agnes' two younger children (from her second marriage) had already been apprehended and taken into custody by CAS. Agnes spoke very little English, and although two separate psychological assessments showed no mental health concerns, she was unable to defend herself.

After discovering she did not have legal status, Toronto Police handed Agnes over to the CBSA. At the time that I was attempting to support her, she was being held at the Toronto Immigrant Holding Centre on Rexdale Boulevard. Through a friend who was able to converse with her in Greek, I was informed that she wanted to arrange visitation with her children at the immigration jail, so she could see her two young children before she was deported. Because CAS had taken her two children into custody as 'crown wards', Agnes would be deported without them. Although the charges in this case had been withdrawn shortly after originally laid, Agnes was de facto criminalised due to her lack of legal immigration status.

The stigma of criminalisation has resulted in a lack of articulation of specific policies around service provision to people living with precarious immigration status in Toronto in both agency and municipal level settings. The Don't Ask Don't Tell campaign and Sanctuary City movement function to challenge this stigmatisation by bringing these issues of injustice into the spotlight and by presenting people living with precarious status as everyday residents of the city: our neighbours, students, friends, community and family members. Lucas, a Portuguese man living with precarious status, characterised the feeling of stigmatisation and the inaccessibility of social rights and community services as a form of depression. He described people with precarious status as, 'just not able to access anything here. Just not being seen as people. You know, as human beings, entitled. Just being seen, I guess, as aliens'. The absence of clearly articulated policies in service organisations places service providers in difficult positions because of the sheer numbers of people coming forward in need of services.

The issue of immigration status and its impact on clients has quickly become a pressing issue in many community service organisations. As Marianne, a housing worker, points out,

> People from all sorts of different agencies and community organizations that never imagined they would be debating immigration, are finding that because there is such a large community of non-status people they have to take that into part of their mandate because it's really an issue everywhere.

In many cases there is no policy to report people who do not have legal status, but there is also no policy *not* to report. This leaves service providers with the challenge of assisting their clients but it also gives them significant power over their clients. Filipa recognised that within her community health centre, 'It's kind of left for interpretation and it depends on the worker, on how sensitive the worker is to being inclusive around this issue.'

For example, in order to access social housing in Toronto, all members of a household must have legal status, and this status must be updated every 12 months. This means that if just one member of the household loses their legal status (e.g. expiration of work visa) the entire family will lose eligibility for this service. However, much lies at the discretion of the staff member at the Toronto Community Housing Corporation. Paola, a social worker, explains,

> I work with an elderly couple in community housing and when they applied for housing they got it because they were both refugee claimants. They have since lost their refugee application. Every year they have to fill out a review form, and this year when it came time to fill it out they were asked for a social insurance number, and their social insurance numbers are expired. So this fellow, who is in his 70s and his wife is quite ill, was going to lose his housing. Now nothing's come of it.... It's really at the discretion of the staff person.

Here we can also see a process of migrant illegalisation at work, wherein tenuous legal status results in a shrinking pool of accessible services and demonstrates the ways in which rights and entitlements are stratified based on various levels of status.

Service providers systematically come up against barriers when trying to access services such as housing or health care for their clients. Filipa notes with frustration,

> My referrals are embarrassing. I refer people to more barriers. They report back to me consistently, saying, 'I went to that agency you referred me to and the minute they asked me for my documents, I just walked out the door'.

Several sympathetic service providers have established networks with workers in other service sectors in order to informally meet the needs of their clients. As a community support worker, argues,

> People need to be able to access services based on their need. That's the number one priority. If someone needs help, needs support, needs a referral, needs housing, then I want to be able to provide that.... The fact that the person has addictions, or mental health issues, or a criminal record, or less than full immigration status is irrelevant to their need.

Due to the informal and precarious nature of many of these networks, many service providers felt it was important to move past an informal or covert approach in order to secure service provision and to take a public stand about the needs that exist within the communities that they are serving.

Fundamental to the Don't Ask Don't Tell campaign is its close work with these service providers, agencies and organisations that do frontline work with people with precarious immigration status. Many community health centres, drop-ins, neighbourhood centres and other agencies have adopted internal Don't Ask Don't Tell policies and have declared their spaces as 'sanctuary zones' within the city, some of which have been unveiled during No One Is Illegal–Toronto's annual march for migrant justice, beginning in May 2007.

'Regularisation from below'

How do the Don't Ask Don't Tell (DADT) campaign and the Sanctuary City movement, through practices of informal citizen-making, challenge the sovereignty of the nation-state via governmentalised borders that emerge at the local level? Launched in March 2004, the Don't Ask Don't Tell campaign affirms the right to public services for all members of the metropolis, and works to ensure that city spaces are welcoming and accessible for all residents, regardless of immigration status. The Sanctuary City movement, on the other hand, complements the Don't Ask Don't Tell campaign through grass-roots mobilisation in neighbourhoods and community-based organisations, developing a migrant justice perspective that foregrounds anti-colonial and anti-capitalist analyses, and politicising new members.

In many instances, a person's immigration status becomes important when they encounter a governmentalised border within the nation-state. The lack of state-issued documentation produces the identity of people with precarious status as 'outsiders' at these internal borders and bars them from necessary services. Consequently, everyday forms of surveillance and repression have a significant impact on the daily lives of people with precarious status in Canada. A municipal policy that prohibits questions about immigration status and denies the ability for city workers or service providers to pass on immigration information to federal agencies circumvents the increased surveillance that racism and discrimination invoke in many situations. The campaign challenges state definitions of migrant illegality that *a priori* criminalise the identity of people living with precarious immigration status through an erasure of legal personhood.

The Don't Ask Don't Tell campaign emerged out of a concern to address barriers facing people living with precarious immigration status in accessing community services. This campaign has brought together directly affected (im)migrants, migrant justice organisations, women's shelters, community health centres and other community groups to work towards 'access without fear' for all residents of Toronto regardless of immigration status. As Filipa noted, 'The quality of life for people living without status is poorer than those with status. This has a huge impact of people's ability to keep jobs, raise kids, and stay healthy.' The Don't Ask Don't Tell campaign works to improve the quality of life for people living with precarious status in the city, thereby confronting and challenging the subordination imposed through governmentalised borders, by promoting increased access to services and social rights. Campaign

140   *J. McDonald*

organisers have argued that this campaign has the potential to pose a significant challenge to the sovereignty of the Canadian nation-state, characterising the campaign as a form of 'regularisation from the ground up' (Mishra and Kamal 2007).

For migrant justice activists affiliated with No One Is Illegal–Toronto, the city is a strategic site for a number of reasons. First of all, the city is a site in which internal governmentalised borders tend to emerge, most often at sites of service provision, such as welfare offices, police stations (although this designation as a site of service provision is questionable), social housing offices, ESL classes, food banks, health centres, hospitals and others. Second, Toronto has become home to almost half of all (im)migrants arriving in Canada (Troper 2000: 1). Finally, Toronto is home to a burgeoning migrant justice movement (Lowry and Nyers 2003, McDonald 2007, Mishra and Kamal 2007).

With events titled 'The City is a Sweatshop' and 'Building a Sanctuary City', the migrant justice organisation No One Is Illegal–Toronto has developed a strong, consistent and strategic focus upon *the city* as a space in which to focus political activism. This is unlike the strategic work of other No One Is Illegal (NOII) groups in Canada, which have maintained a focus upon national issues and federal policies, with Vancouver in particular developing a deep connection, analysis and commitment to indigenous sovereignty work, and Montreal continuing a lot of case-based organising. The campaign in Toronto has made significant gains in terms of access to education, services for women experiencing violence, and, to a lesser extent, police services. Working closely with the Ontario Secondary School Teachers Federation, high school students, parents, staff and community members, under the slogan 'Education not Deportation', the Don't Ask Don't Tell campaign was able to secure a unanimous Don't Ask Don't Tell policy at the Toronto District School Board, and a declaration that all TDSB schools would be sanctuary zones. This policy came after the highly publicised cases of Kimberly and Gerald Lizana-Sossa, two high school students who were arrested by immigration enforcement officers in their school and subsequently deported. The policy at the Toronto District School Board still needs work at the implementation level, as many forms and documents still request status information.

As Navjeet Sidhu, who authored the Community Social Planning Council (CSPC) report, *The Right to Learn: Access to Public Education for Non-Status Immigrants* (2008), noted at a 'City is a Sweatshop' event organised by No One Is Illegal–Toronto in February 2009, 'Many schools are still asking for status information, and status documents are still required to enroll.' The same issue has been found within Toronto Catholic District School Board schools, as outlined in the CSPC report, *Policy without Practice: Barriers to Enrollment for Non-Status Immigrant Students in Toronto's Catholic Schools* (2010). Notably, the TDSB policy has been called into question by the Canada Border Services Agency, who attended a TDSB meeting to argue against its adoption by the school board, which demonstrates the challenge to migrant illegalisation that the Don't Ask Don't Tell campaign has set into motion.

The campaign has also confronted discourses of migrant illegality at the Toronto Police Services Board (TPSB) by challenging the seemingly innate criminality associated with people living without full legal immigration status. Organising leveled at police services came largely out of a noticeably and alarmingly common practice of detaining women who came forward to report sexual or domestic abuse and reporting them to immigration enforcement. Several women that I spoke with discussed this issue as one of the central problems they face living without legal immigration status in Toronto. Jailyn described her scenario, saying, 'I was afraid, afraid when he abused me, [and] I was afraid to call the police. I don't want to because they will send me home one day.' Another woman, Josephine, who was living in women's transitional housing with three children explained,

> I would not call [the police] for anything. One day he almost killed me, choked me with construction boot ties, and I would not call them. One time when I was pregnant with my son, he took me and flung me on the ground, and I was scared of calling them. What will they do with my kids, what will they do with me, you know?

Through these discussions with women living without legal status, it became very clear that women's legitimate fear of the police left them in a position that furthered their vulnerability to exploitation and abuse.

Aiming for a full Don't Ask Don't Tell policy for everyone coming into contact with police – charged offenders, victims and witnesses alike – the campaign has only been able to secure a partial policy, whereby police will not request status documentation from victims and witnesses of crime, 'unless', as the policy states, 'there is a bona fide reason to do so'. Jackie Esmonde, a lawyer at the firm Falconer Charney who spoke at the 'City is a Sweatshop' event organised by No One is Illegal in February 2009, explained the 'bona fide reasons' for which an officer may inquire about status. The first reason accounts for cases in which a victim of a crime may require or seek entrance into the witness protection programme. The second reason refers to cases in which a crown attorney may ask for additional information for 'disclosure' purposes; however, Esmonde argues immigration status should be considered irrelevant in court. The third reason accounts for cases in which status proves necessary to developing a case against perpetrators. The last 'bona fide' reason is when status information is 'essential' for public and/or police safety, which according to Esmonde merely plays into stereotypes of 'dangerous' (im)migrants and is open-ended for wide interpretation.

Esmonde notes that Toronto Police do not have a 'Don't Tell' policy in regard to immigration status, and in her experience, they do tell 'with great relish'. Rather than utilising their discretion in order to protect public interest, she argues, police take it as their legal obligation to inform CBSA, which it is not. The Toronto Police Service claims that their Code of Conduct and oath of office forces officers to notify immigration authorities should they come across people who do not have legal immigration status. The lack of a 'Don't Tell' component,

142   *J. McDonald*

and the provision for 'bona fide reasons' to inquire into status, render the TPSB policy virtually useless, as people living with precarious immigration status continue to have justifiable fears in accessing police services. As Esmonde notes, the policy was originally intended to protect women and other marginalised people who may be experiencing violence and abuse, but this policy does not protect victims or witnesses of crime. Instead, intimate partners, employers, landlords, family members and other people continue to hold status information as a means to gain power over women and other marginalised groups. The implementation of this relatively weak policy leaves much to be desired. The campaign will continue to mobilise for a stronger policy that affirms access to police services without fear of deportation or detention for all residents of the city. Unfortunately, there are many reasons why racialised and poor people fear police in Toronto, and having precarious immigration status is just one of these.

Working to affirm the right of all city residents to use public services, the campaign poses an important challenge to state definitions of migrant illegality by working towards creating communities that are not dependent upon formal citizenship as a marker of belonging. The notion of 'regularisation from below' challenges and circumvents state power by initiating local, community-based movements addressing the production of migrant illegality within these spaces, such as service provision – addressing the substantive basis of citizenship rights. The campaign exists alongside the demand for 'status for all', which is in essence a demand to the state to start a regularisation programme. This is predominantly because proponents of the DADT campaign recognise that, historically, regularisations in Canada have left out certain groups, and indeed have reconfigured illegality rather than eradicating it. The Sanctuary City movement and campaigns such as DADT in Toronto address the needs of those people who enter the country or become illegal after the regularisation deadlines have passed. The DADT campaign is one avenue to secure a form of social inclusion and social rights for persons excluded from regularisation, who miss regularisation deadlines, and who are living in the city prior to when a regularisation programme occurs. In the current political climate, it does not seem likely that an inclusive regularisation will be put into practice anytime soon.

Conclusions: building a sanctuary city

As David Harvey notes, the question of 'What kind of city do we want to live in?' is inextricably connected to the questions, 'What kind of people do we want to be?' and 'What kind of humanity do we want to create amongst ourselves?' (2007: 2). Harvey is part of a broad group of community activists and organisers who have developed the Right to the City[2] initiative in New York City. The initiative emerged in 2007 as a response to gentrification and the displacement of low-income, LGBTQ and youth of colour from neighbourhoods across New York City. The Right to the City initiative has now become a national alliance of racial, economic and environmental justice organisations across the US. A central principle of this initiative is immigrant justice, which affirms 'The right

Building a sanctuary city   143

of equal access to housing, employment, and public services regardless of race, ethnicity, and immigration status and without the threat of deportation by landlords, ICE, or employers' (Right to the City 2010). Local organising is key to movement-building within the initiative, as is the powerful idea 'that everyone, particularly the disenfranchised, not only has a right to the city, but as inhabitants, have a right to shape it, design it, and operationalise an urban human rights agenda' (Right to the City 2010). Similarly, Imran, a community organiser with No One Is Illegal, acknowledges that the campaign may not change federal immigration policy; however, its importance lies in its ability to change the ways in which people interact with one another locally and to develop a shift in ideas around community and belonging. The campaign aims to create city spaces in which people can work, live and play freely, to create a city that is a safe space for all. In a sense, these spaces can be understood as semi-autonomous zones in which city dwellers are enabled to re-imagine their relationship to the state and to national space. In this way, migrant illegality is challenged through a re-imagining of city space and a reconfiguration of what it means to belong, to be members of communities, and to have responsibility for the spaces in which we live.

While cities often seem like naturalised spaces where people live and interact, it is important to understand that cities are *produced*. This means that change is possible and often inevitable. Building a sanctuary city is about creating accessible spaces in which people can live safely and securely, without fear, with equitable rights to services and with the ability to engage in urban politics and civic activity. By creating spaces that are accessible and safe (as possible) for people living with precarious status, the Sanctuary City movement, and the complementary Don't Ask Don't Tell campaign, enable a higher quality of life for all members of our city's communities. This movement does this by disrupting immigration laws that seek to create legal distinctions between human beings in crude attempts to re-frame certain groups of people as having less or no access to political, legal or social rights. As Squire and Bagelman point out (Chapter 8 of this volume), the Sanctuary City movement in the UK mobilises a tactic of taking sanctuary rather than seeking sanctuary. Similarly, the Sanctuary City movement in Toronto works to take and re-make city spaces through practices of active citizenship that exceed statist conceptions of formal citizenship. Governmentalised borders emerge to subordinate and at times exclude people with precarious status from accessing social rights and entitlements, and are challenged and confronted when community organisations refuse to enable these governmentalised borders by creating policies, practices and social movements that ensure services are provided to all residents of the city regardless of immigration status.

Sassen points out that 'the global city is a strategic site for disempowered actors because it enables them to gain presence, to emerge as subjects, even when they do not gain direct power' (1998: xxi). This emergence of active citizenship within cities enables a challenge to state definitions of migrant illegality and the spatial and governmentalised borders that reinforce and reproduce processes of illegalisation. As scholars of citizenship and migrant justice activists have long argued, systems of immigration reinforce hierarchical classification.

144 *J. McDonald*

Members of No One Is Illegal–Toronto recognise this by characterising their work as 'regularisation from below', as fighting for justice not only at the national or state level but also locally. At the same time, the importance of legal status in securing both legal and social rights must be acknowledged. Sassen argues that the denationalisation of urban space, along with the formation of new claims made by transnational actors, raises the question 'Whose city is it?' (1998: xx). The idea of a 'sanctuary city' provides one answer to this question: the city belongs to all who inhabit it, and its residents belong in the city.

Notes

1 Countries which are thought too dangerous for someone to be removed to are considered to be on 'moratorium' for removals, often due to continued civil war, political upheaval and other ongoing political disruptions.
2 www.righttothecity.org/.

Bibliography

Balibar, E. (2004) *We, the People of Europe?* Princeton: Princeton University Press.

Bejan, R. and N. Sidhu (2010) *Policy Without Practice: Barriers to Enrollment for Non-Status Immigrant Students in Toronto's Catholic Schools*, Toronto: Community Social Planning Council of Toronto Report.

Dean, M. (1999) *Governmentality: Power and Rule in Modern Society*, London: Sage Publications.

De Genova, N. (2002) 'Migrant "Illegality" and Deportability in Everyday Life,' *Annual Review of Anthropology*, 31: 419–447.

Foucault, M. (1988) 'Technologies of the Self' in L.H. Martin, H. Gutman and P.H. Hutton (eds) *Technologies of the Self*, Amherst: University of Massachusetts Press, 16–49.

Foucault, M. (1991) 'Governmentality' in G. Burchell, C. Gordon and P. Miller (eds) *The Foucault Effect*, Chicago: University of Chicago Press, 87–104.

Goldberg, D.T. (2002) *The Racial State*, Oxford: Blackwell Books.

Harvey, D. (2007) 'Neoliberalism and the City,' *Studies in Social Justice*, 1 (1): 1–12.

Hobbs, H. (1994) *City Hall Goes Abroad: The Foreign Policy of Local Politics*, London: Trentham Books.

Holston, J. (1998) 'Spaces of Insurgent Citizenship' in L. Sandercock (ed.) *Making the Invisible Visible: A Multicultural Planning History*, Berkeley: University of California Press, 37–49.

Holston, J. and A. Appadurai (1999) 'Cities and Citizenship' in J. Holston (ed.) *Cities and Citizenship*, Durham, NC: Duke University Press, 1–18.

Isin, E. (2002) *Being Political: Genealogies of Citizenship*, Minneapolis: University of Minnesota Press.

Li, T. (2002) 'Ethnic Cleansing, Recursive Knowledge, and the Dilemmas of Sedentarism,' *International Social Science Journal*, 54 (3): 361–371.

Lowry, M. and P. Nyers (2003) ' "No One Is Illegal": The Fight for Refugee and Migrant Rights in Canada,' *Refuge* 21 (3): 66–74.

Magnusson, W. (1996) *The Search for Political Space: Globalization, Social Movements, and the Urban Political Experience*, Toronto: University of Toronto Press.

McDonald, J. (2007) 'Citizenship, Illegality and Sanctuary' in V. Agnew (ed.) *Interrogating Race and Racism*, Toronto: University of Toronto Press, 112–134.

Mishra, M. and F. Kamal (2007) 'Regularization from the Ground Up: The "Don't Ask, Don't Tell" Campaign,' *New Socialist* 61 (Summer).

National Immigration Law Center (2004) 'Annotated Chart of Laws, Resolutions and Policies Instituted Across the U.S. Against State and Local Police Enforcement of Immigration Laws,' available at www.nilc.org/immlawpolicy/LocalLaw/Local_Law_Enforement_Chart_FINAL.pdf (accessed 27 February 2004).

Nyers, P., S. Zerehi and C. Wright (2006) '"Access Not Fear": Non-Status Immigrants and City Services,' *CERIS Report*, February 2006.

Painter, J. and C. Philo (1995) 'Spaces of Citizenship: An Introduction,' *Political Geography*, 14: 107–120.

Right to the City (2010) 'What Are We For?', available at www.righttothecity.org/what-we-do.html (accessed 10 July 2010).

Sassen, S. (1998) *Globalization and its Discontents*, New York: The New Press.

Sharma, N. (2001) 'On Being Not Canadian: The Social Organization of "Migrant Workers" in Canada,' *The Canadian Review of Sociology and Anthropology*, 38 (4): 415–440.

Sidhu, N. (2008) *The Right to Learn: Access to Public Education for Non-Status Immigrants*, Toronto: Community Social Planning Council of Toronto Report.

Soysal, Y. (1994) *Limits of Citizenship*, Chicago: University of Chicago Press.

Stolcke, V. (1995) 'Talking Culture: New Boundaries, New Rhetorics of Exclusion in Europe,' *Current Anthropology*, 36 (1): 1–24.

Tesfahuney, M. (1998) 'Mobility, Racism and Geopolitics,' *Political Geography*, 17 (5): 499–550.

Troper, H. (2000) 'History of Immigration to Toronto Since the Second World War,' *CERIS Working Paper*, 12 March 2000.

Varsanyi, M.W. (2006) 'Interrogating "Urban Citizenship" *vis-à-vis* Undocumented Migration,' *Citizenship Studies*, 10 (2): 229–249.

Interviews

Filipa, Community health care worker and participant in the Health Services and Emergency Services for Non-Status People focus group, Toronto, 28 June 2005 (interview carried out by Jean McDonald).

Jailyn, Person with precarious status living in Toronto, 11 August 2005 (interview carried out by Jean McDonald).

Lucas, Person with precarious status living in Toronto, 20 July 2005 (interview carried out by Jean McDonald).

Luciana, Person with precarious status living in Toronto, 20 July 2005 (interview carried out by Jean McDonald).

Marianne, Community housing worker and participant in the Housing, Shelters and Food Banks for Non-Status People focus group, Toronto, 23 June 2005 (interview carried out by Jean McDonald).

Paola, Social worker and participant in the Housing, Shelters and Food Banks for Non-Status People focus group, Toronto, 23 June 2005 (interview carried out by Jean McDonald).

Terry, Community support worker and participant in the Housing, Shelters and Food Banks for Non-Status People focus group, Toronto, 23 June 2005 (interview carried out by Jean McDonald).

8 Taking not waiting

Space, temporality and politics in the City of Sanctuary movement[1]

Vicki Squire and Jennifer Bagelman

In 2007 Sheffield in England became a City of Sanctuary with the support of the City Council and over 70 local organisations. While Sheffield was the first city in the UK to achieve official status as a City of Sanctuary, it is by no means the only city or town to do so. The formation of a city or town as a City of Sanctuary is based on the commitment of member organisations and groups, as well as on support from local politicians and the active participation of refugees and refugee groups. In June 2010 a national network of local groups in 17 towns and cities throughout the UK formed part of this 'movement to build a culture of hospitality for people seeking sanctuary in the UK', the primary aim of which is to 'influence policy-makers and public attitudes throughout the country' (City of Sanctuary 2009). While the network does disseminate information about campaigns that support its overarching aims and objectives, City of Sanctuary explicitly avoids political lobbying or campaigning in favour of a more subtle process of transforming culture. This effectively consists of a grass-roots approach to political change, which is based on creating a culture of sanctuary or hospitality at a local level through coalition-building and through the development of opportunities for building personal relationships between local people and those seeking sanctuary (Barnett and Bhogal 2009: 83).

As the first official UK City of Sanctuary, Sheffield serves as a key site for the emergence of a proliferating network that challenges many of our assumptions about the meaning and practice of sanctuary. If we interpret the network as a movement that forms part of a broader political response to state policies and practices that limit the ability of non-citizens to move to and settle within the UK, City of Sanctuary can be understood as challenging policing and border controls that criminalise many migrants and asylum seekers. Thus it might be described as contesting a *statist* logic, which is characterised by the struggle to divide people into the categories of 'citizen' and 'non-citizen' and to render the state as a unified space through the containment and expulsion of its 'excessive' elements. However, a second logic also comes into play in sanctuary practices; namely a *pastoral* logic which is characterised by the struggle to draw hierarchical distinctions between 'protector' and 'protected' as well as between those who are 'worthy' of protection and those who are not. What is critical about City of Sanctuary from our perspective is that the movement troubles both statist and

Taking not waiting 147

pastoral assumptions about sanctuary, which come together in defining non-citizen migrants as apolitical whether through a process of criminalisation or through a process of victimisation. Such assumptions are evident in many historical accounts of sanctuary, and we argue that they risk being implicitly reaffirmed in recent Foucauldian renderings of sanctuary. Our chapter seeks to trouble statist and pastoral readings of sanctuary by considering the implications of sanctuary practices that are not contained within a territorially-bound space and that constitute subjects which do not conform to the hierarchical distinction of s/he who is to be protected and s/he who protects. Rather than comprehensively unpacking the potentialities and limitations of City of Sanctuary's politics, the chapter thus limits its focus to an exploration of the ways in which the activities of the movement prompt a reconceptualisation of sanctuary beyond a statist and pastoral frame.

So how does City of Sanctuary trouble the assumptions of statism and pastoralism? The analysis developed in this chapter suggests that this occurs in two ways. First, the activities of City of Sanctuary potentially challenge the statist assumption that sanctuary is contained within sites that fall out of the standardised spatial order of the state, because sanctuary is enacted in much more diffuse terms across the urban environment. Second, such activities potentially challenge the assumption that sanctuary implies an unequal relationship of pastoralism, because they create the conditions by which those taking sanctuary enact themselves as political subjects in their own right.[2] Important in this regard is that City of Sanctuary's activities cannot adequately be understood in spatial terms as practices that occur within a contained site, nor can they be understood in political terms as activities in which distinctions between protector and protected are standardised in line with those of citizen and non-citizen. The activities of City of Sanctuary are thus critical not simply because they mobilise sanctuary in terms that do not fit with the logic of containment which a statist politics implies, but also because they challenge a pastoral politics of care or protection that is associated both with the hierarchical relationship between protector and protected and with the distinction between those who are worthy of protection and those who are not. That such a challenge is posed to both statism *and* pastoralism is important, we want to suggest, because the pastoral logic ultimately reinforces a statist logic by constituting the non-citizen migrant as apolitical through a politics of care or protection. This depoliticisation can be interpreted as the inverse of the process by which non-citizen migrants are constituted as apolitical through a politics of security and criminalisation (Squire 2009a). While we acknowledge that City of Sanctuary certainly can be said to practice protection or care in these terms, what we also want to point to here is the potential for moving beyond such a politics of care in the movement's emphasis on opening up access and routes for participation for those taking sanctuary in the city. A key intervention of this chapter is thus to point to the ways in which the politics of City of Sanctuary cannot in any simple way be reduced to a series of relations in which the sanctuary 'provider' occupies a privileged position over those taking sanctuary.

148   *V. Squire and J. Bagelman*

When sanctuary is practiced not through the closing off of a (mythical) site devoid both of violence and politics, but through the opening up of access to various sites and participation within various activities, opportunities are provided for movements and interactions that challenge the dichotomy of the incapacitated or irresponsible (non-citizen) 'victim' versus the capacitated or responsible (citizen) 'provider'. Such practices are not understood here in terms that privilege mobility analytically, but are theorised in relation to movements and interactions that emerge in and through seemingly fixed sites. We introduce the notion of 'mobile enclaves of sanctuary' in this chapter as a means for understanding these dynamic social and political sites. Specifically, we consider how movements through, and interactions within, such sites can be understood as creating the conditions for 'unexpected' relations that challenge the hierarchical standardisations associated with statist and pastoral renderings of sanctuary. While we indicate that City of Sanctuary creates the conditions for an increasingly mobile form of policing that is grounded in relations of statism, pastoralism, hospitality and care, we thus also show how the activities of the movement create opportunities for a more radical challenge to such renderings of sanctuary. The political significance of City of Sanctuary in this regard is that the movement creates the conditions for sanctuary practices that cut through depoliticising depictions of refugees as victims seeking protection as well as through depoliticising depictions of asylum seekers as criminals 'abusing' the 'hospitality' of the 'host'.

The significance of City of Sanctuary

Key in understanding the political significance of City of Sanctuary is that it is a movement – or perhaps more accurately a network – that emerges in a context whereby refugees and asylum seekers have become widely stigmatised within the UK. Asylum has formed the focus of intense political and social scrutiny over the past two decades, when fears about rising numbers have often been at the forefront of debate (Squire 2009a). Public opinion toward asylum has often been negative in this regard, while the popular press has been hostile both to asylum seekers and to migrants whose status is irregular (Innes 2010). Asylum and immigration policies have, in this context, been torn between heavy restrictions and limited liberalisations. On the one hand, border controls have been intensified with the aim of inhibiting unauthorised entrance, while measures such as the withdrawal of asylum seekers' rights to work have reduced the capacity for many to participate within 'host' communities. On the other hand, the opening of labour markets to groups such as EU nationals and limited numbers of highly skilled migrants has moved policy in a more liberal direction (see Spencer 2003). Based on a separation of migration into its 'productive' or 'harmless' and its 'unproductive' or 'problematic' elements, this policy response has contributed over recent years to the development of a harsh environment for refugees and asylum seekers who have been subject to various processes of criminalisation (Schuster 2003).

Taking not waiting   149

Despite the role of policy in constituting a harsh environment for many refugees and asylum seekers, the development of integration and cohesion policies might be interpreted as part of an attempt to create a more welcoming environment for migrants at large. While local authorities and agencies are increasingly responsible for the task of implementing integration and cohesion policies, asylum seekers are often disqualified as subjects of integration and cohesion due to the wider framing of such policies (see Squire 2011b).[3] In this context, voluntary-sector groups often tend to fill in the gaps of integration and cohesion policies by providing services and opportunities for those who fall outside the remit of public support (see Zetter *et al.* 2003). City of Sanctuary in this regard might be seen as extending the remit of integration and cohesion policies in terms that are both disruptive and conservative at the same time. On the one hand, the activities with which the movement is involved would seem to exceed the limitations of existing policies by creating opportunities for the formation of relations that are otherwise rendered illegitimate by institutionalised policies and practices. On the other hand, the movement would inadvertently seem to play host to the practice of governing migrants even where that is not the explicit aim. Indeed, there is a particular risk of bringing to bear categories of worthy/unworthy or legitimate/illegitimate, as well as a danger of importing a series of statist categories that depoliticises migrants by engaging in practices of integration and cohesion (see Squire 2011b).This would suggest that a series of critical questions needs to be asked about the politics of City of Sanctuary, in addition to paying attention to the potentialities of such a movement in opening up sanctuary practices beyond their statist and pastoral limitations.

The struggle to transform the conditions for refugees and asylum seekers across cities and towns of the UK is thus a complex and difficult process. City of Sanctuary is a movement that was initiated by religious groups, and that was set up with the aim of extending a positive vision of sanctuary through promoting relationships between local people and people seeking sanctuary (see Darling 2010). The formation of a city or town as a City of Sanctuary is based on the commitment of member organisations and groups, as well as on support from local politicians and the active participation of refugees and refugee groups. In order to qualify 'officially' as a City of Sanctuary, a city or town has to achieve the following four goals:

- resolutions of support from a significant and representative proportion of local groups and organisations;
- the support and involvement of local refugee communities, and refugee representation on the local City of Sanctuary working group;
- a resolution of support from the City Council (or other Local Authority);
- a strategy, agreed by the main supporting organisations, for how the city is to continue working towards greater inclusion of refugees and people seeking sanctuary.

(Barnett and Bhogal 2009: 79)

150 *V. Squire and J. Bagelman*

Nevertheless, much work goes on in creating a city or town as a place of sanctuary even before formal status is gained, such as through creating employment opportunities for those denied the right to work or who are unable to enter the job market based on their migration history, as well as through the organisation of cultural events that bring together various local residents. City of Sanctuary in this regard might be read as challenging the exclusionary politics of asylum by creating opportunities for the formation of solidaristic relations between those who are authorised subjects of cohesion and integration and those who are not, albeit in a partial and at times a potentially problematic sense. In order to address the political significance of the movement in relation to the theorisation and practice of sanctuary, however, we first need to consider further how statist and pastoral assumptions are manifest in contemporary and historical accounts of sanctuary.

Seeing sanctuary like a state

The main argument that we develop in this chapter is that the relations constituted in and through the 'mobile enclaves' within which City of Sanctuary operates trouble statist and pastoral accounts of sanctuary. But what precisely do we mean when we speak of a statist account of sanctuary, and how does pastoralism relate to this? Statism entails an ontological assumption regarding political order as organised according to a unified and transcendental principle of sovereignty. This conception of statism draws on James Scott's (1998) work on 'seeing like a state', which has been developed by Warren Magnusson (2011) to illuminate ways in which the fixation on a singular form of sovereignty fails to acknowledge multiple authorities and power relations. These multiple authorities and power relations are, Magnusson suggests, complex, overlapping and contradictory, thus creating heterogeneous political orders that are contextually specific. In contrast to this, a statist politics entails a struggle to construct political space and time through the imposition of discrete 'containers' that are controlled and organised according to a hierarchical logic of simplification or standardisation. The logic of pastoralism might be interpreted as relating to this where the statist categories of non-citizen and citizen are mapped onto categories of protected and protector. Nevertheless, while various containments are central to statist renderings of political order, it is important to note that statism also functions as a more flexible set of mobile practices. Indeed, as authors such as Bartleson (2006) and Deleuze and Guattari (1988) have suggested, statism does not operate simply through processes of bordering *qua* containment. It also works through bordering practices that modulate flow and movement itself (Bigo 2002). Yet what interests us here is not merely the way in which statism (re)territorialises certain types of movement through new modes of ordering, such as through the localisation of control. We are also interested in exploring how these complex (re)orderings are contested through the practices and activities of City of Sanctuary. In so doing, we challenge the naturalisation of statism that is evident in many historical accounts of sanctuary, while raising questions about the limitations of Randy Lippert's Foucauldian account of sanctuary in terms of its ability to address sanctuary as a political site of contestation in its own right.

Taking not waiting   151

Historical accounts of sanctuary

The notion of sanctuary as a territorially contained space is but one strand of sanctuary – a strand that is nonetheless often presented as the central story of sanctuary. This understanding emphasises the sanctuary as a *temenos*, meaning in Greek a 'place that is cut off' (Pedley 2005: 29). Life inside sanctuary from this perspective is conceived of as sacred, untouchable and pure; removed not only from violence but also from movement and indeed political life. This spatial understanding of sanctuary as a place 'cut off' serves to cement an image of those seeking sanctuary as similarly cut off; those 'inside' sanctuary are positioned 'outside' the public or political realm. Indeed, a statist account often perceives sanctuary-seekers to be passive victims (if not risky threats) who await salvation from those who are not contained within the space of sanctuary: namely, citizens. Moreover, it is the 'agency of sanctuary providers', those deemed to be providing rather than depending on the 'physical protection' of sanctuary, which tends to be the central focus of much research into sanctuary (Lippert 2005: 15–16). In contemporary accounts of sanctuary this territorialised demarcation separating those inside from those outside often reifies a split between those deemed to be irregular and those deemed to be regular. From a statist perspective, the former are immobilised and rendered apolitical, while the latter are granted free movement in the granting of hospitality to subjects whose existence depends on the generosity of others.

The association of sanctuary with specific locales has a long history. Reflecting on the pre-modern era, Philip Marfleet claims that sanctuary was practised through 'sites of cosmological significance – locations sanctified by deities or by those empowered by them – which were inviolable' (2007: 138). These sites were often relatively broadly defined locations of geo-religious significance, such as islands, mountains, valleys and caves. Despite this more amorphous notion of spaces of sanctuary, however, the association of sanctuary with more narrowly-defined religious buildings is evident in the linguistic association of sanctuary with *sanctuarium* (the Roman notion of an inviolable area of the temple) and *sanctum* (the early medieval European notion of a place of the sacraments in the Christian church), to which Marfleet draws attention. These entail both some sense of an *enclosed* space of sanctuary as well as a distinction between s/he who receives sanctuary and s/he who provides sanctuary. The concept of sanctuary as developed out of *sanctuarium* and *sanctum* thus brings to bear an unequal relation in which the recipient is under the protection of the provider. In the Roman and Judaeo-Christian tradition this was conceived of in terms of the 'helpless' slave or prosecuted criminal receiving protection from the all-consuming power of God offered through the church within 'sacred' sites. In this history an unequal relation is thus constitutive of sanctuary practices, which are necessarily conceived of as emerging within an enclosed space out of which the recipient is perceived to be at risk of violence.

Indeed, sanctuary is often said to have officially emerged in 392 CE with the early Roman law of Theodosius, who stipulated that 'victims' (initially slaves

152 *V. Squire and J. Bagelman*

complaining of maltreatment) who 'sought sanctuary in churches could not be removed by force' (Price 2009: 32; see also Cox 1911; Lippert 2005). This has become a recognised origin-story within the sanctuary literature, and as such it is often taken for granted that sanctuary 'is the name given to church-based asylum', a practice which provides physical 'shelter' to the helpless (Price 2009: 32). This historical definition and conception of sanctuary is evoked and reproduced in a number of contemporary readings of sanctuary, including Charles Cox's *Sanctuaries and Sanctuary Seekers of Medieval England*. Cox acknowledges earlier informal expressions of sanctuary, yet places emphasis on Theodosius' legal articulation when it was formally recognised by the state as a practice designed to protect those 'in danger of life or limb' within church walls (Cox 1911: 2). While the sanctuary literature has more recently gestured at the ways in which sanctuary has moved beyond religious sites, an emphasis on the 'wall', or enclosure, often remains pervasive.[4] Sanctuary both as a concept and as a practice would in this sense seem to have been articulated in terms that run parallel with dominant understandings and practices of citizenship as a regime; specifically with an approach which is characterised by a struggle to order subjects legally and spatially and a related struggle to 'split' mobility through fixing the boundaries between those who have the right to move freely within and across space, and others who are denied such a right. Sanctuary in these terms is, to put it simply, a statist project.

Statist rationalities?

While many historical accounts tend to reduce a complex set of practices to pastoralism through rendering sanctuary in statist terms, a Foucauldian approach facilitates a more complex account by fleshing out the heterogeneous power relations that are constitutive of sanctuary practices. Randy Lippert's (2005) influential analysis of *Sanctuary, Sovereignty and Sacrifice* is illuminating in this regard, because it shows how pastoral, sovereign and governmental power relations become intertwined in contemporary church sanctuary incidents. Arguing that the former two rationalities have recently been overshadowed by a scholastic obsession with governmentality in the Foucauldian literature, he explores how the three rationalities of power overlap and work together in the case of sanctuary.

The first rationality of power that Lippert addresses is governmental power, which constitutes freedom as an instrument of power and control. Governmental power does not operate from above by directing subjects, but instead operates through processes of normalisation and responsibilisation whereby subjects are presented with the free choice to act responsibly (Lippert 2005: 63). Power from a governmentality perspective is thus largely devolved individually, with citizens increasingly governing themselves through technologies and forms of knowledge that monitor, evaluate and reform (Cruikshank 1999). Sanctuary might be read from this perspective, Lippert implies, as a space carved out by 'responsible' individuals who seek to help 'helpless' migrants that have been abandoned

Taking not waiting   153

by the state to become responsible in their own right (see also Rose 1992). While sanctuary incidents are often assumed to be a direct resistance to the sovereignty of the state, Lippert suggests that such incidents may be better understood as a modality of government through which the governing of refugees is practiced through the 'responsibilisation' of 'self-regulating liberal citizens' (Lippert 2005: 138). In this respect Lippert indicates that sanctuary incidents do not so much challenge a statist politics as reinforce this type of politics, implicitly reaffirming the territorialised logic of inside/outside and the hierarchical relations of legal/illegal or citizen/non-citizen that such a politics involves. Indeed, Lippert contends that governmentality has not displaced state sovereignty but rather suggests that the two are intertwined in contemporary sanctuary incidents.

Similarly, Lippert demonstrates that pastoral power remains central to sanctuary incidents, despite the widespread assumption that such a rationality has faded in the wake of advanced liberalism. Lippert identifies three key characteristics that are constitutive of pastoral power, which in many respects do not undermine governmental power. First, pastoral governance constitutes 'authority in the figure of a shepherd' (Lippert 2005: 90). As Foucault notes: 'The shepherd must be informed of the material needs of each member of the flock and provide for them when necessary' (Lippert 2005: 95). Second, pastoral power is inexorably linked with the notion of sacrifice. Lippert alludes to Foucault's statement that 'pastoral power is not merely a form of power which commands; it must also be prepared to sacrifice itself for the life and salvation of the flock' (Lippert 2004: 359). Third, pastoral power cannot function without shepherds 'becoming informed' of the needs of members of the flock; that is, by 'making them reveal their innermost secrets' (Lippert 2005: 96). Lippert emphasises Foucault's suggestion that the shepherd 'must know what is going on, what each of them does – his public sins. Indeed, he must know what is going on in the soul of each one, that is: his secret sins, his progress on the road to sainthood' (Lippert 2005: 96). Lippert refers to this final quality as 'individualising and intimate knowledge' (ibid.), indicative of the way in which pastoral and governmental powers are intertwined in complementary ways in contemporary sanctuary incidents.

Lippert suggests that sanctuary entails the coupling of these pastoral rationalities with a liberal rationality – that is, a marriage of governing through freedom and governing through need. Important from our perspective, however, is that this intertwinement of governmental and pastoral creates a population which is *nevertheless divided*. The rationalities of governmental and pastoral power do not constitute each subject equally. Indeed, the sanctuary incidents that Lippert addresses distinguish between 'provider' and 'recipient' in ways that create a distinction between responsibilised and irresponsiblised subjects, which might also be understood in terms of the divide between 'legal' citizens and the 'illegal' migrants (see Inda 2011). 'Illegal' migrants in this regard might be interpreted as subjects who have a different experience of power, for they 'cannot be considered affiliated to civilised communities because they are [conceived of as] incapable of managing themselves as subjects … or they are considered a threat … to political order' (Rose 1996: 341). As Nicholas Rose

154 *V. Squire and J. Bagelman*

argues, those deemed to be 'less receptive to responsibilisation strategies' face different and 'more intensive strategies' of control (ibid.). An account that points to the intertwined strategies of pastoral and governmental power in this regard thus allows us to see how the subjects of sanctuary are hierarchically divided and ordered in complex ways.

For Lippert, this intertwinement of governmental and pastoral power cannot be understood in separation from sovereign power. Sovereign power, Lippert argues, functions largely through the 'control of territory' (Lippert 2005: 68). If governmentality and pastoralism are rationalities that function through the gaining of (official and personal) information, then sovereignty *qua* territorialisation can in some respects be conceived of as a condition of possibility for these practices. Indeed, Lippert contends that the borders enacted to surround a given space of sanctuary enable providers to keep track of recipients (Lippert 2005: 75). This effectively enables citizens to organise, gain data and assist migrants in need as it is through the bordering of space that the migrant may be tracked, known and therefore supposedly protected and cared for more efficiently (see also Cruikshank, 1999). Lippert's Foucauldian approach is thus important in drawing out the complexity of the power relations which are enacted through sanctuary incidents and in showing how heterogeneous rationalities are contingently intertwined in ways that (re)order the subjects of sanctuary in statist terms. In particular, Lippert's analysis is crucial in pointing to the various ways in which sanctuary practices become involved in the governing of migrants in terms that reinforce a notion of the non-citizen migrant as apolitical.

Despite the critical insights of Lippert's Foucauldian account of sanctuary incidents, however, we want to suggest that this type of analysis risks overlooking some of the more dynamic interactions and unexpected relations that emerge in 'mobile enclaves' whereby sanctuary is both taken and enacted. It could perhaps be argued that Lippert's reading of sanctuary further embeds an unequal or hierarchical relationship between provider and recipient by dividing those 'inside' sanctuary from those 'without' in the public or political realm (Lippert 2005: 16). While Lippert's discussion of sanctuary incidents needs to be read in relation to a particular form of anti-deportation activism, it is nevertheless important to consider how this type of analysis of sanctuary can reify a relationship of pastoralism and care in which those who are to be protected are effectively denied political capacity or voice. This is perhaps accentuated in research that gives voice to providers only, and which tends to support a pastoral-governmental politics of care by presenting 'recipients' as victims requiring protection. The temporal emerges here as a spatialised question in terms of 'when might they become political?' with those within the contained space of sanctuary implicitly posed as *waiting* for political life to begin. In this regard, the statist-pastoral spatial ordering of subjects is transformed into a statist-pastoral temporal order in which those authorised to move are distinguished from those who are not yet ready to do so. Such an analysis of sanctuary in this sense would seem to risk reaffirming statist and pastoral distinctions while overlooking some of the more dynamic interactions and unexpected relations that an analysis of 'mobile enclaves' might provide.

Sanctuary on the move?

While this chapter draws upon and acknowledges the critical insights of Lippert's Foucauldian analysis of sanctuary in terms of its emphasis on the intertwinement of heterogeneous rationalities of power, it also takes as a starting point the observation that a more dynamic rendering of sanctuary might be gleaned from an analysis of the practices of the City of Sanctuary movement. City of Sanctuary is an interesting case, because its practices are not confined to an enclosed or contained space, such as the church as a sacred space of protection. Rather, the movement's struggle to constitute the city as a space of sanctuary brings to bear a dynamism that a statist frame of reference is unable to grasp (see Darling 2010; Squire 2011b). Indeed, more dynamic enactments can be found littering historical practices of sanctuary, suggestive of the partiality of a conception of sanctuary that assumes spatial containment or enclosure.[5] The practices of City of Sanctuary might be conceived of in relation to these alternative histories of sanctuary. Rather than functioning in or through the logic of containment, the activities of City of Sanctuary operate through what we call 'mobile enclaves of sanctuary', which open up possibilities for unexpected relations that challenge statist and pastoral renderings of sanctuary. The notion of mobile enclaves of sanctuary thus brings to the fore the inherent dynamism of social sites that are often assumed to be static and unchanging (e.g. Jensen 2009). These sites, we suggest, create the conditions for the emergence of relations that cut through depoliticising pastoral depictions of those taking sanctuary as victims who are worthy of protection, along with the statist distinction between citizen and non-citizen on which such depictions largely rely.

Mobile enclaves of sanctuary

A focus on City of Sanctuary would seem to demand a more diffuse and relational account of the sites of sanctuary than that provided by the historical and contemporary analyses introduced above. For City of Sanctuary activists, it is the city or town that forms the key site to be constructed as a place of sanctuary, and this is thus seen as requiring a much broader range of interventions across the urban environment than that associated with conventional church-based sanctuary practices (see Darling 2010). Instead of protecting sanctuary seekers in fixed spatial sites, City of Sanctuary promotes a culture of hospitality toward those taking sanctuary across diverse sites, such as local businesses or workplaces, community cafés and religious congregations. This entails a range of practices, such as the placing of signs on the window sills of various community buildings, shops, student unions and offices around Sheffield which bear the words: 'We welcome asylum-seekers and refugees' (interview with Craig 2009: 32). Practices such as these can be interpreted as constituting a wider range of relational sites through which sanctuary is practised, and would seem to blur the boundaries between hospitality and sanctuary by enacting protection in the form of welcome at sites across the urban environment. Yet what we want to

156   *V. Squire and J. Bagelman*

emphasise alongside this practising of sanctuary across dispersed sites is the way in which the hierarchies of citizen/non-citizen and protector/protected that inform statist and pastoral accounts of sanctuary are troubled through the enactment of sanctuary in 'mobile enclaves'.

What we refer to as a mobile enclave of sanctuary is perhaps apparent if we consider the Terminus Initiative in Sheffield, which is a community initiative set up by a local church group associated with City of Sanctuary. The Terminus Initiative includes a Conversation Club and a community café. The former is a site whereby those seeking sanctuary can meet with each other and with more 'established' residents to practice speaking English, and the latter is a site which is largely run by migrants and asylum seekers for local residents at large. As such, these are less adequately conceived of as fixed sites that contain those 'seeking' sanctuary, than they are as hubs that allow local residents to meet and interact, regardless of their social position or legal status (Barnett and Bhogal 2009: 35). As one of the founders of the City of Sanctuary movement points out, the sanctuary café is important as an initiative because, like other City of Sanctuary activities, it effectively creates opportunities for 'greater interaction' between local residents (interview with Inderjit 2009: 17). This is important in challenging policies and practices that limit the rights of migrants in moving to and settling in the city, because the practice of sanctuary is premised upon the creation of relational sites that operate according to a logic of open access rather than closed borders. Specifically, we want to stress the significance of this type of activity as creating opportunities for interactions and relations that trouble statist distinctions between those authorised to move and interact and those who are not, as well as pastoral distinctions between those worthy of protection and those in a position of providing protection.

Mobile enclaves of sanctuary can be interpreted as sites that are constituted through the movements and interactions of those taking sanctuary, and are politically significant because they entail the enactment of sanctuary in terms that are not prescribed by the practices of 'providers'. For example, Sheffield in itself as a 'city of sanctuary' can be interpreted as a mobile enclave that refuses the logic of closed borders by opening up its urban environment to the movements and interactions of those taking sanctuary. Whether or not the City of Sanctuary movement directly challenges statism and pastoralism in this regard is less important from the perspective developed here than the 'minor' practices that open up the potential for those taking sanctuary to challenge the closures and hierarchical distinctions associated with an exclusionary politics of asylum (Squire 2011b; Squire and Darling forthcoming). Our analysis of the Terminus Initiative indicates that those taking sanctuary in Sheffield are neither rendered immobile through their containment within fixed sites nor left dependent upon the movement and political advocacy of those 'providing' sanctuary. Those taking sanctuary in Sheffield engage with others in dynamic ways through their interactions within, and movements across or between, mobile enclaves of sanctuary such as the Conversation Club or sanctuary café. For instance, an asylum seeker describes her experiences working at the Terminus Café and the

Taking not waiting   157

interactions and relations that are constituted through such a site: 'We are cooking a load of food for other[s] ... together and then one day they invited immigration and the police to interview. And me, I talk, they eat also my food, cooking – they enjoy' (interview with Adolphine 2009: 6). What is significant about this example from our perspective is that it allows us to see how mobile enclaves of sanctuary such as that of the Terminus Café entail movements and interactions that would appear unexpected from a statist and pastoral perspective. Adolphine here describes how the relations of 'host' and 'guest' are reversed in the café, with Adolphine able to speak in her own voice as 'host' to those who would from a statist perspective be deemed as her interrogators. Such an account is thus indicative of the constitution of sites of open access and equal participation by which those taking sanctuary relate to others in terms that are unimaginable where sanctuary is conceived of in terms of contained spaces and pastoral mechanisms.

One way in which we might understand the political significance of these relatively open, equal and relational sites of sanctuary is in relation to the notion of 'proximate diversity'. This notion is used by various urban studies scholars to describe how diverse actors and activities are brought together in shared spaces of the city, thereby generating a complex set of relations which often challenge discrete categorisations (Allen 2000; Jacobs 1961; Magnusson 2011). In terms of our focus on the way that an analysis of mobile enclaves of sanctuary challenges statist and pastoral accounts of sanctuary, what is most interesting about these complex relations of proximate diversity is that they trouble any singular account of sovereignty imposed from above or below. This means that legal distinctions between citizens and non-citizens become ineffective, while political distinctions between the protector and the protected and between the worthy and the unworthy begin to unravel (see also Nyers 2010). This is evident in the claim of one interviewee, for example, who describes her experience of a Conversation Club associated with City of Sanctuary as follows: 'You cannot come to a Conversation Club and not be changed' (interview with Myra 2010: 5). The notion of proximate diversity in this regard is one that is inherently relational.

The critical importance of this notion of proximate diversity is further evident if we consider the case of an asylum seeker who was interviewed as a participant of City of Sanctuary (see Squire 2011b). What is striking about this particular example is that the asylum seeker in question works as a radio broadcaster in Sheffield and in this capacity described a situation in which he interviewed the local Mayor on the issue of asylum on a local radio show (interview with Ouattara 2009). Already, we can see how the movement of this individual into the city invokes a relatively complex set of diversities, with the individual in question simultaneously occupying both a position of legal, social and economic marginalisation (as asylum seeker) as well as a position of social status (as broadcaster). The individual in question effectively challenges the assumption that his status as asylum seeker relegates him to a position of one who is denied the right to work and political voice, and points to the ways in which this brings him closer to others in the following way: 'one of my friends, who was working

158   *V. Squire and J. Bagelman*

here voluntarily [at the Radio Station] … he never knew I was an asylum seeker and he was always against them. But the day I tell him about ourselves, he was in tears' (interview with Ouattara: 15). The story that this interviewee tells us is indicative of the creation of unexpected relations in a context whereby the movements and interactions of those taking sanctuary refuse to conform to (or exceed) existing political categorisations. This is politically significant because it allows us to see how an analysis of the proximate diversities that are constituted through mobile enclaves of sanctuary can challenge the unequal relations by which non-citizen migrants are defined as apolitical, whether through a process of victimisation or of criminalisation.

Unauthorised takings of sanctuary

So if the mobile enclaves of sanctuary and proximate diversities that these entail create the conditions for unexpected relations that trouble simplistic distinctions between citizens and non-citizens, between the protected and protector, and between the worthy and unworthy, then how precisely does this play out in the practices and politics of City of Sanctuary? It is here that the subtle intertwinement of sovereign, governmental and pastoral rationalities of power needs to be carefully unpacked. To suggest that City of Sanctuary might most critically be understood in terms that refuse statism and pastoralism is not to say that its practices are entirely devoid of the sovereign, governmental or pastoral rationalities of power that Lippert outlines. For example, the very articulation of City of Sanctuary as 'a movement to build a culture of hospitality for people seeking sanctuary in the UK' (City of Sanctuary 2009) clearly invokes an unequal logic of pastoral care. It also draws lines between citizens and non-citizens in terms that affirm the assumptions on which a rationality of sovereign power rests. To suggest that City of Sanctuary is a post-statist movement or network would thus clearly be a step too far.

Indeed, City of Sanctuary might also be seen through a governmental lens as devolving authority to 'responsible' communities. This is evident in the first criterion of qualification as a City of Sanctuary, whereby a city or town must gain 'resolutions of support from a significant and representative proportion of local groups and organisations' (Barnett and Bhoghal 2009: 79). It is not difficult to see how we might interpret the activities of City of Sanctuary as invoking a governmental rationality that is bound up with a 'responsibilising' power-knowledge complex. For example, in order to 'build a culture of hospitality for people seeking sanctuary in the UK', a strong emphasis is placed on facilitating personal testimonies (City of Sanctuary 2009). Where these are invoked to facilitate protection and hospitality there is always a risk that such testimonies invoke governmental-pastoral rationalities in which those seeking sanctuary are divided into the simplified categories of responsible or 'worthy' victim and irresponsible or 'unworthy' threat.

Nevertheless, we want also to draw attention here to the ways in which the activities of City of Sanctuary facilitate movements and interactions that

Taking not waiting   159

challenge such sovereign, governmental and pastoral rationalities, along with the social and political relations that they entail. In particular, we want to highlight the ways in which these 'excessive' relations challenge a hierarchical statist distinction between citizen and non-citizen, along with a series of simplifications that have become bound up with such distinctions. As one of the founding members of City of Sanctuary suggests, it is impossible to draw clear-cut lines between migrants and those seeking sanctuary: 'Thus the distinction only loosely holds in practice despite the clear focus on sanctuary within the movement' (interview with Craig 2009: 8–9). Indeed, a series of simplified distinctions break down in the activities of City of Sanctuary: the distinction between citizens and non-citizens; the distinction between those who are responsible or worthy and thus authorised to move or interact and those who are not; and the distinction between those who are the recipients of sanctuary and those who are its providers. After all, mobile enclaves of sanctuary produce complex interactions through which unexpected social and political relations challenge hierarchical statist simplifications along with the exclusionary politics that they so often invest.

There are various ways in which this occurs. We have already seen how City of Sanctuary's facilitation of voluntary work for those taking sanctuary in the city challenges the exclusions of contemporary asylum policy, where asylum seekers are denied the right to work. In so doing, the hierarchies of inclusion/exclusion that a statist politics implies are overturned and the potential for mutual exchange is opened up in creative ways.[6] Similarly, voucher exchange programmes in which asylum seekers exchange supermarket vouchers for cash challenges exclusionary policy initiatives that deny those seeking sanctuary the opportunity to move across and engage within urban spaces in equal terms. Activities such as these should not in any simple way be interpreted in terms of a more inclusive politics, in our opinion. To reduce such interventions to a politics that seeks to bring that which is excluded to the 'inside' of community would be to remain within a statist frame of reference. Rather, what is important about these activities is that they entail a claiming of the right to move around and interact or undertake exchanges within the city regardless of one's status. This claiming of a 'right to the city' through presence (see Lefebvre 1996) and regardless of status might be observed in the activities of sanctuary gardeners, for example, with the activity of 'community gardening' constituting a mobile enclave of sanctuary in which statist assumptions do not hold.

Clearly, the struggle to create a city of sanctuary in which status does not play a role has its limits. Ultimately the constitution of mobile enclaves of sanctuary does not effectively guard against the violences of state practices of forced (im)mobility, such as detention, deportation and dispersal (see Schuster 2005). Nor do activities such as voucher exchanges and sanctuary gardening effectively challenge exclusionary asylum policies (see Squire 2009a). However, such sites and activities do contribute to the creation of disruptive or 'unexpected' relations that open to question the assumptions upon which the political divisions and legal categories which inform such policies and practices are based (see also

160   *V. Squire and J. Bagelman*

Squire 2009b). Importantly, they also shift attention from practices of *seeking* sanctuary to practices of *taking* sanctuary, thus troubling the distinction between 'recipient' and 'provider' along with the distinction between participants who are able move or act 'responsibly' and those who are not yet ready to do so.

Indeed, we would suggest that the temporality of *taking rather than waiting* is critical in understanding the political and temporal significance of the sanctuary practices that emerge through an analysis of City of Sanctuary. This emphasis allows us to expose how those taking sanctuary have a voice in the movement in the present, rather than having to wait to be spoken for:

> We play an active role.... And the problem is that we have to make people understand about asylum [seeker]s and refugees so by doing that they have to know the refugee themselves and send them to speak to the [people of] Sheffield, and this is what City of Sanctuary has done.
>
> (interview with Ouattara 2009: 9)

The centrality of the voices of those taking sanctuary within the movement is critical in understanding how its activities tend to function according to a principle of equality (Rancière 1999), rather than simply conforming to the uneven logic of hospitality (Squire and Darling forthcoming). This is reflected in one participant's description of the movement, for example, where she describes how the City of Sanctuary allows her 'to be part of a group who look after me and [I] look after [them] too' (interview with Adolphine 2009: 5). Moreover, the practice of sanctuary through a temporality of taking rather than waiting can also be read into the development of a town or city as one of sanctuary prior to its official recognition as such. The launching of a town or city as a City of Sanctuary does not await the agreement of local authorities, as one participant describes:

> We didn't er, wait for the Council to decide it and different organisations decided that the city should be called City of Sanctuary, they make it clear to the Lord Mayor, they sent a letter and petitions, and he saw them and these people – I mean the Sheffield wanted it to be called Sheffield, City of Sanctuary. And he just have to follow it.
>
> (interview with Ouattara 2009: 7)

City of Sanctuary in this regard might be read as enacting sanctuary in terms that facilitate the claiming a 'right to the city' regardless of status and official authorisation, specifically through a temporality of taking not waiting.

So where does this leave us when it comes to providing an alternative lens through which to view sanctuary practices, instead of the statist and pastoral approach which we examined in the first part of this chapter? Our analysis suggests that scholars such as Randy Lippert are right to point to the multiple rationalities of power that are at play in contemporary sanctuary practices. However, such an analysis would seem to miss a critical dimension of heterogeneity which exceeds the statist frame. We conceive this heterogeneity in the movements and

Taking not waiting 161

interactions of those taking sanctuary which, through the proximate diversities of mobile enclaves of sanctuary, create a series of disruptive and unexpected relations that trouble the assumptions of statist and pastoral accounts of sanctuary. This element of heterogeneity might be situated within a broader 'politics of migration', which exceeds a 'politics of control' that struggles to capture or contain movements that are deemed to be unauthorised (see Squire 2011a). It might also be captured through a distinction between 'major' and 'minor' practices of sanctuary (Squire 2011b; see also Balibar forthcoming). Rather than accepting statist and pastoral distinctions as given, those taking and enacting sanctuary through City of Sanctuary challenge the assumptions about who is authorised to move and (inter)act politically. In other words, they prompt a rethinking of sanctuary 'on the move' that undermines distinctions between protector and protected and between citizen and non-citizen, thus urging us all to 'see like a city' with all the ambiguities and complexities that this entails (Magnusson 2011). This is important when it comes to questions of migrant subjectivity, because it allows us to uncover the politics that an exclusionary politics strives to cover through categorisations of a statist and pastoral form (Squire 2009a).

Conclusion

This chapter has made the case for a reconceptualisation of sanctuary through an analysis of the activities of the City of Sanctuary movement in Sheffield, UK. Critiquing historical analyses which present the space of sanctuary as a contained space and which present hierarchical relations between those who protect and those who are to be protected as clear-cut and incontestable, we have shown how Randy Lippert's Foucauldian account of the intertwined rationalities of power serves as a welcome intervention in our understanding of contemporary sanctuary practices. However, we have also drawn attention to the shortcomings of such an approach in challenging a statist and pastoral frame of reference. Specifically, we have made the case for an approach that both takes into account these various rationalities of power as they are played out in the activities or practices of City of Sanctuary, and also pays critical attention to the ways in which such practices create the conditions for movements and interactions that contest or exceed statist and pastoral framings of sanctuary. The analysis in this chapter conceptualises these contestations in terms of the taking and enactment of sanctuary across dynamic relational sites or 'mobile enclaves', through which 'unexpected' relations are created that trouble the hierarchical statist and pastoral categories of citizen/non-citizen and recipient/provider.

The contested politics that this chapter points to thus cannot be captured within a singular frame, just as the rationalities of power at play in contemporary sanctuary practices cannot be reduced to a logic of sovereignty whereby authority is granted to the state. This is not to say, however, that the politics of City of Sanctuary can in any simple way be understood as a pluralised alternative to statism, for this would be to leave unchallenged the distinctions of a singular frame. It is for

162 *V. Squire and J. Bagelman*

this reason that we suggest that an analysis concerned with the political signifi-cance of City of Sanctuary requires an approach that is open to those elements that are heterogeneous to statism and pastoralism. This heterogeneity might be one that an approach based on 'seeing like a city' allows us to address through an emphasis on mobile enclaves and proximate diversities. Such analytical categories allow us to see how the enactment of sanctuary entails a disruptive politics of movement or mobility that exceeds the confines and standardisations of statist and pastoral rationalities. This is important, we argue, because it allows us to see how non-citizen migrants who take sanctuary in cities such as Sheffield challenge the proc-esses of victimisation and criminalisation through which they are constructed and governed as 'apolitical' subjects. Contestations of a statist and pastoral politics of sanctuary in this regard are critical because they engage a temporality of taking not waiting, through which those taking sanctuary refuse to engage as criminals or victims and instead constitute themselves as political beings in their own right.

Notes

1 The authors would like to thank all of the participants of the workshop 'Putting Citi-zenship in Motion: Migrant Activism, Mobile Citizenship and the Politics of Move-ment', which was held at the Institute on Globalization and the Human Condition, McMaster University, Canada, during October 2009. In particular, thanks are extended to our discussant, William Walters, and to the organisers of the workshop and editors of this collection, Peter Nyers and Kim Rygiel, whose insightful comments have been invaluable in our development of the arguments in this essay.

2 The analysis in this chapter draws on a series of in-depth qualitative interviews with a total of ten organisers and participants from Sheffield City of Sanctuary, which were carried out in the spring and summer of 2009 and in June 2010. It also draws upon a doc-umentary analysis of material written by organisers, as well as upon observations of meetings with participants from each of the mobilisations in question. Thanks are extended to Louise Richards, whose support with carrying out these interviews has been invaluable. Thanks also to Gabi Kent, Director/Producer for Angel Eye Media. Full details of these interviews are provided at the end of the Bibliography of this article.

3 Such a conception is evident, for example, in the fact that integration policy is offi-cially orientated toward refugees and immigrants rather than toward migrants or asylum seekers (see National Strategy for Refugee Integration, 2004).

4 Certainly it would appear that the walls of sanctuary have expanded (to include hospi-tals, schools, etc.) but it is largely assumed that enclosure itself is the condition of pos-sibility for sanctuary. This is evident in Randy Lippert's work *Sanctuary, Sovereignty and Sacrifice* wherein sanctuary is defined as a space in which migrants 'actually enter and remain in physical protection' (2005: 16).

5 Before sanctuary was enshrined in Roman law the practice was 'already recognised and well established', and in fact was not delimited to the confines of a particular build-ing, religious or otherwise. For instance, a form of sanctuary was afforded to those who fled to an unenclosed statue of a caesar, or to those who clung to an 'image of god while grasping a broken twig or wool, the signs of a supplicant' (Price, 2009: 31). These more disparate practices have, however, often been displaced or lost under the formal, state-recognised definition of 'sanctuary', which was originally provided by Theodosius and which places emphasis on the walled church.

6 See Aradau, Huysmans and Squire (2010) for a discussion of the importance of exchange in relation to mobility.

Taking not waiting   163

Bibliography

Allen, J. (2000) 'On Georg Simmel: Proximity, Distance and Movement' in *Thinking Space*, London: Routledge, 54–70.

Aradau, C., H. Huysmans and V. Squire (2010) 'Acts of European Citizenship: A Political Sociology of Mobility' *Journal of Common Market Studies* 48 (4), 945–965.

Barnett, C. and I. Bhogal (2009) *Becoming a City of Sanctuary: A Practical Handbook with Inspiring Examples*, Plug and Tap.

Bartelson, J. (2006) 'The Concept of Sovereignty Revisited' *European Journal of International Law*, 17: 463–474.

Bigo, D. (2002) 'Security and Immigration: Towards a Critique of the Governmentality of Unease' *Alternatives: Global, Local, Political*, 27 (1): 63–92.

City of Sanctuary (2009), available at www.cityofsanctuary.org (accessed 4 June 2009).

Commission on Integration and Cohesion (2007) *Shared Futures*, Wetherby: Crown Copyright.

Cox, C.J. (1911) *The Sanctuaries and Sanctuary Seekers of Mediaeval England*, London: George Allen & Sons.

Cruikshank, B. (1999) *The Will to Empower: Democratic Citizens and Other Subjects*, Ithaca: Cornell University Press.

Darling, J. (2010) 'A City of Sanctuary: The Relational Re-imagining of Sheffield's Asylum Politics' *Transactions of the Institute of British Geographers*, 35: 125–140.

Deleuze, G. and F. Guattari (1988) *A Thousand Plateaus: Capitalism and Schizophrenia*, London: Athlone Press.

Inda, J. (2011) 'Borderzones of Enforcement: Criminalization, Workplace Raids, and Migrant Counter-Conducts' in V. Squire (ed.) *The Contested Politics of Mobility: Borderzones and Irregularity*, London: Routledge.

Innes, A.J. (2010) 'When the Threatened Become the Threat: The Construction of Asylum Seekers in British Media Narratives' *International Relations* 24 (4): 456–477.

Jacobs, J. (1961) *The Death and Life of Great American Cities*, New York: Random House.

Jensen, O.B. (2009) 'Flows of Meaning, Cultures of Movements – Urban Mobility as Meaningful Everyday Life Practice' *Mobilities* 4: 139–158.

Lefebvre, H. (1996) *Writings on Cities*, ed. and transl. E. Kofman and E. Lebas, London: Blackwell.

Lippert, R. (2004) 'Sanctuary Practices, Rationalities and Sovereignties' *Alternatives* 29: 533–555.

Lippert, R. (2005) *Sanctuary, Sovereignty and Sacrifice: Canadian Sanctuary Incidents, Power and Law*, Vancouver: University of British Columbia Press.

Magnusson, W. (2011) *Seeing Like a City: Towards a Political Ontology of Urbanism as a Way of Life*.

Marfleet, P. (2007) 'Refugees and History: Why we Must Address the Past' *Refugee Survey Quarterly* 26 (3): 136–148.

Nyers, P. (2010) 'Duelling Designs: The Politics of Rescuing Dual Citizens' *Citizenship Studies* 14 (1): 47–60.

Pedley, J. (2005) *Sanctuaries and the Sacred in the Ancient Greek World*, Cambridge: Cambridge University Press.

Price, M. (2009) *Rethinking Asylum: History, Purpose and Limits*, New York: Cambridge University Press.

Rancière, J. (1999) *Dis-agreement*, Minneapolis: University of Minnesota Press.

Rose, N. (1992) 'Governing the Enterprise Self' in P. Heelas and P. Morris (eds) *The Values of the Enterprise Culture: The Moral Debate*, London: Routledge, 141–164.

Rose, N. (1996) 'The Death of the Social? Re-Figuring the Territory of Government' *Economy and Society* 25 (3): 327–356.

Schuster, L. (2003) *The Use and Abuse of Political Asylum in Britain and Germany*, London: Frank Cass.

Schuster, L. (2005) 'A Sledgehammer to Crack a Nut: Deportation, Detention and Dispersal in Europe' *Social Policy and Administration* 39 (6): 606–621.

Scott, J. (1998) *Seeing Like a State: How Certain Schemes to Improve the Human Condition Have Failed*, New Haven, CT: Yale University Press.

Spencer, S. (2003) 'Introduction' *Political Quarterly* 74 (1): 1–24.

Squire, V. (2009a) *The Exclusionary Politics of Asylum: Migration, Minorities, Citizenship*, Basingstoke: Palgrave.

Squire, V. (2009b) 'Mobile Solidarities: The City of Sanctuary Movement and the Strangers into Citizens Campaign', available at www.open.ac.uk/ccig/news/mobile-solidarities-the-city-of-sanctuary-movement-and-the-strangers-into-citizens-campaign (accessed 2 May 2011).

Squire, V. (2011a) 'The Contested Politics of Mobility' in V. Squire (ed.) *The Contested Politics of Mobility: Borderzones and Irregularity*, London: Routledge.

Squire, V. (2011b) 'From Community Cohesion to Mobile Solidarities: The City of Sanctuary Network and the Strangers into Citizenship Campaign' *Political Studies* 59 (2), 290–307.

Squire, V. and J. Darling (forthcoming) 'Enacting Rightful Presence: Justice and Relationality in City of Sanctuary' [paper in preparation for *International Political Sociology*].

Zetter, R., D. Griffiths and N. Sigona (2003) 'Social Capital or Social Exclusion? The Impact of Asylum Seeker Dispersal on Refugee Community Organizations' *Community Development Journal* 40 (2): 169–181.

Interviews

Andrew, Volunteer, asylum seeker and participant of City of Sanctuary, 23 June 2010 (interview carried out by Gabi Kent, Director/Producer for Angel Eye Media).

Craig, National Co-ordinator and co-founder of City of Sanctuary, 30 March 2009.

Diane and Myra, participants of Conversation Club, 23 June 2010 (interview carried out by Gabi Kent, Director/Producer for Angel Eye Media).

Inderjit, co-founder of City of Sanctuary, 4 April 2009.

Joy and Adolphine: Joy, local minister, co-organiser of the Terminus Initiative and participant of City of Sanctuary, with Adolphine, asylum seeker and participant of the Terminus Initiative café, 4 June 2009.

Ouattara, broadcaster, asylum seeker and participant of City of Sanctuary, 20 June 2009.

Robert, Chair of Assist and participant of City of Sanctuary.

Rodrigo, Volunteer, refugee and participant of City of Sanctuary, 23 June 2010 (interview carried out by Gabi Kent, Director/Producer for Angel Eye Media).

9 Undocumented citizens?

Shifting grounds of citizenship in Los Angeles[1]

Anne McNevin

Recent developments in the US state of Arizona have focused international attention on increasingly localised strategies of border policing against irregular migrants. In 2010, Arizona legislators introduced a law (SB 1070) that criminalises undocumented presence and compels police to check the status of anyone reasonably suspected of being in the state without the necessary papers. As federal law-makers equivocate over immigration reform, SB 1070 is in keeping with trends whereby numerous municipal administrations are taking immigration enforcement into their own hands. Many cities in the US deploy their police as proxy-immigration agents and have devised municipal ordinances to sanction employers or landlords hiring or leasing to those who cannot prove lawful residence (Campbell 2007; Varsanyi 2008; Weissman *et al.* 2009). The trend towards localisation is not confined, however, to 'enforcement' approaches. Equally controversial has been the response from other jurisdictions to the Arizona initiative. Several cities, including Los Angeles, have placed bans on official travel to Arizona and on business dealings with Arizona-based companies.

The furore over SB 1070 arises in part over the potential for Latino *citizens*, in particular, to face discrimination on account of 'looking like' a predominantly Mexican undocumented population. Yet it also reflects different approaches to the public policy dilemmas associated with a structurally integrated undocumented population. Administrators contend, for example, with growing numbers of 'mixed status' families where the citizen/alien distinction divides parents from children and spouse from spouse (in 2008 such families tallied to 8.8 million people across the US; Passel and Cohn 2009: 8). Police forces struggle to maintain law and order when sectors of the community are fearful to report crimes or act as witnesses on account of immigration status. Many local economies are built on businesses where undocumented migrants are a large part of the workforce. Against this backdrop, enforcing the line between citizens and aliens does not necessarily serve the interests of citizens in practical terms.

An approach more attuned to the complexity of the citizen/migrant divide became apparent in an interview I conducted with Felix, field organiser for the Los Angeles City Council's 13th District, which takes in the central gateway areas for the city's most recent migrants. As we talked over breakfast, some of

166   *A. McNevin*

those migrants were making their living selling hot cups of *champurrido* from carts on street corners. Others were making their way to the car-parks of home-improvement stores where day-labour markets operated. Felix was musing on the ways in which 'undocumented citizens' (he used the term deliberately) could be encouraged to participate in local economic development. For Felix, this question, rather than the issue of immigration enforcement, was the starting point for LA City Council. The approach, he suggested, was a pragmatic and humane one: how can we legitimise the work being done by the City's undocumented residents? What can the Council do to make it safe, clean and dignified to sell breakfast on the street or to negotiate a day's work from a car-park? How can these informal sectors be made less threatening to other local businesses and residents (interview, 20 May 2009)?

A series of Council initiatives in recent years add substance to Felix's account. Since the late 1990s, the Council has tendered for community organisations to run day-labour centres, providing shade and amenities for workers. The centres encourage day-labourers to collectively set minimum wages and to establish a fair rotation system when work is in short supply. In 2008, the City passed an ordinance that compelled new home-improvement stores to provide services for day-labourers before they would be granted a permit to operate (LA City Council 2008). In the same year, the City endorsed a campaign to improve deplorable wages and working conditions for thousands of car-wash workers, widely known to be largely undocumented migrants, and to audit the City's car-wash contracts with respect to workers' demands (*California Chronicle* 2008). The City offered its premises as a neutral site for negotiations between car-wash workers and employers. It has also sponsored workshops to inform undocumented students in local high-schools of their eligibility for higher education in the state of California (Villaraigosa 2009).[2]

In this chapter, I interpret these council initiatives as a mode of public recognition of the place of undocumented migrants in the civic life of Los Angeles. These and other examples of public recognition are one dimension of contemporary citizenship dynamics occurring at the level of the city. The other dimension relates to public acts initiated by undocumented migrants themselves. Together, public modes of recognition and acts of contestation are transforming the terms of political association in ways that challenge prevailing norms of citizenship. The challenge occurs not only on account of the incorporation of undocumented people, but also on account of the spatial and temporal reference points for doing so. In what follows, I reflect upon a shifting ground that constitutes both 'the where' and 'the when' of political belonging as moving targets. I suggest an approach to theorising citizenship that captures its mobility, in this sense. More specifically, I reflect upon three examples (student activism, worker cooperatives and parent mobilisations) where undocumented migrants in Los Angeles are engaged in acts of citizenship. These examples encompass outspoken demands that 'undocumented citizens' be recognised in formal terms as well as more modest negotiations with the institutions and relationships that shape community and civic engagement. From this vantage point, I argue that undocumented

Undocumented citizens? 167

migrants are becoming citizens in unlikely ways and I contribute to a growing field of scholarship that takes the local-urban setting as a laboratory for contemporary citizenship struggles.

Theorising citizenship and space

Critical scholars of citizenship have built a compelling case for citizenship to be understood as a dynamic social relation as opposed to a static legal status conferred unidirectionally from 'above' to 'below' (Joseph 1999; Isin 2002; Ehrkamp and Leitner 2003; Secor 2003; Oboler 2006; Isin and Nielson 2008). Understood in this way, citizenship emerges *in practice*, in the claims and counter-claims of what it means to belong, in the repetitive acts through which people are marked as one of us or one of them and places as ours or theirs. Citizenship is about *being there*, legitimately, in public space, and *being seen* to be there. It involves, on one hand, demands to be recognised and, on the other, external recognition of one's place in the civic sphere. Citizenship is thus shaped, in part, by the strategies through which its outsiders resist their social positioning. These strategies are what Engin Isin (2008) refers to as 'acts of citizenship' – acts which rupture the given nature of citizenship and constitute citizens in new ways.

Drawing on the 'spatial turn' in social theory, critical studies have also theorised citizenship as a spatial relation. This is to say that 'the where' of citizenship (as much as 'the who' and 'the what') is the result of ongoing *political* negotiation. In many studies, cities feature prominently as places in which national-territorial norms of citizenship are being reconfigured (Pincetl 1994; Garcia 1996; Holston and Appadurai 1996; Isin 2000; Bauböck 2003; Staeheli 2003; Sassen 2004; Earnest 2007; Hanley *et al.* 2008). This emphasis reflects, on one hand, the re-scaling of state space associated with neoliberal restructuring and uneven development both within cities and across national territories (Sassen 2000; Brenner 2004). In this context, cities generate stark disaggregation in substantive access to citizenship rights and play host to fierce disputes over distribution of limited public resources. On the other hand, this emphasis reflects new subjective relations across urban, transnational and trans-local landscapes that are transforming the spatial parameters of political community and civic engagement (Smith 2001; Ehrkamp and Leitner 2006; Smith and Bakker 2008). Such approaches have generated important empirical findings on the changing 'topographies of home' (Staeheli and Nagel 2006) that provide spatial groundings for contemporary acts of citizenship (see also Soguk 2008). As such, they have shed crucial light on the co-implication of emerging citizen-subjects and situated places in which globalisation 'happens'.

These critical studies intersect with what Sheller and Urry (2006) describe as a 'new mobilities paradigm' in the social sciences. The shift is paradigmatic, they argue, because it challenges the privilege ascribed to stasis over movement in fundamental categories of social science inquiry, including space and citizenship. While the spectrum of scholars I draw on here may not necessarily

168   A. McNevin

subscribe to a paradigm shift or to mobility as the central analytic in their work, they are all engaged to varying degrees with the empirical mobilities that shape the world around us (migration, in particular) and with challenges to the onto-logical starting points that structure inquiry (transitioning, for instance, from coherent migrant/citizen subjects to dynamic, in-process and socially constituted acts of citizenship). For Sheller and Urry, the point is to understand how mobil-ity is crucially tied to the exercise of power, both at the level of material experi-ence (the ability to be mobile) and at the level of inquiry (shifting designations of what counts as valid objects of investigation). Forms of immobility (border controls, for example, or static geographic registers that frame social science inquiry) are just as important to investigate as forms and degrees of mobility.

Citizenship, space and (im)mobility, approached from these critical perspec-tives, come together around the subject of irregular migrants – those with undoc-umented, ambiguous or insecure forms of immigration status. An emerging field of 'border studies' investigates border policing against irregular migrants enacted in new kinds of mobile spaces from militarised border zones at territory's edge to ambiguous offshore island jurisdictions where would-be migrants are detained, to virtual borders brought into being by administrative and policing functions operating well within or beyond the border as such (for an overview see Parker and Vaughan-Williams 2009). Here, the focus rests upon specific spatial technologies that de-territorialise and re-territorialise borders at once and apply them inconsistently for different kinds of human traffic. This is a rich body of literature that captures the centrality of emerging spatial imaginaries to dynamics of citizenship with specific regard to techniques of illegalisation. While such work invokes a sense of citizenship as practice, its focus is neverthe-less upon the practice of closure rather than on acts of contestation which seek to open citizenship to new formulations. The latter is the focus of a growing body of literature which draws attention, on one hand, to the practices which consti-tute certain types of people as 'illegal' and thus as intruders on citizens' turf. On the other, it shows how irregular migrants resist this categorisation and claim a legitimate presence in the places to which they have come (Pincetl 1994; De Genova 2005; Varsanyi 2005, 2006; Balibar 2006; McNevin 2006, 2011; Nyers 2006, 2008; Moulin and Nyers 2007; Beltrán 2009; Squire 2009).

This chapter builds on literature focused on irregular migrants' acts of citi-zenship whilst drawing implicitly on a broader orientation towards mobility. As a way of pushing at the limits of this work, it is useful to engage with Monica Varsanyi's notion of 'grounded' citizenship (2006: 239), developed in relation to empirical work closely related to this chapter. Drawing on both urban and agent-centred formulations of citizenship, Varsanyi investigates three examples (voting rights, the *Matrículas Consulares* or identity documents provided to expatriate Mexicans, and the provision of drivers' licences) whereby local government agencies in the US context 'recognise' undocumented people. On the basis of what she calls 'de facto consent for the formal membership of [undocumented people]' (2006: 240) Varsanyi makes a normative case for 'grounded' citizen-ship, whereby:

Undocumented citizens? 169

full membership would not be dependent upon an *explicit* consent to enter
and remain in a bounded community … but instead upon the mere reality of
presence and *residence* in a place. As an unbounded model of citizenship,
there would be no necessary difference in status between insiders and outsiders, and in this sense, legal status would cease to be a defining
characteristic.

(Varsanyi 2006: 239)

Grounded citizenship provides a normative route to 'lock-in' political membership through a grounded sensibility that has real substance in local institutions
with the power to confer a range of citizenship rights on undocumented people.
The empirical material I outline below might be taken to support Varsanyi's
notion of grounded citizenship. However, I want to suggest that certain acts by
undocumented people might also engender a more mobile sense of the places in
which citizenship is made meaningful and, in turn, a more mobile sense of citizenship itself – one that rests less on grounded-ness than on *shifting* grounds of
political belonging. What I am trying to get at is a tension between two important aspects of contemporary citizenship struggles. Varsanyi and other scholars
of urban transformation highlight new modes of citizenship that emerge 'in-
place' and challenge us to conceptualise places and political acts in new ways.
But if citizenship is indeed a dynamic practice, then we need to leave space for
that part of it that cannot be grasped in advance – that genuinely creative and
disruptive moment that engenders citizen-subjects in unforeseeable ways that
may be incommensurable with the spatial (territorial) baggage that remains
attached to the language of citizenship. My intention is therefore to explore
whether the notion of mobility allows us to acknowledge (but not to 'know' or
'fix') that excess of subjectivity, excess of space, and excess of practice that
inhere in acts of citizenship but evade recognition from within existing conceptual limits.

Citizenship in-place: Los Angeles

Los Angeles is an exemplary case of a global city transformed in recent decades
by the shift to a post-Fordist economy and a starkly polarised labour market. As
demand has grown for cheap migrant labour in expanding service-sector indus-
tries, supply has been aided by structural changes in origin countries which dis-
place workers from rural areas and traditional forms of employment. In many
countries of Central America, migrating north is a culturally and institutionally
embedded process and a crucial element of both state development and commu-
nity/family income earning strategies (Rocco 1997; Sassen 2000; Donahoe 2005;
Fernández-Kelly and Massey 2007, Delgado Wise and Márquez Covarrubias
2008; Phillips 2009). As a gateway city for much of this migration, Los Angeles
is heavily integrated, with a process of restructuring and division of labour with
decidedly global dimensions, as much as it is the site of more specific migration
histories, federal restructuring trajectories, regional dynamics and cumulative

170   *A. McNevin*

cultural ties (Monahan 2002; Keil 1998; Smith 2001). Los Angeles County is currently home to an estimated one million undocumented migrants, close to 700,000 of whom are likely to be working on any typical day (Pastor and Ortiz 2009: 26, 36). Space permits only a cursory account of the trans-local positioning that constitutes Los Angeles as a migrant metropolis. It is important, however, to emphasise the way in which place specificity necessarily shapes associated citizenship dynamics.

The specific conditions faced by low-wage migrant workers in Los Angeles gave rise to labour organising strategies in the 1990s that contextualise current 'acts of citizenship'. The innovative 'Justice for Janitors' campaign played a pioneering role in mobilising undocumented service workers (Gutierrez de Soldatenko 2005; Narro 2005–2006; Savage 2006). By the mid-2000s a surging Latino vote had transformed the political landscape in local and state fora such that immigrant rights (regardless of citizenship status) were of central concern to the fastest-growing group of constituents (Hayes-Bautista 2004). Momentum peaked most dramatically in 2006 when hundreds of thousands of people took to the streets of Los Angeles in the largest of nationwide demonstrations opposing legislation that aimed to criminalise undocumented presence. Graphically illustrating the leverage of a largely Spanish-speaking migrant rights movement, the demonstrations attracted scholarly attention as performative enactments of citizenship and crucial symbolic moments in the formation of a counter-public (McNevin 2007; Beltrán 2009; Staeheli *et al.* 2009).

In light of this progressive momentum, much has changed in the tone of public debate. Commenting over 16 years ago on earlier examples of undocumented migrant activism, Stephanie Pincetl observed that 'Los Angeles is *fighting* the presence of non-Anglo nonwhite undocumented immigrants rather than developing ways to *validate* the dynamism of such communities, their imagination, and entrepreneurial spirit' (1994: 919, emphasis added). Pincetl was doubtless discouraged by widespread support in the mid 1990s for anti-immigrant initiatives (such as California's infamous Proposition 187). Today, in stark contrast to this history, and in contrast to enforcement trends in other US cities, numerous examples exist in which the City of Los Angeles is pragmatically and inclusively disposed towards undocumented migrants.[3] Precisely because of this pragmatism, there is every reason to be cautious in interpreting these trends as substantive modes of public recognition. Given Los Angeles' nodal position in a global division of labour, it seems reasonable to suggest that quasi forms of recognition for undocumented people simply provide more effective ways of sustaining the cheap and flexible workers that capital requires. From this perspective, it is no surprise that elected officials and local business leaders have come together in opposition to federal immigration workplace raids, or that advocates for migrants encourage local authorities to view undocumented residents proactively as an 'emerging market' worthy of economic and community development investments. For Nicola Philips, such gestures are part of an unspoken strategy to entrench existing divisions of labour, albeit with minor modifications to wages and working conditions (Phillips 2009). Others have likewise interpreted undocumented migrants' struggles as acts of citizenship only insofar as they fall in line with the mutation of citizenship from welfare to neoliberal models (Chavez 2008: 176). Accordingly, we might question whether manifestations of 'grounded citizenship' in the Los Angeles context have more to do with instrumentality and exploitation than with recognition and inclusion.

Yet, even a pragmatically driven approach to undocumented residents provides enabling conditions for more profound challenges to citizenship norms. By claiming certain kinds of rights and recognition, undocumented migrants engage in subject-producing practices with political effects that go beyond the success or failure of the immediate issue at hand (wage-claims or legalisation, for example). Their struggles are at once *reactions to* their marginalised condition and *productive of* new forms of citizenship. Council initiatives simultaneously generate an atmosphere of ambiguity in which it is possible to push at the limits of citizenship in new and unpredictable ways. This is the kind of ambiguity that makes it possible for Felix to speak of 'undocumented citizens' and to expect that his meaning will be understood, even if the term is contested. Elsewhere in the world, or elsewhere in the country, the term simply wouldn't make sense. In Los Angeles, however, it resonates with an actually existing (if partial and vulnerable) expression of political belonging and one that is forged between the push and pull of public modes of recognition and acts of citizenship.

To develop this case I outline in the following section three sites of contestation where undocumented migrants are pushing at the limits of what it means to belong. These examples were gathered between February and May 2009 when I visited several community, migrant and labour organisations in central Los Angeles, and engaged with undocumented migrants in various capacities such as union organising, community development, legal assistance and educational advocacy.

Three sites of contestation

Underground undergrads

In April 2009, some 20 students held a mock graduation ceremony in the grounds of UCLA. The event was the culmination of a series of actions over the course of a week that had drawn attention to undocumented students on campus. Many of the students participating were soon to graduate and faced the prospect of being unable to use their qualifications or to work at all on account of their immigration status. Most of these students had grown up in the US, had attended Californian high-schools and did not necessarily have other countries to which they could say they unambiguously belonged. Some were the children of visa over-stayers; some had more complex forms of status, caught in the gaps of administration systems which rendered them undeportable. Various flags pinned to their backs – Mexican, Korean, US and others – reflected this ambiguity as well as the multiple home-lands and transnational affiliations that shaped the students' identities. Dressed in graduation robes, they held mock certificates that simply read: 'What Now?'

172   *A. McNevin*

The event constituted a public outing of undocumented status. Students openly declared their legitimate right to be present, to be students, to work and to contribute to the places they called home. They also sought recognition as full and active members of society – literally as citizens, regardless of their formal status:

> I am an undocumented student. I am also a daughter, a sister, a girlfriend, a Bruin,[4] and an American. But that might shock some of you a little bit, how can I be undocumented and American? It's an interesting paradox. But I am American, in loyalty, in culture, in speech, in education, in values. The only thing that says I am not American is a piece of paper with some numbers and letters.... This immigrant has *always* been American.

In this personal testimony, read out at the mock graduation, Bina, a third-year student of sociology and Spanish, directly contests the documents, laws, and regulations that mark her as alien in contradistinction to the American she declares herself to be. Her position is clear: such conventions simply lack legitimacy so long as they dispute her claim to belong.

After the event, students explained that it had taken several years to reach the kind of collective confidence it took to speak out so openly. Their activism comes with considerable risks to themselves and to their families. One former student recalled a number of cases where students who spoke up about their status were harassed by anti-immigrant groups in emails and phone-calls (interview, 8 May 2009). When Tam Tran, a UCLA student, testified before Congress in regard to her situation, her family was subsequently arrested by federal immigration agents, detained overnight and released subject to electronic monitoring (Madera *et al.* 2008). Countering the fear inspired by the potential for seizure and sanction was one of the main tasks of a support group founded in 2003 on the UCLA campus: Improving Dreams, Equality, Access, and Success, or IDEAS. IDEAS is now one of 29 such groups operating throughout California. The group aimed to overcome the isolation that many undocumented students felt, unaware that others like them were on campus. More concretely, the students aimed to disseminate information about college eligibility to undocumented high-school students, to fundraise for college expenses in lieu of the formal right to work, and to advocate for state and federal legislation (DREAM Acts) that would open pathways to formal citizenship for undocumented students. Bina explains the affirming and radicalising effect of joining the association:

> Oh it was so good. It's like any feeling that an outcast has when she realises that there are other people like him or her. It's ecstatic. But I do confess, the best thing was realizing that if these people could be politically active and nothing bad was happening to them, then I could do it too ... until I started going to IDEAS ... I had no idea that we actually did have a political avenue that we could travel to become active, and that we could do things, and

could talk about it [our status] in certain ways, and that there were people who wanted to listen. I thought it was some sort of alien situation. Like now if I don't have to I don't say 'illegal alien', I don't say 'illegal immigrant' so my whole terminology has changed.... I say 'undocumented'.

(interview, 12 May 2009)

For Bina, joining IDEAS not only gave her the confidence and strategic direction to focus her political energies, but changed the terms of reference through which she framed her sense of belonging and entitlement. By shifting her language from 'illegal' to 'undocumented' the narrative that explained her status also transformed from a story of illicit border-crossings to one of bureaucratic fallibility. This shift in subjectivity profoundly affects the strategies employed by undocumented students to advocate for their rights. Specifically, it provides the grounding to move from an underground presence to a publicly open one.

A key strategy of the students' campaign is to emphasise the extent to which they are integrated into mainstream US society. The stories they tell are of young people who have grown up effectively *as* Americans and share with their 'regular' classmates a set of skills and experiences that prime them for an exceptional civic contribution. The case made is one of social utility and cultural consistency: these are highly skilled youth that the economy needs, fully at ease in mainstream institutions and thus culturally non-threatening. The approach therefore reinforces existing cultural norms applying to US citizenship. At the same time, however, students like Bina insist that they are *already* citizens, regardless of immigration status. In doing so, they directly challenge formal measures of citizenship for their failure to account for the diverse modes of political belonging that are increasingly possible. The students publicly embody the messiness and movement that constitute relations to place, jurisdictions, homelands and communities and that cannot be captured by fixed territorial identities. Their actions work simultaneously to resist and renew prevailing modes of citizenship.

Magic cleaners

In a small office in the northern suburbs of Los Angeles, I attended a meeting to confirm three new members of the Magic Cleaners business cooperative. The cooperative is a limited liability company formed under Californian law and an economic development project of community organisation, Institute for Popular Education of Southern California, or IDEPSCA. Magic Cleaners' members are equal owners in the business and income earned is split after operating costs have been covered. Members thus avoid paying high commissions for agency placements; they can independently negotiate the clients they do business with and the conditions under which they work. The business takes seriously the harsh effects of cleaning substances on the health of its members. Those involved had previously suffered from repeated exposure to toxic chemicals. Using only environmentally friendly products, Magic Cleaners have created a targeted niche as a green cleaning service.

174   *A. McNevin*

This legal business entity generates a space of employment that is difficult to categorise according to prevailing assumptions about formal and informal economies and who does what work where. Magic Cleaners' owner-members cannot be legally employed by others but there is nothing to stop them from starting a business under Californian law, which does not require a social security number in order to do so.[5] Clients engage the business, rather than the workers directly, and the exchange takes place entirely within the formal economy. The cooperative generates an avenue of social recognition that bridges the divide between legitimate and illegitimate status. 'Being in the cooperative', one member explains, 'clients have learnt to respect us, because the company is backing us up.' In discussion, members express pride in their work and in their status as business owners. They now feel more secure in their work and can plan with more certainty for the future (interview, 6 May 2009). Moreover, working as Magic Cleaners, migrant women are integrated into administrative systems in a cultural and ideological context that rewards entrepreneurs as model civic subjects. Their story invokes an enterprising spirit and a pioneering immigrant work-ethic that has long framed the tradition of US citizenship and continues to provide the essential leverage for a broader campaign for immigrant rights *as workers*. To police these business owners over immigration compliance now raises the spectre of economic *dis*-investment.

Magic Cleaners express a far less passionate relation to their formal status than students like Bina. On the question of how they identify, one business owner simply states that she is 'Mexican until I get the papers' (interview, 6 May 2009). She and her colleagues are conscious of building a solid track-record of legitimate business activity, tax-paying and so on, in support of future applications for residency and citizenship that are likely to rest on demonstrations of 'good character'. Their approach to citizenship in its conventional form is thus largely pragmatic and lacks the level of affect that makes Bina's claims to citizenship so compelling. From Magic Cleaners I have the distinct impression that papers alone, though essential to secure their future, cannot so easily capture the legitimacy they might feel about where and who they are in the world, or the relations to places and people that provide them with the grounding to know where they belong. There was neither the urge to justify their 'place' in these terms nor an attempt to articulate an alternative register of status – perhaps on account of what they recognised as my own implication in an analytics that was insufficient to the task of conveying multiple and everyday sovereignties. Our encounter was always invested with expectations and assumptions about citizens and aliens. The premise of our meeting, at least from my perspective, was to think about citizenship from the standpoint of its outsiders. Hence Magic Cleaners appeared in and through that encounter as what citizens are not. The encounter, in this sense, re-made the alien subject even as it worked towards reconstituting citizenship in alternative 'undocumented' terms (on this point see Ahmed 2000: 3–9). Our meeting demanded, at the very least, a reflexive orientation towards the 'excess' of belonging that evades perception from within analytics that shape inquiry into citizenship. It suggested, moreover, the necessity of leaving theoretical space for acts of contestation and political subjectivities that resist subordination to the concept of citizenship, however broadly interpreted.

Undocumented citizens?   175

Parents for educational justice

When Mario and Louisa saw their children struggling with school, they wanted to intervene. As migrant parents, they witnessed their children ignored and belittled by their teachers on account of poor English language skills. Mario and Louisa felt that the school was failing to respond to the needs of its majority Spanish-speaking students. They started talking with other parents and quickly discovered that the problem was systemic, extending well beyond their own children's schools. The result, some 10 years later, is Asociación de Padres de Pasadena Luchando por la Educación (Pasadena Parent Association Advocating for Equitable Education, or APPLE), a parent-led organisation that has pushed for reform in public education in the Pasadena Unified School District. At the time I spoke to Mario and Louisa, 58 per cent of the district's students in 29 schools were Latino and 22 per cent were English language learners. District averages on student achievement hid a more disaggregated reality. In different high schools in recent years graduation rates varied from 96 to only 57 per cent. In the 2007–8 school year, only 53 per cent of English language learners who entered Year 12 completed graduation requirements (Pasadena Unified School District: www.pusd.us/). Yet thanks to the efforts of APPLE the District Board has recognised English Learners as one of its key priorities and is obligated to translate official school documents into languages other than English.

When parents began to seek changes in their children's education they faced three major obstacles. First, as immigrant parents, many had no prior experience of the US school system and many had had only rudimentary schooling in their own countries of origin. As such they were unfamiliar with the structure of school administrations, the location of decision-making power, and the curriculum and educational pathways available to their children. Second, parents faced a language barrier in that non-English speakers had no formal avenues to consult with school administrations. Third, parents were fearful of speaking out as many were undocumented and either assumed that their status outweighed any rights they may have as parents or feared the exposure that public acts of protest would attract.

Working with several community organisations, parents organised workshops to discuss how they could overcome their fears, mobilise as a community, approach school authorities and present a case for reform. They embarked on comprehensive training sessions on the structure of the school system and on advocacy skills. According to Mario and Louisa, the workshops and training were an important part of building the confidence and knowledge to demand a voice in the schools. Crucially, the first demand made by parents was changes to the language of negotiation. They insisted that all written and spoken information provided to parents be available in Spanish. Mario explains:

> Whenever we went to the school district or even the school we always found the answer – we don't speak Spanish. Well [our position was that] you have

to. You have to speak Spanish because we have many things to tell you. We have many things to say but we have this barrier of the language.

(interview, 22 May 2009)

As concerned parents attempting to improve their children's educational outcomes, Mario, Louisa and their co-campaigners might be said to be playing a traditional civic role through the social reproduction of households and families and by raising productive citizens. Yet their activism is also indicative of non-traditional parents in terms of the demand that public institutions adapt to non-traditional cultural and linguistic needs. These parents compel authorities to recognise Spanish speakers; to listen to broken English with patience, purpose and respect; and to find a more equal mode of communication. All parties are transformed by this experience.

APPLE's next strategic step was to position parent representatives in key decision-making bodies where they could exert real influence. After much initial resistance, APPLE secured the District Board's approval to deliver a curriculum to parents with a view to encouraging participation in school committees. By 2007, APPLE had secured parent participation in the committees of over 25 per cent of district schools (IDEPSCA: www.idepsca.org/apple). Here in these committees, parents were recognised – regardless of language or immigration status – as active members and decision-makers within the public school system.

Mario is now attempting to bring the Pasadena model to other areas of the city. He is working to organise parents in the downtown Pico Union neighbourhood, which is a low-income gateway for recently arrived and undocumented migrants. In broadening the struggle, Mario is linked to other initiatives, prompted when service-sector unions realised that their membership was comprised of parents with children in some of the lowest performing schools in the city. Union staff wondered whether the numbers of parents within their membership might be strong enough to build a potentially powerful base from which to campaign. For Mario the task is primarily about building a sense of attachment, investment and community among the parent population:

we are going to start working with parents trying to define what is a community, what is the role of the parents in the school, what kind of power do we need to be there and to advocate for the students. Because a community doesn't exist until you build it ... we can talk about neighbourhood but not a community ... a community needs to mean something.

(interview, 22 May 2009)

Mario's emphasis on community-building reflects the interplay between neighbourhood places, cultural ties, associational networks and the 'work' that it takes for marginalised groups to enter into the public. While 'the public' may be imagined and discursively created, membership within it nevertheless brings a degree of legitimacy to rights-based claims. Building community (in the sense of harnessing pre-existing ties, proximity and shared interests) is a crucial

Undocumented citizens? 177

stepping-stone for 'outsider' groups to generate resources with which to confront relative strangers and 'insider' groups with a counter-public presence. Such encounters destabilise prevailing categories – citizen/non-citizen, legal/illegal – that shape the uncertain terrain of political belonging in Los Angeles and beyond.

Shifting grounds of citizenship

What can be said in general of these three examples in terms of acts of citizenship? The first thing to notice is a politics of presence – an embodied taking-up of public space. The students provide the most dramatic example in this regard by openly 'outing' themselves. Like other public outings in other social movements – gay rights activism comes to mind – the students place their bodies on the line, inviting public scrutiny precisely on account of the status that marks them as outsiders. In doing so they contest processes of illegalisation and openly declare the legitimacy of their presence. While parents do not raise their immigration status in the course of their educational activism, they also insist on taking up public space. A central part of their strategy is simply *to be there*, at the table, in school committee meetings and in representations to the School District Board, declaring by their presence their legitimate role as parties to negotiation regardless of immigration status. Magic Cleaners too have carved out a space for themselves in the formal economy. While this is a much more abstracted place than school meeting rooms or university campuses, it nevertheless (and increasingly) shapes norms of civic engagement.

If seizing public space is an embodied process, it is also place-specific. It sends a message that we are here, as we are, in this place – this campus, this school, this workplace and this city which we mark, however subtly or dramatically, as our own. Public space – and a space in the public – is enacted through face-to-face exchanges between students and academics, business owners and clients, workers and union officials, parents and school board members, residents and councillors. Across this array of exchanges, new subjectivities are forming. Through expressions of belonging to local communities as parents, workers, students and so on, a 'becoming' of the citizen takes place. When these actions are incorporated into daily routines (working, studying, parenting) in shared institutions (businesses, schools, universities, assemblies) and backed by support from local officials, business leaders and community sectors, a cumulative momentum is generated that transforms what it means to be part of a civic life.

The case of Magic Cleaners, in particular, prompts a range of questions about the gendered dimension of emerging citizen subjectivities. Magic Cleaners' work occurs in the largely domestic spaces of private households. It reminds us, perhaps more clearly than the other case studies in question, that politics happens in intimate and mundane settings which may have little of the drama and visibility of mass protests, for instance. I do not want to buy into rigid distinctions between public and private space, not least because of the compelling case that feminists have made for the central role of domestic and care work in the

178   *A. McNevin*

contemporary transnational political economy (Chang 2000; Peterson 2003). I do want to consider, however, how the gendered specificity of domestic work impacts upon emerging subjectivities. What role does gender play in the kind of ambivalence expressed by Magic Cleaners' owner-members in relation to legality and citizenship? Is there a connection between gendered migrant work and more 'mobile' accounts of political belonging? Los Angeles remains a fruitful site from which to investigate these questions which require further research. Inspired by the model set by Magic Cleaners, staff at the Pilipino Workers Center in downtown Los Angeles are investigating options for a care-givers' cooperative. IDEPSCA has also recently established gardening cooperatives amongst day-labourers that are geared towards demand for a 'green' skilled workforce that will flow from municipal low-impact development initiatives. These examples are fertile ground for exploring the intersection between gendered work (domestic and care-giving versus gardening), mobile migrant labour, new sites of civic engagement (environmental activism) and emerging citizen-subjectivities.

This research agenda implies that the study of citizenship necessitates place-based approaches which capture at once the significance of embodied encounters *and* their positioning within complex trans-local geographies. There is substance here for Varsanyi's notion of grounded citizenship in practice. Yet it seems to me that, both as a conceptual starting point and a normative aspiration, 'grounded citizenship' may not take us far enough in terms of capturing the dynamic constitution of the places and subjects in and through which political belonging takes form. From undocumented migrants in Los Angeles, I have the impression of a practice of citizenship where the ground necessarily shifts. By this, I mean more than the movement of migrants and the re-constitution of citizen-subjects through different jurisdictions (from Arizona to Los Angeles for instance). These are clearly important 'grounds' to consider. However, the shifting grounds I have in mind are brought into being by strategic acts (such as building a community of parents or operating a business) that are not necessarily permanent or self-consciously 'civic'. Such acts may morph into others which build new kinds of communities for certain types of purposes, establish new modalities of membership across formal/informal lines and connect in transitory or fundamental ways with social ties in other places. Such acts both contract and expand the spatial and temporal horizons of citizenship in ways that subvert Cartesian reference points for political belonging. They challenge us to radically reconceptualise political space. This is a different proposition from rethinking the way we inhabit or transit through spaces that are already there (say, the city of Los Angeles), prior to our passage through them. That passage reconstitutes the space that makes politics possible and may do so in ways that do not cohere with subject or status coherence, that is, with that which can be included or excluded in socio-spatial terms in the first place.

A different way of saying this is to imagine a political practice that leaves open the possibility of opting out of citizenship as a mode of resistance. Such a practice would expose the limits of citizenship in prevailing *or altered* forms, to

Undocumented citizens? 179

reflect the range of political subjectivities and practices that are possible and/or desirable. I am thinking here of a refusal to justify one's political subjectivity in terms that make sense within existing socio-spatial vocabularies and conceptual limits (on this point see also Walters 2008). Both Magic Cleaners and the undocumented parents are engaged in acts which disrupt citizenship norms yet which are not in themselves aimed at gaining legal or conventional citizen-status. To be sure, there is a broader migrant community with which they are engaged which is actively working towards legalisation as an element of immigration reform. Yet the acts in question also suggest ambivalence towards legality as a political strategy. Might they also engender a sense of citizenship as a transient practice, deployed instrumentally and partially – a practice that undermines the link between stasis and status? Could this practice challenge the conceptual routing of citizenship in a progressive notion of time, whereby acts of citizenship necessarily move in a linear direction towards fuller modes of inclusion – however spatially grounded they might be?

At this stage, these are speculative ideas about the intersection of mobility and citizenship, prompted by the emergence of what Felix calls 'undocumented citizens'. It is nevertheless important to raise some notes of caution in pursuing this line of inquiry. Whether in relation to citizens or undocumented migrants, instability of status is usually interpreted negatively in terms of vulnerability to the whims of sovereign power. In this respect, undocumented migrants in Los Angeles and elsewhere are subject to ever more innovative and invasive techniques of sovereign border control that continue to shape the broader US (and global) political landscape. To be clear, I remain profoundly aware of the dangers and hardships that arise on account of insecure citizenship and immigration status. Any attempt to theorise a mobile citizenship must take those realities seriously and avoid slipping into politically ill-considered abstractions. That said, it is equally important to understand how sovereign logic has constituted instability *as* insecurity and rendered unstable subjects objects of surveillance and policing. Might there also be radical and emancipatory dimensions of this kind of instability? Answers to these questions require considerable empirical and theoretical research into mobile (acts of) citizenship. This chapter and its snapshots of undocumented citizens in Los Angeles are intended as exploratory pointers in this direction.

Notes

1 Thanks to Vicki Squire, Kim Huynh, Angharad Closs Stephens, Barry Hindess, Andy Scerri and three anonymous reviewers of an earlier draft, as well as to the editors of this volume, for close readings and helpful suggestions for revision.
2 State Assembly Bill 540, passed in 2000, makes undocumented high-school graduates eligible for in-state college tuition, avoiding the higher fees associated with out-of-state or foreign residence.
3 In addition to the examples outlined in the introduction to this chapter, the Los Angeles Police Department (LAPD), for instance, works on the basis that it's bad public policy for a large cohort of the population to be fearful and mistrustful of police. A policy known as Special Order 40 prevents officers from initiating any action for the purpose

180   *A. McNevin*

of eliciting a person's immigration status. The Department makes it known within immigrant communities that it's safe to cooperate with police as a witness or a victim of crime without the threat of apprehension and deportation. This works, in effect, as a Don't Ask Don't Tell policy and limits the extent to which police cooperate with immigration authorities.

4 Bruins are the sports teams for the University of California, Los Angeles.
5 The documentation required was two forms of identification (a passport and IDEP-SCA's organisational ID card) and an Individual Taxpayer Identification number. The latter is issued by the Internal Revenue Service to those ineligible for a Social Security Number, regardless of immigration status.

Bibliography

Ahmed, S. (2000) *Strange Encounters: Embodied Others in Post-coloniality*, London and New York: Routledge.

Balibar, E. (2006) 'Strangers as enemies: Further reflections on the aporias of transnational citizenship,' *Globalization Working Papers* 06/4, Hamilton, ON: Institute on Globalization and the Human Condition, McMaster University.

Bauböck, R. (2003) 'Reinventing urban citizenship,' *Citizenship Studies* 7 (2): 139–160.

Beltrán, C. (2009) 'Going public: Hannah Arendt, immigrant action, and the space of appearance,' *Political Theory* 37 (5): 595–622.

Brenner, N. (2004) *New State Spaces: Urban Governance and the Rescaling of Statehood*, Oxford: Oxford University Press.

California Chronicle (2008) 'LA City Council votes unanimously for resolution supporting carwash workers,' 30 July.

Campbell, K.M. (2007) 'Local Illegal Immigration Relief Act ordinances: A legal, policy, and litigation analysis,' *Denver University Law Review* 84 (4): 1041–1060.

Chang, G. (2000) *Disposable Domestics: Immigrant Women Workers in the Global Economy*, Cambridge, MA: South End Press.

Chavez, L.R. (2008) *The Latino Threat: Constructing Immigrants, Citizens and the Nation*, Stanford: Stanford University Press.

De Genova, N. (2005) *Working the Boundaries: Race, Space and 'Illegality' in Mexican Chicago*, Durham, NC: Duke University Press.

Delgado Wise, R. and H. Márquez Covarrubias (2008) 'Capitalist restructuring, development and labour migration: The Mexico–US case,' *Third World Quarterly* 29 (7): 1359–1374.

Donahoe, M.C. (2005) 'Economic restructuring and labor organizing in Southeast Los Angeles, 1935–2001' in E.C. Ochoa and G.L. Ochoa (eds) *Latino LA: Transformations, Communities, and Activism*, Tucson: University of Arizona Press, 83–108.

Earnest, D.C. (2007) 'From alien to elector: Citizenship and belonging in the global city,' *Globalizations* 4 (2): 137–155.

Ehrkamp, P. and H. Leitner (2003) 'Beyond national citizenship: Turkish immigrants and the (re)construction of citizenship in Germany,' *Urban Geography* 24 (2): 127–146.

Ehrkamp, P. and H. Leitner (eds) (2006) *Rethinking Immigration and Citizenship: New Spaces of Migrant Transnationalism and Belonging*, special issue, *Environment and Planning A* 38.

Fernández-Kelly, P. and D.S. Massey (2007) 'Borders for whom? The role of NAFTA in Mexico–U.S. migration,' *Annals of the American Academy of Political and Social Science* 610 (1): 98–118.

Garcia, S. (ed.) (1996) *Cities and Citizenship*, special issue, *International Journal of Urban and Regional Research* 20.

Gutierrez de Soldatenko, M.A. (2005) 'Justice for janitors Latinizing Los Angeles: Mobilizing Latina(o) cultural repertoire' in E.C. Ochoa and G.L. Ochoa (eds) *Latino Los Angeles: Transformations, Communities, and Activism*, Tucson: University of Arizona Press, 225–245.

Hanley, L.M., B.A. Ruble and A.M. Garland (eds) (2008) *Immigration and Integration in Urban Communities: Renegotiating the City*, Washington, DC, and Baltimore: Woodrow Wilson Center Press and Johns Hopkins University Press.

Hayes-Bautista, D.E. (2004) *La Nueva California: Latinos in the Golden State*, Berkeley, Los Angeles and London: University of California Press.

Holston, J. and A. Appadurai (eds) (1996) 'Cities and citizenship,' special issue, *Public Culture* 8.

Isin, E.F. (ed.) (2000) *Democracy, Citizenship and the Global City*, London and New York: Routledge.

Isin, E.F. (2002) *Being Political: Genealogies of Citizenship*, Minneapolis and London: University of Minnesota Press.

Isin, E.F. (2008) 'Theorizing Acts of Citizenship' in E.F. Isin and G.M. Nielson (eds) *Acts of Citizenship*, London and New York: Zed Books, 15–43.

Isin, E.F. and G.M. Nielson (eds) (2008) *Acts of Citizenship*, London and New York: Zed Books.

Joseph, M. (1999) *Nomadic Identities: The Performance of Citizenship*, Minneapolis and London: University of Minnesota Press.

Keil, R. (1998) *Los Angeles: Globalization, Urbanization and Social Struggles*, Chichester: John Wiley & Sons.

Los Angeles City Council, Permit Process/Day Laborer Operating Standards/Home Improvement Stores, Ordinance No. 180174, introduced 23 June 2008.

Madera, G., A.A. Mathay, A.M. Najafi, H.H. Saldívar, S. Solis, A.J.J. Titony, G. Rivera-Salgado, J. Shadduck-Hernández, K. Wong, R. Frazier and J. Monroe (eds) (2008) *Underground Undergrads: UCLA Undocumented Immigrant Students Speak Out*, Los Angeles: UCLA Center for Labor Research and Education.

McNevin, A. (2006) 'Political belonging in a neoliberal era: The struggle of the Sans-Papiers,' *Citizenship Studies* 10 (2): 135–151.

McNevin, A. (2007) 'Irregular migrants, neoliberal geographies and spatial frontiers of "the political",' *Review of International Studies* 33 (4): 1–20.

McNevin, A. (2011) *Contesting Citizenship: Irregular Migrants and New Frontiers of the Political*, New York: Columbia University Press.

Monahan, T. (2002) 'Los Angeles studies: The emergence of a specialty field,' *Cities and Society* 14 (2): 155–184.

Moulin, C. and P. Nyers (2007) '"We live in a country of UNHCR": Refugee protests and global political society,' *International Political Sociology* 1 (4): 356–372.

Narro, V. (2005–6) 'Impacting next wave organizing: Creative campaign strategies of the Los Angeles worker centers,' *New York Law School Law Review* 50 (2): 465–513.

Nyers, P. (2006) *Rethinking Refugees: Beyond States of Emergency*, New York and Milton Park: Routledge.

Nyers, P. (2008) 'No One Is Illegal between city and nation' in E.F. Isin and G.M. Nielson (eds) *Acts of Citizenship*, London and New York: Zed Books, 160–181.

Oboler, S. (2006) 'Redefining citizenship as a lived experience' in S. Oboler (ed.) *Latinos and Citizenship: The Dilemma of Belonging*, New York: Palgrave Macmillan, 3–30.

182   *A. McNevin*

Parker, N. and N. Vaughan-Williams (2009) 'Lines in the sand? Towards an agenda for critical border studies,' *Geopolitics* 14: 582–587.

Passel, J.S. and D. Cohn (2009) *A Portrait of Unauthorized Immigrants in the United States*, Washington, DC: Pew Hispanic Center.

Pastor, M. and R. Ortiz (2009) *Immigrant Integration in Los Angeles: Strategic Directions for Funders*, Program for Environmental and Regional Equity and Center for the Study of Immigrant Integration, University of Southern California, commissioned by the California Community Foundation, January 2009.

Peterson, V.S. (2003) *A Critical Rewriting of Global Political Economy: Integrating Reproductive, Productive and Virtual Economies*, London and New York: Routledge.

Phillips, N. (2009) 'Migration as development strategy? The new political economy of dispossession and inequality in the Americas,' *Review of International Political Economy* 16 (2): 231–259.

Pincetl, S. (1994) 'Challenges to citizenship: Latino immigrants and political organizing in the Los Angeles area,' *Environment and Planning A* 26: 895–914.

Rocco, R. (1997) 'Citizenship, culture, and community: Restructuring in southeast Los Angeles' in W.V. Flores and R. Benmayor (eds) *Latino Cultural Citizenship: Claiming Identity, Space and Rights*, Boston: Beacon Press, 97–123.

Sassen, S. (2000) *Cities in a World Economy*, Thousand Oaks, London and New Delhi: Pine Forge Press.

Sassen, S. (2004) 'The repositioning of citizenship' in A. Brysk and G. Shafir (eds) *People Out of Place: Globalization, Human Rights and the Citizenship Gap*, London and New York: Routledge, 191–208.

Savage, L. (2006) 'Justice for janitors: Scales of organizing and representing workers,' *Antipode* 38 (3): 645–666.

Secor, A.J. (2003) 'Citizenship in the city: Identity, community, and rights among women migrants to Istanbul,' *Urban Geography* 24 (2): 14–168.

Sheller, M. and J. Urry (2006) 'The new mobilities paradigm,' *Environment and Planning A* 38: 207–226.

Smith, M.P. (2001) *Transnational Urbanism: Locating Globalization*, Malden and Oxford: Blackwell Publishers.

Smith, M.P. and M. Bakker (2008) *Citizenship Across Borders: The Political Transnationalism of El Migrante*, Ithaca, NY, and London: Cornell University Press.

Soguk, N. (2008) 'Transversal communication, diaspora, and the Euro-Kurds,' *Review of International Studies* 34 (1): 173–192.

Squire, V. (2009) *The Exclusionary Politics of Asylum*, New York and Houndmills: Palgrave Macmillan.

Staeheli, L.A. (ed.) (2003) *Cities and Citizenship*, special issue, *Urban Geography* 24 (2).

Staeheli, L.A. and C.R. Nagel (2006) 'Topographies of home and citizenship: Arab-American activists in the United States,' *Environment and Planning A* 38: 1599–1614.

Staeheli, L.A., D. Mitchell and C.R. Nagel (2009) 'Making publics: Immigrants, regimes of publicity and entry to "the public",' *Environment and Planning D: Society and Space* 27: 633–648.

Varsanyi, M. (2005) 'The paradox of contemporary immigrant political mobilization: Organized labor, undocumented migrants, and electoral participation in Los Angeles,' *Antipode* 37 (4): 775–795.

Varsanyi, M. (2006) 'Interrogating "urban citizenship" vis-à-vis undocumented migration,' *Citizenship Studies* 10 (2): 229–249.

Varsanyi, M. (2008) 'Immigration policing through the backdoor: City ordinances, the "right to the city," and the exclusion of undocumented day laborers,' *Urban Geography* 29 (1): 29–52.

Villaraigosa, A.R. (2009) 'Mayor Villaraigosa announces opening of over 40 "cash for college" financial aid workshops throughout Los Angeles,' press release, Office of the Mayor, City of Los Angeles, 2 February.

Walters, W. (2008) 'Acts of demonstration: Mapping the territory of (non-)citizenship' in E.F. Isin and G.M. Nielson (eds) *Acts of Citizenship*, London and New York: Zed Books, 182–206.

Weissman, D.M., R.C. Headen and K.L. Parker (2009) 'The policies and politics of local immigration enforcement laws: 287(g) program in North Carolina,' American Civil Liberties Union and Immigration and Human Rights Policy Clinic, February 2009.

Index

Page numbers in **bold** denote figures.

access to citizenship 41–2, 44
access without fear campaign 15
Acién, E. 100
active citizenship 129, 130, 131, 143
activism 8–9, 11–12, 119–20
activist citizenship 10
acts of citizenship 81, 119, 121–2, 167, 170–1
acts of contestation 166
Adepoju, A. 76
Adolphine 156–7
advocacy 49–50
Agamben, G. 110, 118
agency 14–15, 110, 117–18, 121
Algeria 23, 25, 33
Almería 97, **98–9**
amnesty, Brazil 64–5
Anderson, B. 47
Anderson, Benedict 76
Anderson, Bridget 3, 5, 13
Andrijasevic, R. 5
anti-deportation campaigns 79
anti-Frenchness 29, 30
anti-racism 79
anti-racist discourse, France 27
anti-terrorist legislation, France 25
Appadurai, A. 129–31
Arendt, Hannah 42, 120
Aristotle 62
Arizona 165
Asociación de Padres de Pasadena Luchando por la Educación (Apple) 175–7
Asociación Pro Derechos Humanos de Andalucía (APDHA) 14, 92–7, **93**; terminology 102; *see also* sex workers
assimilation 23
asylum 14–15, 148–9
Australia 115–17, 121, 123, 126
authorities, multiple 150

Bagelman, J. 15, 131
Balibar, E. 31–5, 76, 81, 130
banlieues, as spaces of jihad 25–6
bare life 118
Barnett, C. 149, 158
Barreto, Luiz Paulo 65

Benani, Souad 33
Benchellali, Mourad 25
Benziane, Sohane 33
beurs 26, 27
Bhogal, I. 149, 158
biopower 133
Blair/Brown government 44–6
Blédardes 34
Bonelli, E. 102
border controls 13–14, 73, 111, 148
border studies 168
bordering 150
borderland, Europe as 31
borders: complexity 12; conceptualisation 2; governmentalised 133, 139–40, 143; as ideological 76; power of 76–7; between public and private 80–1; rejection of 82; and rights 3; of sanctuary 154; volatility 86
Borders, Immigration and Citizenship Act (2009) (UK) 46–7
Brace, L. 78
Brasilia protest 57–8
Brazil 13, 64–5; *see also* Palestinian refugees, Brazil
Britishness 44–6
Brown, Gordon 44
Burundi 112

Cairo 122
Calavita, K. 113
'Call Yourself British' campaign 44
camps 110, 111, 118
Canada 79, 83–4, 129, 134–6, 140
capitalism, and immobility 75–6
catastrophe prediction 82
Cesari, J. 22, 24, 25, 26, 27, 28, 29, 31
Ceuta 113–14
child protection 136
Chirac, Jacques 23
cities 129–31, 140, 143
citizen/migrant divide 165
Citizens UK 48
citizenship 1; becoming claim-making subjects 126; civil practice 22; construction 81, 130; dynamics 166; freedom and protection 67;

Index 185

French ideal 24–5; and human rights 78–82; movement and mobility 28; as set of multifaceted practices 21; shifting grounds 177–9; as spatial relation 167–9; as transcendent 34; transnational 35–6; as undesirable 11; as unstable 21
citizenship policy, developments in 42
citizenship spaces 9–12
citizenship-rights-based approaches 81
City of Sanctuary movement 15, 139, 143, 146, 148–50, 158, 160–2
City of Sanctuary, Sheffield 146–8, 155–7
city politics 15
civil liberties 77
civil society action 49–50
coalition government, United Kingdom 47
Code of Nationality (France) 23–5
coerced immobility 75–6
cohesion 149
Cole, P. 82
colonialism 23–4, 25
Commission for Racial Equality (UK) 43
Commission on Integration and Cohesion (UK) 43
commoning 85–6
CONARE 60
confederate imaginary 24
contestation 9
Control Orders (UK) 77
Cox, C. 152
criminalisation 76, 136–7, 147, 148, 165
criminality, of refugees 66
critical security studies, of refugees 58–9

D'Andrade, W. 58
da Silva, Luis Inacio Lula 64–5
day-labour centres 166
De Genova, N. 134
de-identification 10
Designated Areas (Tanzania) 111–12
detention, Australia 116
deterrence, and border control 111
deterritorialisation, of religion 30
diasporic identity 20
distinctions, breaking down 158
domestic violence 141
Don't Ask Don't Tell 10, 83, 136, 139, 143

earned citizenship 13, 43–7
earned regularisation 45
Edkins, J. 120, 123, 124
education 175–7
Einaudi, J.-L. 23
Ellerman, A. 9
equality 31, 86
ethnography 96; see also Asociación Pro Derechos Humanos de Andalucía (APDHA)
Europe, as borderland 31
European integration 113
exclusion 64, 81–2, 130–1
Ezekiel, J. 33

facilitators 102
family regrouping laws (France) 23

Fanon, F. 32
fear, refugees' 60–1
Felix 165–6
feminism 34–5, 79, 123–4
foreign national prisoners 81
formal citizenship 130
Fortress Europe 113
Foucault, M. 124, 132, 153
France 23–4, 29, 31–5
France, Muslim communities 12–13, 20–2, 22–6, 26–31
Freedman, J. 32
freedom 5, 66
freedom vs. protection 55, 58–65, 66–7
French National Federation of Muslims (FNMF) 29
Frenchness, rejection of 29, 30

Gabaccia, D. 80
Garaizábal, C. 102
gender 31–5, 80
gender-blindness 33
gendered violence 33
gendered work 178
gift exchange logic 62–3, 65
Giscard d'Estaing, Valéry 25
global city 143
global social movements 118
globalisation, and mobility 2–7
globalised Islam 33
Goldberg, D.T. 133
Goldsmith Citizenship Enquiry 2008 44
González, E. A. 14
governmental power 152–4
governmentalised borders 133–4, 139–40, 143
governmentality 132
gratitude 54, 60–2
grounded citizenship 168–9, 178
Grove-White, R. 13

habitus 119, 121
Harvey, D. 142
hau 65
headscarves 32; see also veil
Hindess, B. 4, 11
Hobbes, Thomas 62
Holston, J. 129–31
Home Office 44
hope, legitimacy of 60
hospitality 155, 158
house-bars 14, 97, **98–9**, 100–1
human rights 78–82
human trafficking 78–9, 101–4
humanitarianism, and securitisation 9
Huysmans, J. 118
hybridisation, of identity 27

identification, need for 133
identity 20, 27
ideology 13–14, 29, 30–1
illegal status 74
illegalisation 132–9, 141
Immigrant and Refugee Protection Act (IRPA) (Canada) 134

186 Index

immigration policies 73–4, 77, 129, 134
immigré, meaning of term 24
immobility 168
inclusion 130–1
individualism 30
informal citizenship 42
ingratitude 63, 66
Institute for Popular Education of Southern
  California (IDEPSCA) 173
insurgent citizenship 130
integration policies 149
irregular migration 6
Isin, E. 10, 47, 49, 81, 119, 121, 124, 126, 167
Islam, securitisation 22–6
Islamic activism, France 28–30
Islamic Armed Group (GIA) 25
Islamic radicalisation, France 27–9

Jelloun, T.B. 26–7
Johnson, H. 14–15
Juliano, D. 102, 103
Justice for Janitors 170

Kamanga, K. 111
Kelkal, Khaled 25
Kemp, A. 34
Khosrokhavar, F. 25, 27, 29, 30, 31
Kirkemann Boesen, J. 51

labour, and spatial practices 79
labour solidarity 79–80
labour unions 79–80
language requirement, United Kingdom 44
Lavenex, S. 113
law of gratitude 60
Law on Everyday Security (France) 26
Lefebvre, H. 158
Lewis, M. 7, 8
liberal rationality 153
Libya, as transit point 105–6
Linebaugh, P. 85
Lionnet, F. 21, 36
Lipietz, A. 20
Lippert, R. 152–4
Lizana-Sossa, Kimberley and Gerald 140
Lloyd, C. 31
localisation 165
logic of gratitude 62–4
Los Angeles: acts of citizenship 170–1;
  Asociación de Padres de Pasadena Luchando
  por la Educación 175–7; council initiatives
  166; Magic Cleaners 173–4, 177–8; overview
  169–70; summary and conclusions 177–9;
  undocumented students 171–3

Maccanico, Y. 105
McDonald, J. 15
McNevin, A. 10, 16
mafias 102, 103–4
Magic Cleaners 173–4, 177–8, 179
Magna Carta Manifesto 85
Magnusson, W. 150
Majuelos, F. 100
Maoris, gift exchange logic 65

March for Equality and Against Racism
  (France) 26
Marfleet, P. 151
marginalisation 25, 28–9
Martin, D.G. 124
Martin, T. 51
Massey, D. 11
Mauss, Marcel 62, 65
Maxey, L.J. 124
Mazumdar, S. 76
Melilla 113–15, 125
Memmi, A. 24, 31
Mexico Declaration and Plan of Action 56
Mezzadra, S. 122
migrant activism 8–9, 11–12; Australia 115–17,
  121, 123; context and overview 109–10;
  feminist theory 123–4; France 26–31; limits
  and possibilities 35–6; moments 123–6;
  moments in the field 110–17; non-citizens as
  initiators 121–3; political activism 117–21;
  Spain 113–15, 121, 123; Tanzania 111–12,
  120–1, 123
migrant agency 10
migrant citizenship 2, 7–9, 14–16
migrant communities, political activity 42–3
migrant illegality 132–9, 141, 143
migrant mobilisations 21, 49–50
Migrant Voice 50
migrants 75, 79–80; *see also* undocumented
  migrants
Migrants' Rights Network (MRN) 43
Migrants' Rights Scotland (MRS) 50
migration 73, 74–7
Migration Act (Australia) 116
migration controls, and rights 3
Migration Policy Institute (US) 45
minor transnationalism 12–13, 21
mobile enclaves of sanctuary 146–7, 155–8
mobility 3, 5, 6–7, 74–5, 76
mobility rights 2–7, 133–4
mobility turn 6
moments of madness 119, 123, 124
moral exchange 62
Morocco 113–15
Moulin, C. 13, 122
Mouvement des Indigènes de la République
  (MIR) 34–5
multiculturalism, United Kingdom 43
municipal policy 131
muslimwoman 31–5

Nanas-Beurs 32–3
Napoleon III 24
nation-state-centrism 75
national citizenship, inclusivity 41
nationalism, universal legitimacy 76
naturalisation 41–2, 43, 45
Neilson, B. 122
Neither Whores Nor Submissives (NPNS) 33
Neocleous, M. 67, 68
networks, of transit 102, 104
new life in the UK test 44
new mobilities paradigm 167
No Borders 13–14, 73–4, 82–6

No One Is Illegal 15, 140
non-citizen migrants 9
non-citizen Others 79
non-citizen subjectivities 4
non-citizens, agency of 110
normalisation 152
normative maleness 31
norms, disruption of 179
Nyers, P. 60, 61, 118, 120, 121, 122

open borders 82
others, non-citizen 79
Ouattara 157–8, 160

Pacific Solution 116
Painter, J. 130
Palermo protocol 4
Palestinian refugees, Brazil 13; background to
  protest 56; Brasilia protest 57–8; context and
  overview 54–6; expectations 57; freedom vs.
  protection 58–65; gratitude 60; settlement
  programme 56–7; summary and conclusions
  66–9
pan-Islamism 29, 30–1
Papadopoulos, D. 10, 75, 76
Papon, Maurice 23
Paris Massacre 1961 23
Parti des Indigènes de la République (PIR) 35–6
Pasqua Laws 23–5
passivity 81
passports 75
pastoral power 153–4
pastoralism 146–7, 150, 158
personal testimony 158
Philips, N. 170
Philo, C. 130
Pin-Fat, V. 120, 123, 124
Pincetl, S. 170
place-based approaches 178
points systems 4, 134
political activism 117–21
political activity, migrant communities 42–3
political agency 14–15, 117–18
political engagement, mobility of 21
political exclusion, *banlieues* 28
political subjectivities 1–2, 3, 33–4
politics, as disagreement 125
politics of presence 177
Pontecorvo, G. 32
Poor Laws (England) 75
populations, internal management 4–5
porteuses de bombes 32
poverty 25
power 120, 152–4, 158–9
power hierarchies 36
power relations 150, 152–4
presence 177
privatisation, of religion 30
probationary citizenship 45
'Program of Social and Sanitary Mediation with
  Women in Contexts of Prostitution 95–6
property rights 85
protection, as gift 60, 61, 62–3
protection vs. freedom 55, 58–65, 66–7

protest 7–9, 57–8, 78–82
proximate diversity 157
public policy, dilemmas 165
public recognition 166
public space, presence in 177

quality of life 139

racist attacks, France 26–7
Rancière, J. 11, 125
rationalities of power 152–4, 158–9
ratonnades 23
reciprocity 61, 64
Refugee Action Coalition 116
Refugee Control Act (1998) (Tanzania) 111
refugees: Canada 135; critical security studies
  58–9; fear 60–1; freedom vs. protection 55;
  humanitarianism and securitisation 9; as
  political subjects 67; representations of 120;
  and resistance 7–9; resistances 61;
  responsibility of 67–8; right to hope 60;
  Tanzania 111; UN definition 59
regularisation campaigns 65, 79, 139–42
regularisation from below 27, 129, 139–42, 144
regularisation, of status 47–9
regulation, of mobility 3, 6
relationships, of violence 120, 123, 125
religion 30
religious signs, visibility 28
Renegar, V.R. 124
resistances 7–9, 61, 124
responsibilisation 152–3, 158
responsibility, of refugees 67–8
restrictive approach 41, 42
right to difference 27
right to have rights 66
right to resemblance 27
Right to the City 142–3, 158, 160
right-wing movements, France 27
rights 42, 130
rights based approaches 49–50, 51
rights of persons 85–6
rights to work 148, 158
Roberts, R.C. 62
Rose, N. 153
routes and transportation, sex workers 104–5
Roy, O. 30, 33

Said, E. 126
Sajed, A. 12–13
Salafism 30
sanctuary 15; historical accounts 151–2;
  meaning and practice 146–7; mobile enclaves
  146–7, 155–8; political significance 157; as a
  state 150–4; statist rationalities 152–4;
  unauthorised 158–61
sanctuary cities 129, 131, 142–4; *see also* City
  of Sanctuary; Toronto
Sanctuary, Sovereignty and Sacrifice 152–4
Sans Papiers 82
Sassen, S. 130, 143
schools 140, 175–7
Scott, J. 150
secularism (France) 24

188 *Index*

securitisation 5, 9, 21–6
security–liberty equilibrium 60
service provision 132, 134–6
services, access to 15, 133, 136
sex workers 4, 14; cost of journey 106; decision to migrate 101; hopes and aims 106–7; migratory process 101–7; modes of access 102–3; numbers 106; overview of 101; routes and transportation 104–5; summary and conclusions 107; transit and arrival in Spain 97–101; *see also* Asociación Pro Derechos Humanos de Andalucía (APDHA)
Sharma, N. 3, 13, 134
Sheffield *see* City of Sanctuary, Sheffield
Sheller, M. 167–8
Shih, S.-M. 21, 36
Sidhu, N. 140
Silverstein, P. 26, 27, 31
social exclusion, *banlieues* 28
social housing, Toronto 138
social relations, and space 12
Soguk, N. 122, 124
Soja, E. 11
Solidarity Resettlement Program 56
SOS Racisme 27
sovereign power 110
sovereignty 65, 82, 118, 150
Sowards, S.K. 124
Soysal, Y. 130
space 12, 167–9
spaces of abjection 9–10
Spain 113–15, 121, 123; *see also* Asociación Pro Derechos Humanos de Andalucía (APDHA); sex workers
spatial practices, and labour 79
Squire, V. 6, 15, 131
state of exception 110
statism 146–7, 150, 158
status 4, 47–9, 74
Stephenson, N. 75
stigmatisation 137
Stolcke, V. 130
Stora, B. 24
strangement 59
Strangers into Citizens campaign 43, 48–9
students, undocumented 171–3
subject formation 133
subjectivities 3–4, 5, 9–12

Tabligh wa Dawa 29
Tam Tran 172
Tanzania 111–12, 120–1, 123, 125
Tarrow, S. 123
temporality 77, 160
temporary foreign worker programmes 4
temporary protection 111
terminology 102
Terminus Initiative (Sheffield) 156–7
territorialisation, of relationships and subjectivities 76
territory of strangement 59
terrorism, France 25–6

Tesfahuney, M. 134
'The Path to Citizenship' 44–5, 46
Theodosius 151–2
Toronto 138, 139–42, 143
Toronto Police Services Board (TPSB) 141–2
trades unions 79–80
transit, sex workers 97–101
transnational citizenship 41
transnationalism 35–6
transpolitics 31
transportation and routes, sex workers 104–5
travel regulations 4
Tsianos, V. 10, 75

UK immigration 13; anxiety about 44; coalition government 47; context and overview 41–3; earned citizenship 13, 43–7; earning citizenship 47–9; liberalism 43; points-based test 46; qualifying period 45; rights based approach 49–50; summary and conclusions 51
Ulloa, M. 102
umma 29, 31
undecidability 67
undocumented citizens 166, 171
undocumented migrants 16, 47–9
undocumented students 171–3
ungrateful refugees 55
UNHCR, view of Palestinian refugees 58
Union of Islamic Organisations in France (UOIF) 29
United Kingdom 43, 44, 47
United States 79, 83, 131
universal, crisis of 35
Urry, J. 167–8

Van Wees, H. 61, 63
Varsanyi, M. 168–9
veil 31–2, 34; *see also* headscarves
victimhood, of refugees 66
victimisation 147
Vigipirate (France) 25
violence 33, 120, 123, 126
volunteering 45, 158
voucher exchange 158
vulnerability 78–9, 141

wage labour, and gender 80
Walsh, Renée 136
Walters, W. 81, 82
Walzer, M. 76
Weil, P. 24
women bomb-carriers 32
women, violence against 33
Woolas, Phil 46
workers' rights 79
Working Group on Prostitution 95–7
Wright, C. 3, 13

zero immigration 24
Zolberg, A.R. 119, 124